The Representation of Business in English Literature

D1291275

Introduced and edited by
Professor Arthur Pollard

Geoffrey Carnall
Professor Angus Easson
Dr John Morris
Professor Arthur Pollard
Dr Allan Simmons
Professor W.A. Speck

Published by The Institute of Economic Affairs
2000

First published in October 2000 by
The Institute of Economic Affairs
2 Lord North Street
Westminster
London SW1P 3LB

PR
830
.C633
R47
2000

IEA Readings 53
All rights reserved
ISSN 0305-814X
ISBN 0-255 36491-1

Printed in Great Britain by
Hartington Fine Arts Limited, Lancing, West Sussex
Set in Times Roman 11 on 12 point

Contents

FOREWORD

John Blundell

AT FIRST GLANCE it might seem a little out of the ordinary for the Institute of Economic Affairs (IEA) to publish a collection of essays on the representation of business in English literature over the past three centuries, however good those essays may be.

However, the mission of the IEA is to broaden public understanding of the functioning of a free economy. Thus a very significant part of its work has to do with understanding the processes by which public opinion evolves and, against such analysis, to consider how the free economy is viewed, why it is so viewed, and how such a view might be improved.

When the IEA's founder, the late Sir Antony G. A. Fisher, met with future Nobel Laureate F. A. Hayek at the London School of Economics and Political Science (LSE) in the summer of 1945[1], Hayek was between *The Road to Serfdom* and *The Intellectuals and Socialism*. The former was his call to arms, the latter his blueprint for change. In that blueprint he lists the types of people he believes make up the class of 'intellectuals'.[2] Before doing so, however, he makes these points:

- before you try making such a list yourself 'it is difficult to realise how numerous it is'; try it now yourself before going any further – list all the intellectual professions you can think of;
- the 'scope' for the 'activities' of this 'class' or group constantly increases in modern society; and
- 'how dependent on it (that is, the class of intellectuals) we have become.'

---

[1] See *Hayek, Fisher and The Road to Serfdom*, my Introduction to the IEA's November 1999 reprint of the Reader's Digest *Condensed Version of The Road to Serfdom*, pp. xi-xix. It was at this meeting that Hayek told Fisher '...reach the intellectuals, the teachers and writers, with reasoned argument. It will be their influence on society which will prevail and the politicians will follow.'

[2] In a letter to Fisher of 5 January 1985 Hayek confirms that this essay 'gives a clear account of what I had then in mind in giving you the advice I did'. Hayek later in that letter claims to have found the essay 'pleasantly good' on his rereading of it.

Hayek's list then goes on as follows:

- 'journalists, teachers, ministers, lecturers, publicists, radio commentators, *writers of fiction* (my emphasis), cartoonists, and artists – all of whom may be masters of the technique of conveying ideas but are usually amateurs so far as the substance of what they convey is concerned'; and
- 'many professional men and technicians, such as scientists and doctors, who through their habitual intercourse with the printed word become carriers of new ideas outside their own fields and who, because of their expert knowledge of their own subjects, are listened to with respect on most others'.

To Hayek the term intellectual is not very satisfactory because it does not give a full picture of the size of this group of 'secondhand dealers in ideas'. This lack of a precise term he thinks has deterred serious study of the role of such people. He also attempts his own definition which has always delighted me, ever since I first read it as an undergraduate at the LSE.

In Hayek's view, when someone is performing the intellectual function he or she is *not* an 'original thinker' nor a 'scholar or expert in a particular field'. In performing intellectual work he or she does *not* 'possess special knowledge of anything in particular' and 'need *not* even be particularly intelligent'. What the intellectual does have is 'the wide range of subjects on which he can readily talk and write' and 'a position or habits through which he becomes acquainted with new ideas sooner than those to whom he addresses himself'.

Hayek presents a bleak picture. He is clearly saying that this large class of intellectuals consists of two categories. In the first are the people who are expert at conveying ideas but are complete and utter amateurs when it comes to substance and need not even be particularly intelligent. In the second are people who are the true experts in a particular small area; unfortunately this gives them the standing such that they are listened to with respect in all kinds of other areas well outside their areas of competence.

Hayek often told the story of how he nearly turned down the award of the Nobel Prize for Economic Science in 1974 because he feared the impact on him of being asked to comment on anything and everything under the sun with people hanging on, and possibly acting on, every word. Likewise former world number one ranked golfer David Duval (whose tour nickname is 'the intellectual' because he says he both reads, and understands the ideas behind, the novels of Ayn Rand), was staggered at the range of questions, from astronomy to zoology, put to him while he enjoyed that top spot. Fortunately for both golf and society he was sufficiently intelligent to laugh off such inquiries.

Hayek's point about the intellectual not needing to know too much was brilliantly illustrated in *Don't Quote Me: Hi, My Name Is Steven, and I'm A Recovering Talking Head* by Dr Steven Gorelick in *The Washington Post* Outlook Section, Sunday, 27 August 2000. Dr Gorelick is special assistant to the President at the City University of New York's Graduate School and University Center and his Outlook piece was condensed from the 21 July issue of the *Chronicle of Higher Education.*

Gorelick is an expert on how communities on the one hand, and news organisations on the other hand, respond to high-profile violent crimes. Over a ten year period he found that having the Dr title, an academic job and being the kind of person who keeps up with the issues of the day, he experienced 'expertise creep' and was soon commenting on topics far outside his general area of expertise.

His moment of truth came when he was asked, 'Should adopted children be encouraged to locate their birth parents?' He framed a suitable response in his mind: 'It is probably not possible for an adult to form a complete, integrated personality without knowing fundamental facts about his or her personal history'. Suddenly he realised he 'knew absolutely nothing about adoption'. He declined to comment and ever since has taken 'the pledge' under which he refuses to be given a platform as an expert on something he knows nothing about. One would think this would be easy. Why would people want your view on something you know nothing about? He reports it is hard as the telephone rings with requests for his views on euthanasia, socialisation and military readiness.

In the Hayekian vision of change there are experts and original thinkers or scholars, that is, firsthand dealers in ideas. But we are 'almost all ordinary men' outside our specialist fields and thus terribly dependent on the class of intellectuals or secondhand dealers in ideas, including novelists, for access to the ideas and work of the experts. The intellectuals truly are the gatekeepers of ideas 'who decide what views and opinions are to reach us, which facts are important enough to be told to us, and in what form and from what angle they are to be presented. Whether we shall ever learn of the results of the work of the expert and the original thinker depends mainly on their decision'.

Time and again IEA authors have turned to the theme of what makes public opinion from *Not from benevolence:Twenty years of economic dissent*[3] to *The Emerging Consensus? Essays on the interplay between ideas, interests and circumstances in the first 25 years of the IEA;*[4] and from *Ideas, Interests and Consequences*[5] to *British Economic Opinion: A Survey of A Thousand Economists.*[6] A recent Liberty Fund video, in its *Intellectual Portrait* series, in which Lord Harris and Arthur Seldon are interviewed about the IEA's influence on opinion, is in the same tradition, and, as this Readings concerns itself with 'writers of fiction', mention must also be made of Michael Jefferson's chapter, 'Industrialisation and Poverty: In Fact and Fiction' in *The Long Debate on Poverty.*[7]

In the chapters that follow one is faced with a rather damning picture of prodigiously wasteful, yet Scrooge-like businessmen who are abnormal and antagonistic; corrupt, cunning and cynical; dishonest, disorderly, doltish, dumb and duplicitous; inhumane, insensitive and irresponsible; ruthless; unethical and unprincipled; and villainous to boot. Direct data, loved by economists, are not available, but in the closely related field of TV entertainment some relief is to hand.[8] The Washington DC-based Media Institute tracked the portrayal of businessmen in 200 episodes of 50 prime time TV programmes. It found that:

- 'Over half of all corporate chiefs on television commit illegal acts ranging from fraud to murder.'
- 'Forty-five percent of all business activities on television are portrayed as illegal.'
- 'Only 3 percent of television businessmen engage in socially or economically productive behavior.'

---

[3] Hobart Paperback 10, Institute of Economic Affairs, 1977, 2nd Impression 1977.

[4] Hobart Paperback 14, Institute of Economic Affairs, 1981

[5] Readings 30, Institute of Economic Affairs, 1989.

[6] Research Monograph 45, Institute of Economic Affairs, 1990.

[7] Readings 9, Institute of Economic Affairs, 1972, 2nd Edition 1974.

[8] Hayek was of course writing at the very dawn of television and were he writing today he would surely have included this medium.

- 'Hard work is usually ridiculed on television as 'workaholism' that inevitably leads to strained personal relationships.'[9]

Put another way, 97 per cent of business is either illegal (Crooks) or duplicitous (Conmen) or foolish (Clowns) and those who practice it have rotten marriages and unhappy kids... of course they would have because they are all emotionally atrophied. Would the data for our novelists be any different? I doubt it.

The only possible TV bright spot is small business. Here the protagonist is not so much a vicious, corrupt, murdering drug dealer masquerading as a city banker, as a dumb, inept, social climber, way out of his league and subject to ridicule. So it is not much of a bright spot.

And in *The Businessman in American Literature* (University of Georgia Press, 1982), Emily Stipes Watts lights on a similar vein, namely 'small, private businessmen' but even then openly admits that 'four sympathetic protagonists...created by three important post-1945 novelists do not compose a dominant trend.' (p. 149). Indeed, less than 20 years later, my US bookstore could not find one of the four titles and was unsure of another.

In some fields of literature, the portrayal of business is more positive. Popular writers such as Neville Shute and Dick Francis between them populate some three score or more high selling books with lots of self employed small business characters who are heroic yet humble; problem-solving and law-abiding; self reliant and self interested but not selfish. Long running British soap operas such as *Coronation Street* and *Eastenders* have their fair share of used car dealers of all types but many of the main characters are utterly respectable smaller business people making wonderful contributions to all the lives around them. It is when one moves to a *Dallas* or to a Booker prize candidate that the picture changes and it is difficult, nay impossible, to point to 'literary capitalism' while 'literary socialism' abounds.

So why is the picture so bleak? Why does the novelist, the writer of fiction, spit at the market, despise its institutions such as private property and the rule of law, and try to bite off the hand that feeds him? Surely Hayek again has part, at least, of the answer for us,

---

[9] *Crooks, Conmen and Clowns: Businessmen in TV Entertainment*: The Media Institute, 1981.

when later in *The Intellectuals and Socialism* he discusses the role of disaffection.

For Hayek, the talented person who accepts our prevailing current norms and institutions faces a wide range of good career paths. However, to those who are 'disaffected and dissatisfied' with the current order 'an intellectual career is the most promising path to both influence and the power to contribute to the achievement of his ideals'.

But Hayek goes further. The top class person not 'disaffected and dissatisfied' is more likely to opt for the scholarly rather than intellectual path whereas his equally able peer who is out to change things will see an intellectual rather than scholarly route as 'a means rather than an end, a path to exactly that kind of wide influence which the professional intellectual exercises.'

Hayek concludes this section by asserting that there is no greater propensity to what he calls socialism among the more intelligent in society than to any other 'ism'. If one gets that impression from the pulpit or in the classroom or from the television or in novels then it is simply because 'among the best minds' there is a higher propensity among the socialists than among, say, the capitalists to 'devote themselves to those intellectual pursuits which in modern society give them a decisive influence on public opinion.'

Should those concerned with the intellectual climate in which business operates be concerned about these scribblers of novels? How should they respond?

The power of fiction to convey a message is beyond question. As Hayek wrote *The Intellectuals and Socialism*, the British Broadcasting Corporation (BBC) was busy establishing a daily 15 minute wireless soap opera set in the mythical country village of Ambridge. Its purpose then was to teach farmers good new agricultural techniques to get the most out of the land in highly rationed post-World War II Britain. Today it is more likely to feature a politically correct lesbian couple on an organic hobby farm wanting to adopt a baby than an ordinary land-owning farmer off to market.

Another BBC offering, the combined 38 episodes of *Yes, Minister*, and *Yes, Prime Minister* by Antony Jay and Jonathan Lynn, are not so much comedy as deeply insightful, highly educational, powerful training movies which have completely altered the way a generation looks at its government. Jay and Lynn's programmes, which were recently voted ninth in a compilation of the 100 best TV shows for the British Film Institute, removed our blinkers.

In the US, commentators from John Chamberlain on ('The Businessman in Fiction', *Fortune*, November 1948, pp. 134-48) have credited 'to some extent' the passage of the 1906 Pure Food and Drug Act directly to Upton Sinclair's depiction of the slaughterhouses of Chicago in *The Jungle*. Chamberlain wondered why, in the face of the incredible impact of his novels, Upton Sinclair continued to write as if nothing had changed, either on the part of the businessman or on the part of the legislators.

Surely the answer is very simple and has close parallels with the so-called 'environment movement' of today. Neither Sinclair nor the leaders of today's 'environment movement' is at all, not remotely, interested in improvement. The idea of a new, improved, kinder, gentler capitalism is utterly alien to them. They want to tear it down and destroy it: the novel or the 'environment movement' is simply a means to an end, the outright destruction of business, the total demise of capitalism.

In both cases – the novelist and the environmentalist – appeasement has never and will never work. Legislation directly addressing Upton Sinclair's worries did not slow him down one jot in the opening decades of the 20th century and likewise with the environmentalists in the closing decades.

So how would I reply to the businessman who says, 'Look, John, we are getting a real bad press here with these writers of fiction. It isn't funny and over the long haul it is damaging our ability to provide our customers with quality products at a good price while simultaneously paying the pension funds who own us a good return. What should we do?'

First, I would urge patience and caution. Three centuries of bad press will not be fixed overnight, and throwing millions of pounds at problems such as this by, say, endowing an Oxbridge Chair of Literary Capitalism is not only futile but also self defeating, as such resources will immediately be captured by the anti-capitalists.

Second, I would say that education is important and I would start a very modest programme of outreach to brand new emerging talent. A day spent visiting a factory or similar capitalist institution would be a positive eye-opener for most, if not all, such talent.

Third, my still modest outreach programme would extend to current leaders, both market-place practitioners and academic theorists, to engage them in whatever way possible.

Lastly, I would argue that incentives do matter, and I would seek to find ways of financially rewarding fiction writers above all who treat business as an honourable, creative, moral and personally satisfying way of life. Some of the pounds spent on appeasing might be better spent on encouraging and rewarding.

Finally a word about the origins of this book. They go back some years now to a series of conversations I had with Fiona Davis, then a policy analyst with the Confederation of British Industry (CBI). Fiona was a regular attender at IEA events and had a degree in English literature from Oxford University. My knowledge of the American literature in this area mentioned above but also including *The Capitalist As Hero In the American Novel* by John ('Jack') R. Cashill (unpublished PhD thesis, Purdue University, August 1982; printed by University Microfilms International, Ann Arbor, Michigan, USA, 1985) led us to discuss the idea of an IEA publication on how business has been treated over the centuries in English literature. Pressures from other commitments stalled Fiona's progress, but serendipitously a favourable reference to Mrs Gaskell's *North and South* in an American magazine brought the name of Professor Arthur Pollard to mind and he caught the baton just in time.

As always, the views expressed in Readings 53 are those of the authors, not the Institute (which has no corporate view), its managing trustees, Academic Advisory Council members or senior staff.

September 2000   JOHN BLUNDELL
General Director
Institute of Economic Affairs

THE AUTHORS

Geoffrey Carnall was taught by C. S. Lewis and Humphry House at Oxford, and worked for a time with a Quaker organisation in India. He later held a lectureship at the Queen's University of Belfast, and then moved to Edinburgh University. For 25 years he was Reader in English Literature there, and is now Honorary Fellow. In 1960 he published *Robert Southey and his Age*, an account of the poet's transformation from an ardent radical to a vehement conservative. He edited and completed John Butt's *The Mid-Eighteenth Century*, the eighth volume of the *Oxford History of English Literature*. He has a long-standing interest in relations between Britain and India, and has edited a symposium on the impeachment of Warren Hastings, as well as editing and completing a history of the Quakers in India by Marjorie Sykes. He is currently writing a biography of Horace Alexander, one of Mahatma Ghandi's English friends.

Angus Easson is Research Professor of English at the University of Salford. He taught at the University of Newcastle upon Tyne and at the Royal Holloway College (University of London), before becoming Foundation Professor of English at Salford in 1977. In 2000, he became Research Professor. He has published widely on Victorian Fiction, including a book on Elizabeth Gaskell and editions of Dickens's *The Old Curiosity Shop* and *Little Dorrit* and of Gaskell's *Mary Barton*, *North and South*, *The Life of Charlotte Brontë*, and *Wives and Daughters*. He is currently working on the representation of domestic space in Victorian literature and is an advisor and contributor to the electronic British Heritage Database.

John Morris teaches English in the Faculty of Arts at Brunel University, where he was formerly Director of English Studies in the Language Centre. He has also lectured for the Universities of Wisconsin, Notre Dame and Oxford. His main research interests concern the impact of technology, commerce and politics on modern literature, language and culture and he is the author of *Writers and Politics in Modern Britain* (1977) and *Exploring Stereotyped Images* (1993). In addition he has contributed essays to *The First*

World War in Fiction (ed. Klein, 1976), *Twentieth Century Suspense*, (ed. Bloom, 1990), *Literature and Culture in Modern Britain* (ed. Bloom and Day, 3 Vols. 1993-2000), *Modern War on Stage and Screen* (ed. Görtschacher and Klein, 1997) and *Stereotypes in Contemporary Anglo-German Relations* (ed. Emig, 2000). John Morris has published poetry and short stories and plans to write more fiction in the future.

Arthur Pollard is Emeritus Professor of English in the University of Hull and has recently also lectured in Church History at that university. He is a graduate in English of the Universities of Leeds and Oxford and in Theology of Hull and London. He taught at Manchester, where he also became Director of General Studies in the Faculty of Arts, before moving to Hull, from where on his retirement he acted as Consultant Professor at Buckingham. Besides a minor specialism in Australian literature, his principal scholarly interests lie in the nineteenth century, where his publications include works on Mrs Gaskell (including her *Letters*, edited with J.A.V. Chapple), Trollope, the Brontes and Thackeray as well as *The Poetical Works of George Crabbe* (with Norma Dalrymple-Champneys) and editing *The Victorians* in The *Penguin History of Literature*. He is also active in local politics and the Church of England.

Allan Simmons is a Senior Lecturer in English Literature at St. Mary's College, Strawberry Hill, a College of the University of Surrey, where he teaches various courses on Modern and Contemporary Literature. He is the General Editor of *The Conradian*, the Journal of the Joseph Conrad Society (UK), devoted to articles and essays concerning the life and works of Joseph Conrad. Dr Simmons has published regularly and widely on the work of Joseph Conrad. His writings address such varied aspects of Conrad's fiction as their Modernist narrative strategies, their implicit post-colonial concerns, and cinematic adaptations of Conrad's novels and short stories. He is the editor of the Centennial Edition of Conrad's novel *The Nigger of the "Narcissus"* for Everyman publishers and a contributor to the *Oxford Reader's Companion to Conrad*. His current projects include co-editing a volume of essays on Conrad's novel *Lord Jim* to mark the centenary of its publication.

W. A. Speck is Emeritus Professor of History at the University of Leeds and President of the Historical Association. His most recent book was *Literature and Society in Eighteenth-Century England: Ideology, Politics and Culture 1680-1820* (Longman, 1998). He is currently working on the life and writings of Robert Southey.

INTRODUCTION
Arthur Pollard
University of Hull

MAKING MONEY IS A DIRTY GAME. That sentence might almost sum up the attitude of English literature towards British business. Few writers have had first-hand experience of the world of commerce and industry. Their world is governed by the imaginative and the spiritual. It is no wonder therefore that they so often despise the other world that they see as materialistic, concerned with the despised but necessary activities of everyday existence, with matters of trade and work and wages and profits. Even if they do not condemn it for its materialism, they will see it as a world where things at best are very ordinary and uninspiring. For the most part, however, concerned as they are with the conflict of vice and virtue, they see business men as profiteers and bullies of their work-people.

As far back as Chaucer, the rogues on the Canterbury pilgrimage include the merchant concealing his debts, the reeve deceiving his lord and the shipman adept at theft and not above murder when it suits his purpose. In later periods a writer here and there may confer occasional favour on a diligent small businessman like Deloney's Jack of Newbury, but a more memorable figure from the Tudor-Stuart period is Massinger's Sir Giles Overreach in *A New Way to Pay Old Debts*, the aptly named stage-counterpart of the notoriously oppressive and ultimately disgraced monopolist, Sir Giles Mompesson. If in this period we find, as R. H. Tawney believed, the beginnings of British capitalism, it would develop amazingly over the next two centuries until with the burgeoning industrial revolution it emerged in recognisably modern form by 1800. It is not therefore until the 19th century and for the most part in the novel, itself often considered a bourgeois manifestation of literature, that we meet business in its various forms as a topic for extensive imaginative consideration.

Authorial attitudes, however, have not changed; imaginative

writers, occupied largely with ethical values, have shown neither sympathy for nor appreciation of materialistic success and the qualities required for its attainment.

As William Speck emphasises, much of the interest in the subject in the early 18th century related to finance. That is not surprising in view of the effect that the South Sea Bubble had on business consciousness, though this, of course, was also the period in which more 'respectable' commercial activity such as the establishment of the Bank of England occurred. Industry also began to develop from the cottage to the factory stage, so that John Dyer in *The Fleece* (1757) could speak, in his ignorance of actual working conditions, of the mill chimneys of Leeds and Birstall with their smoke pouring forth as 'the incense of thanksgiving'! Predominantly, however, England remained agricultural, but with a dramatic transformation affecting this area of the economy also, so that Goldsmith, lamenting rural depopulation caused by the spreading enclosure movement, could write:

Ill fares the land, to hastening ills a prey,
Where wealth accumulates and men decay.

That might be true, but his fellow-poet Crabbe was quick to point out in *The Village* that the rural environment was a place where the garden was not always lovely but more often an abode of poverty, degradation and crime. Similar social effects would later be laid at the door of the new economic order of large-scale industrialism and mass production.

It will be clear from what has already been said that graft, unrestrained greed, and oppression of the poor are among the evils which literature has associated with business. There are yet others, and one which, though in lessening degree, persists into the 20th century is that of class. The self-made man is the envy of those he has outstripped and despised by those with whom his wealth has now provided him the chance to associate, a matter of keeping us 'in our proper stations'. It is beautifully exemplified in Jane Austen and especially in the episode from which Geoffrey Carnall has taken the title of his essay. The rich but vulgar Mrs Elton, daughter 'of a Bristol – merchant, of course, he must be called' (the hesitation and reluctant near-synonym are charged with meaning), snobbishly remarks of a family of her acquaintance: 'How they got their fortune nobody knows. They came from Birmingham which is not a place to promise much. ...One has not great hopes from Birmingham.'

This speech provides a defining moment in our subject. Jane Austen probably agreed with every word her character here spoke, but she questioned the right of Mrs Elton to say it – and the reason was class. The author herself was 'county', she was 'gentry'; her character, despite all her pretensions, is 'trade', and what right has 'trade' to be scornful of Birmingham? Yet Birmingham was not Bristol. Bristol was old, it was merchanting, buying and selling; Birmingham was new, it was the city of Boulton and Watt. Neither, however, was 'county'; both to Jane Austen were 'trade'.

This contempt for 'trade' persisted. We see it in such different contexts as those of Disraeli, Gissing and some of the poems of John Betjeman, but its significance lessens as the extent of engagement with and the degree of concern for business develops in the literature of the 19th century. The range of interest takes in finance and commerce, industry and agriculture. It may be useful to remind ourselves of just some of the examples that the period provided, the massive financial peculation of such precursors of Robert Maxwell as Merdle in Dickens's *Little Dorrit* and Melmotte in Trollope's *The Way We Live Now*, or the trading activities of *Dombey and Son*. There are also the major industrial novels of that single decade 1845-55 – Disraeli's *Sybil*, Dickens's *Hard Times* and Mrs Gaskell's *Mary Barton* and *North and South*. Small-town economic activity often linked to the rural hinterland is illustrated in George Eliot and in Hardy's *The Mayor of Casterbridge*, whilst Hardy supplies a vivid contrast in *Tess of the d'Urbervilles* between the contented prosperity of the Blackmore Vale and the upland starveling acres of Flintcomb Ash.

Whatever the context, it is always fundamentally a matter of men and money. Carlyle, in his idiosyncratic style, points up the conflict between business and literature, between matter and spirit, between life and possessions. The cash-nexus was not really a nexus at all.

> 'Sooty Manchester – it too is built on the infinite Abysses; overspanned by the skyey Firmaments; and there is birth in it and death in it [and there] Brother, thou art a Man, I think; thou art not a mere building Beaver, or two-legged Cotton Spider; thou hast verily a Soul in thee.'[1]

---

[1]   Thomas Carlyle, *Past and Present*, III, Ch. xv.

(Though Carlyle, incidentally, rejected his native Scottish Presbyterianism, it still suffuses his thought and language.) If Jane Austen makes us aware of the relationship of class and business, Carlyle compels us to take account of two other factors – the impact of thoroughgoing materialism on human society and in the reference to 'Sooty Manchester' the effects of industry on the physical environment. In addition, his mention elsewhere in *Past and Present* of Morrison's Pill, a popular quack remedy of the time, illustrates yet another ill in the trading system of the time, one which has its variations in Disraeli's exposure of truck-selling and later in the exploits of Uncle Ponderevo in Wells's *Tono-Bungay*. These examples remind us that fraud is not just bogus finance on a large scale, but quite as often the fleecing of the poor in the very staples of their existence. They are instances of that unrestrained competition which so much occupied Mrs Gaskell in the Manchester settings of her novels. She lived there, and if Jane Austen and Birmingham form one defining moment in our subject, Mrs Gaskell and Manchester mark another. Asa Briggs has called Manchester the 'shock-city' of the 1840s, and in truth what was happening there at that time surpassed the ability of contemporaries either to control or understand. If contempt for business in Jane Austen is rooted in class, in her successors in the mid-19th century contempt sharpened into animosity before the sheer dehumanising effects which industry had brought with it. Population had outpaced the capacity of housing and sanitation. Living conditions for the majority were simply ghastly. We need to remember, however, that this, though an effect of, was not primarily caused by, industry. Mrs Gaskell was very fair about this. She does not underplay the foulness of the environment, but she does not blame the industrialists for it. She does feel deeply for the helpless plight of the workers. John Barton, as she herself stated, is the real inspiration of her first novel, not his daughter, the eponymous heroine. At the same time, like Dickens in *Hard Times*, she noticed the way in which trade-union agitators were quick to exploit the workers in tense industrial situations; and in her later novel, *North and South*, she would take the central character, John Thornton, cotton manufacturer, through a learning process by which he makes the connection between men and money.

Nevertheless, the chronicle of suffering inflicted by industry, as we have it in the 19th-century novel, takes us through sweated labour, class conflict, cut-throat capitalism, bankruptcies and suicides. It is often a grim story of callous individualism where dog eats dog and the devil takes the foremost. And so it continues, but the degree of artistic conviction can sometimes be in inverse proportion to the vehemence of social condemnation. Mrs Gaskell got into trouble with Manchester manufacturers for what they considered to be her bias towards the workers in *Mary Barton*, but in her fair-mindedness she sought to redress the balance in *North and South*.

Perhaps not surprisingly, with their ready sympathy for those who are obviously suffering, creative writers can tend to be too simplistic. Thus Disraeli in *Sybil* has his heroine, the previously unrecognised aristocrat (note class again), resolve matters in what one can only call a fairy-tale solution at the end. In a comparable reversion of what has gone before, Gissing in *Demos* has his hero physically eradicate the new town and factory development and restore the landscape to its pristine pastoral condition! That sort of transformation is difficult to credit, but no more difficult than the relentless catalogue of oppression of the workmen which Robert Tressell describes in his turgid and prolix novel, *The Ragged Trousered Philanthropists* (1914). Mrs Gaskell and Dickens, by their fair-minded portrayal of such sympathetic characters as the enlightened John Thornton and in *Nicholas Nickleby* the Cheeryble brothers, based on the Grants of Ramsbottom (Lancashire), manifest a credibility that is so obviously absent from both the idealised and the excessively condemnatory examples of the industrial novel.

Attitude shows by way of tone. Earnestness was a Victorian characteristic; wit was not. We have to wait until the later years of the 19th century to find this latter faculty deployed upon our subject, though, one has to say, without that deft scalpel-like refinement which Jane Austen always had at her command. Nevertheless, we cannot but admire the effectiveness of Shaw as he makes the glorious impudence of the munitions manufacturer Sir Andrew Undershaft annihilate the ultra-seriousness of his earnest Salvationist daughter, Major Barbara, in the play of that name. Likewise, we appreciate Wells's exposure of Uncle Ponderevo on the one hand and his generous fun at the expense of Mr Polly on the other, whilst Galsworthy's persistent low-key criticism of the materialism of the Forsytes in the saga of that name provides yet another variation in satiric tone: 'Nothing for nothing and remarkably little for sixpence' may be a truism, but it is also a devastating comment on the attitude of mind behind it. Satire is often in one respect at least a confession on the part of the satirist that, though he may condemn, he cannot convert. By the end of the 19th century modern capitalist society had become so firmly established and so complex that criticism, though it might secure the approval of readers, could never be so radical as to threaten the foundations as Manchester manufacturers had once thought it threatened them. That may be one reason why Tressell's vehemence is so much off-key and why the wit of the writers I have mentioned seems more to the point. It speaks better to the mood of the time.

Twentieth-century writers have a different kind of contempt for business from that of their predecessors. Generally speaking, theirs is a development of attitudes first enunciated in the Victorian period and typically expressed by Matthew Arnold, what one might call, to quote from his own phrase from *Culture and Anarchy*, the 'we in Oxford' syndrome, the dislike that intellectual superiority displays for what it regards as uncultured materialism, the denigration of the 'Philistines'. It is there in Forster's contrast of the Schlegels and the Wilcoxes, music against money, in *Howards End*. It is there again in Lawrence's hostile portraits of the manufacturers Gerald Crich (*Women in Love*) and Clifford Chatterley (*Lady Chatterley's Lover*); and once more in T. S. Eliot's 'double whammy' in *The Waste Land* when he condemns the small-house agents' clerk 'on whom assurance sits/As a silk-hat on a Bradford millionaire'. Those who succeed in business are seen as ruthless go-getters, even sinister characters as in some of Conrad's creations, destroyed spiritually by their enslavement to money; whilst of those who are entrapped in the system it is Eliot again who notices the 'death-in-life' of the city workers:

> *A crowd flowed over London Bridge, so many,*
> *I had not thought death had undone so many.*

Nihilistic materialism becomes even more evident as the century progresses, descending, as John Morris concludes his essay by noting, into 'an unprecedented moral quagmire'. This, however, is not just a criticism of business; it is an indictment of the age. In earlier periods criticism had taken the form of protest, outraged by the failure of business to measure up to a set of basic human values. With these values gone, protest has given way to cynicism and despair. Business, like all else, is now seen as operating in the post-modern spiritual vacuum. Literature has lost its bearings and defining moments are no more.

2

EIGHTEENTH-CENTURY ATTITUDES

TOWARDS BUSINESS

W. A. Speck

University of Leeds

IN THE EARLY 18TH-CENTURY, LITERARY REACTIONS TO business activity were largely conditioned by the impact of the Glorious Revolution of 1688 upon society. Above all they were influenced by the rise of the fiscal-military state and by its creation of a special relationship between the government and the City generated by the so-called Financial Revolution.[1] Later, in the middle decades of the century, literary responses to commerce addressed the effects of economic growth and a rising standard of living, which some welcomed as 'progress' but others deplored as 'luxury'.[2] Towards the end of the century incipient industrialisation and class struggle were emerging as themes informing some writings, anticipating the debate between the pessimists and the optimists over the changes wrought by the Industrial Revolution. But the most vociferous literary responses to business activity in the closing decades of the century were responding to the campaign to abolish the slave trade in the British Empire, a campaign which triumphed in 1807.

The term Financial Revolution sums up those measures introduced to underwrite the wars against Louis XIV which occupied the years 1689 to 1697 and 1702 to 1713. These required revenues on a quite unprecedented scale. Moreover, the taxes voted by parliament, although initially adequate for war finance, took time to reach the Treasury. Meanwhile, allies and the armed forces had to

---

[1] See J. Brewer, *The Sinews of Power: War, Money and the English State 1688 - 1783* (1989); P. G. M. Dickson, *The Financial Revolution in England: a study in the development of public credit 1688 - 1756* (1967).

[2] See especially J. Sekora, *Luxury: The Concept in Western Thought, Eden to Smollett* (1977).

be paid and equipped, necessitating the anticipation of revenues. The government therefore resorted to loans secured on the various taxes, at first short term but increasingly long term, until a national debt came into being which depended on faith in the régime's ability to pay the interest. This system of public credit was enshrined in the Bank of England, established in 1694. In return for its privileged financial status the Bank lent £1,200,000 to the Treasury. In 1709 an Act of Parliament increased its capital to £4,402,343 and allowed it to lend another £2,900,000. Other corporations were also involved in the new financial machinery. The East India Company was frequently tapped for loans in return for the confirmation of its privileges. During the 1690s, when there were two companies vying for the government's favours, the state received substantial sums from this source. Thus in 1698, when the 'new' East India company was incorporated, it lent £2,000,000 to the government while in 1708, just before the rival concerns joined to form the United East India Company, a further sum of £1,200,000 was advanced. In 1711 the financial mechanism was completed with the launching of the South Sea Company, which incorporated the state's short-term creditors and transformed some £9,000,000 of debt into the new corporation's stock. These links between the state and the City created a fiscal-military complex which underpinned Britain's newly acquired Great Power status.

Reactions to the New Fiscal-Military State

Reactions to this new financial machinery were mixed. Some welcomed them, but many criticised them. The fiscal-military state created huge vested interests which depended on the success of the novel experiment in public credit. The members of the financial corporations and those who serviced them in the stock exchange, together with the bureaucrats employed in the revenue system, not to mention the armed forces, all had a stake in it. Among those who welcomed its creation were the subscribers to the stock of the three great companies. These numbered around 10,000 individuals, about a third of whom were proprietors of Bank and East India stock. They were overwhelmingly based in London and the Home Counties and derived their incomes largely from non-landed sources. Relatively few landowners had surplus capital to invest in Bank, East India or South Sea stock. Spokesmen for the landed classes were very critical of the 'monied interest', as the investors in government loans were called. Thus J. Briscoe wrote *A Discourse on the late Funds of the Million Act, Lottery Bank and Bank of England shewing that they are injurious to the nobility and gentry and ruinous to the trade of the nation,* in which he argued that they were

'like a canker, which will eat up the gentlemen's estates in land and beggar the trading part of the nation and bring all the subjects in England to be the monied men's vassals.'[3]

In 1709 Henry St John observed that

'we have been twenty years engaged in the two most expensive wars that Europe ever saw. The whole burden of this charge has lain upon the landed interest during the whole time. The men of estates have, generally speaking, neither served in the fleets nor armies, nor meddled in the public funds and management of the treasure. A new interest has been created out of their fortunes and a sort of property which was not known twenty years ago is now increased to be almost equal to the terra firma of our island'.[4]

Jonathan Swift inveighed against this new monied interest the following year in the *Examiner,* observing that

'through the contrivance and cunning of stock jobbers there hath been brought in such a complication of knavery and cozenage, such a mystery of iniquity, and such an unintelligible jargon of terms to involve it in, as were never known in any other age or country in the world'.[5]

He pursued the same theme vigorously in *The Conduct of the Allies.* In it he claimed that in William's reign 'a set of upstarts ... fell upon these new Schemes of raising Mony, in order to create a Mony'd Interest that might in time vie with the Landed'.[6]

By 'a set of upstarts' Swift meant the Whigs who came to power under William III. For the dispute over the conflict of interests

---

[3]   J. Briscoe, *A Discourse on the late funds...* (1696), p. 2.

[4]   Bodleian Library MS Eng. Misc. e. 180 ff. 4-5.

[5]   *Prose Works of Jonathan Swift,* ed. H. Davis (14 vols., 1939-68), Vol. iii (1940), pp. 6 - 7.

[6]   *Ibid.,* Vol. vi (1951), p.10.

allegedly created by the Financial Revolution got caught up in the disputes between the Tory and Whig parties of the later Stuart era. Tories claimed to represent the landed interest and accused the Whigs of cultivating the monied interest. The reality was of course different from the rhetoric. While most landowners probably were Tory, a significant minority were Whigs. And while most investors in the 'funds', as stock in the Bank and the East India Company came to be known, were Whigs, there were nevertheless Tory speculators too. But the rhetoric of party propaganda and polemic has a life of its own quite apart from reality. Thus in the years between 1945 and 1979 the Conservatives were identified with the middle class and the Labour party with the working class, despite the fact that some business and professional voters voted Labour while many more workers voted Conservative.

Certainly Whig writers like Joseph Addison set themselves up as spokesmen for the monied interest. On 3 March 1711 he published an essay in *The Spectator* shortly before an unsuccessful bid by the Tories to wrest control of the Bank of England from the Whigs. It described an allegorical dream in which Mr Spectator saw Public Credit as a beautiful virgin on a throne of gold. Upon the walls were such symbols of English liberty as Magna Carta, the Toleration Act and the Act of Settlement, which she cherished. Her health responded immediately to news reports which were hourly read to her, an allusion to the way that the stock exchange reacted to good and bad news. She was then menaced by six phantoms, Tyranny and Anarchy, Bigotry and Atheism, Republicanism and Jacobitism, the last in the person of the Old Pretender who brandished a sword in his right hand and was rumoured to have a sponge in his left. The sword he pointed at the Act of Settlement, while the sponge was to wipe out the National Debt. At their approach Public Credit fainted, while money bags piled behind her throne. Fortunately she was rescued by such friendly forces as Liberty and the future George I, the Protestant successor.[7]

John Arbuthnot, the Tory creator of John Bull, by contrast, was as critical as Swift of the City and its financial institutions. In his *History of John Bull*, law is an allegory for war, and the celebrated statement 'law is a bottomless pit' is a metaphor for the vast public debt incurred by England in the War of the Spanish Succession. In

---

[7] *The Spectator*, ed. D. F. Bond (5 vols., 1965).

order to finance his law suit 'John began to borrow money upon Bank stock, East India bonds, now and then a farm went to pot'. This put him in the hands of scriveners – financiers who would lend on landed securities:

'such fellows are like your wiredrawing mills, if they get hold of a man's finger they will pull his whole body at last, till they squeeze the heart, blood and guts out of him.'[8]

Not all Whigs were uncritical of the new machinery of public credit. Daniel Defoe could extol the City in his *Tour through the whole Island of Great Britain* and his *Essays* upon Public Credit and Loans and yet deplore *The Villainy of Stock Jobbers*. Other Whig writers deplored not just the unscrupulous manipulation of the financial machinery but the machine itself. Thus in *Cato's Letters*, published in the aftermath of the South Sea Bubble of 1720, John Trenchard and Thomas Gordon attacked the Bank, the East India Company and the South Sea Company. 'The benefits arising by these companies,' they asserted: [9]

'generally and almost always fall to the share of the stock-jobbers, brokers and those who cabal with them; or else are the rewards of clerks, thimble men, and men of nothing; who neglect their honest industry to embark in those cheats, and so either undo themselves and families, or acquire sudden great riches; then turn awkward statesmen, corrupt boroughs where they have not, nor can have, any natural Interests; bring themselves into the Legislature with their peddling and jobbing talents about them, and so become brokers in politicks as well as in stock.'

The bursting of the Bubble, when many who had speculated in South Sea stock were ruined, seemed to confirm the gloomy prophesies of those like Briscoe and Swift who had predicted that the Financial Revolution would be a social disaster. 'The world is turned upside down, topsie turvy', remarked Charles Gildon; 'those who had plentiful fortunes are now in want, and those that were in

---

[8] J. Arbuthnot, *The History of John Bull*, ed. A. W. Bower and R. A. Erikson (1976), pp. 11, 38, 64.

[9] J. Trenchard and T. Gordon, *Cato's Letters* (4 vols., 1755), Vol. iii, pp. 206-13.

want, have now got plentiful fortunes.'[10]

While most of these Cassandras were Tories, a significant voice amongst the critics of the City's new institutions and their involvement with the Bubble was that of opposition or Country Whigs like Trenchard and Gordon. They were moved to write *Cato's Letters* by the débâcle. In them they called for those responsible to be brought to justice, including corrupt politicians as well as the Directors of the South Sea Company. 'Shall a poor pick pocket be hanged for filching away a little loose money,' they demanded, 'and wholesale thieves who rob nations of all that they have be esteemed and honoured?' They even published a letter, allegedly from the public hangman, 'asserting his right to the necks of the overgrown brokers'.[11]

What they shared with Tories was a suspicion of the Court, meaning the ministry and its adherents in the City, whom they accused of conspiring to create a government machine which would benefit monied and military men at the expense of the landed interest and the rest of the mercantile community. Since in their view the constitution was sustained by the stake landowners had in society and the economy, the new interests of money and the expanded machinery of the state brought into being to sustain a standing army threatened to subvert the constitutional freedoms enjoyed by freeborn Englishmen. They were resisting the growth of the military-fiscal state.

'Civic Humanism'

The rhetoric which they employed to articulate this resistance has also been identified as 'civic humanism'. The leading historian of this ideology is Professor J. G. A. Pocock.[12] He traces its pedigree to Machiavelli's cynical exposure of the motives of politicians, and how men in power constantly endeavour to become more powerful. Virtuous citizens must therefore be perpetually vigilant to resist moves by those in authority to undermine their liberty. These Machiavellian notions were transmitted into English political

---

[10] C. Gildon, *All for the better; or the world turned upside down* (1720), p. 3.

[11] *Cato's Letters, op. cit.*, Vol. i, pp. 131-44.

[12] See especially, J. G. A. Pocock, *The Machiavellian Moment: Florentine Political Thought and the Atlantic Revolution* (1975).

discourse in the 18th century through the medium of James Harrington's *Oceana*, written in the mid-1650s as a solution to the problem of preserving the English republic. His investigation of English history in the previous two centuries had led him to the conclusion that power was ultimately based on landed property. Thus he argued that, before the advent of the Tudors, there had been what he termed a Gothic constitution in which the power of the Kings, the Lords and the Commons had been more or less equal. This was because the Crown, the nobility and the gentry had each owned roughly similar amounts of land. Between 1485 and 1640, however, the Crown and the nobility had alienated land to the Commons. This shift in landed wealth caused an accompanying shift in the balance of power, from the Crown and the Lords to the Commons. The readjustment resulted in the Civil War. As Harrington put it, the dissolution of the Gothic constitution caused the war, not the war the dissolution of the constitution. He was concerned to prevent a similar seismic movement which would cause the Commonwealth to collapse, and proposed an agrarian law which would stop men from acquiring enough landed property to threaten the stability of the republic.

With the Restoration in 1660 the Gothic constitution was restored. In constitutional theory the Crown, Lords and Commons were again equally balanced forces. This was regarded as a perfect polity, since at any time two of the three could offset the tendency of a third to acquire more power. Thus the Crown and the Lords could combine to defeat a bid by the Commons to create a democracy, the Crown and the Commons could between them prevent the Lords from aspiring towards oligarchy, and the Lords and Commons could defeat the Crown's bid for tyranny. During the 1680s, however, the Crown came near to erecting an absolute monarchy by keeping parliament in abeyance. The Glorious Revolution was therefore held to have restored equilibrium. The Country writers, however, urged that the subjects should exercise eternal vigilance to prevent it being overturned again. They argued that it was threatened by the development of the fiscal-military state. The growth of the armed forces posed a direct threat, while the Financial Revolution threatened it indirectly. Thus the Court's special relationship with the City gave it opportunities to corrupt the independence of parliament and ultimately of the electorate. The South Sea Bubble narrowly averted the complete subversion of the constitution. Hence the hostility of Country rhetoric to the new machinery of public credit.

Professor Pocock sees this rhetoric in the form of civic humanism as the dominant paradigm of the period before the French Revolution. It certainly was influential, not least in the ideology of colonial resistance to British claims of sovereignty in the War of American Independence. But there were other ideological stances less inimical to the institutions of public credit. As we have seen, Addison and Defoe both welcomed the City's relationship with the state. Bernard Mandeville was another who positively advocated the advantages of the fiscal-military state. His *Fable of the Bees* took issue with those who criticised it for being a means of corrupting the constitution. Mandeville did not deny that it was corrupt – on the contrary, he depicted it as being soused in corruption up to the ears. But where its critics saw this as a source of weakness he asserted that it was a source of strength. As he expressed it in a notorious paradox, 'private vices, public benefits'. The paradox he explained by asserting that such vices as lust and envy generate consumer demand which stimulates the economy.

Debate on 'Luxury': Standards and Quality

Mandeville was contributing to a debate which went beyond the pros and cons of public credit to the question of whether economic growth in general was beneficial to society. This debate centred round the word 'Luxury' in the sense of demands for commodities which drove up the standard and the cost of living. Mandeville was quite convinced that it was beneficial. Luxury 'employed a million of the poor'. It was particularly the conspicuous consumption of the aristocracy whose demand for buildings, furniture, equipages and clothes stimulated the urban economy. Above all, it was the insistence of upper-class women on luxury goods which swelled the demand for them: '...the variety of work that is performed and the number of hands employed to gratify the fickleness and luxury of women is prodigious.'[13]

Swift was convinced that Luxury was detrimental to social well-being. He got Gulliver to complain that he wore 'the workmanship of a hundred tradesmen; the building and furniture of my house employ as many more; and five times the number to adorn my wife'.

---

[13] B. Mandeville, *The Fable of the Bees*, ed. P. Harth (1970).

He was particularly scathing about the extravagance of women, asserting that 'this whole globe of earth must be at least three times gone round, before one of our better female Yahoos could get their breakfast, or a cup to put it in', while

> 'in order to feed the luxury and intemperance of the males, and the vanity of the females, we sent away the greatest part of our necessary things to other countries, from whence in return we brought the materials of diseases, folly and vice to spend among ourselves'.[14]

The dispute over luxury was thus at bottom a debate about the impact of overseas trade on society. Reactionaries like Swift deplored its allegedly corrosive effect on manners and morals, while progressive thinkers like Mandeville welcomed its contribution to improving the standard of living and the quality of life. Among the enthusiasts for the burgeoning commercial activity in the middle of the 18th century was the poet John Dyer, who published a georgic poem in four books, *The Fleece*, in 1757. It celebrated the providential ordering of the global economy, whereby God had distributed different resources throughout the world, the exchange of which between nations benefitted mankind. Commerce was therefore part of the divine plan, and did not deserve aristocratic disdain.

> *To censure Trade*
>
> *Or hold her busy people in contempt,*
>
> *Let none presume.*

The bulk of the *Fleece* was an encomium on the textile industry. Describing the district around Leeds, Dyer observed that 'all is joy; And trade and business guide the living scene'. Among the more reactionary was John Brown, who published a celebrated *Estimate of the Manners and Principles of the Times* in 1756. In it he claimed that there were three stages of commerce. The *first* was confined to the exchange of necessities. The *second* was concerned with trade in conveniences. The *third* exploited demand for luxuries. Where the first two stages were beneficial the third was pernicious since it eroded morality and rendered a nation effeminate. Brown was convinced that it had already corrupted the English aristocracy and

---

[14] J. Swift, *Gulliver's Travels*, ed. H. Davis (1956), pp.19-20, 56, 252-54.

threatened to corrupt the middle and lower orders. By 1763 an anonymous tract, *The Tryal of the Lady Allurea Luxury*, lamented that 'almost every order of people amongst us, even to the meanest of the mechanics, are seduced by her malice'.

The novelist Tobias Smollett joined in the debate. His *Complete History of England*, as well as his novels, can be read as a diatribe against the rising tide of luxury provoked by excessive demand, especially from females. Thus in the *History* luxury is vividly portrayed as a tidal wave which swept in with the Revolution of 1688 and inundated the country under the Hanoverians until by 1748 'an irresistible tide of luxury and excess' had 'flowed through all degrees of the people, breaking down all the mounds of civil polity and opening a way for licence and immorality'.[15] Similar sentiments are expressed in all his novels but above all in *Humphrey Clinker*. Matthew Bramble was taken aback by the prodigal size of London. 'There are many causes that contribute to the daily increase of this enormous mass', he observed, 'but they may be all resolved into the grand source of luxury and corruption.' This was attributed by Lismahago to 'the sudden affluence occasioned by trade' which 'forced open all the sluices of luxury and overflowed the land with every species of profligacy and corruption'. The contagion had even reached his native Scotland.

> 'The Scots, not content with their own manufactures and produce, which would very well answer all necessary occasions, seem to vie with each other in purchasing superfluities from England, such as broadcloth, velvets, stuffs, silks, lace, furs, jewels, furniture of all sorts, sugar, rum, tea, chocolate and coffee.'[16]

Like Mandeville and Swift, Smollett attributed the rise of luxury above all to the insatiable demand of women for a luxurious life style, giving several examples in the novel of wives who had ruined their husbands by living beyond their means. The sexism was quite explicit, for the classical figure Luxuria was a female. Luxury was accused of emasculating society and making it more effeminate.

---

[15] T. Smollett, *The continuation of the complete History of England* (4 vols., 1760-61), Vol. i, p. 56.

[16] T. Smollett, *The Expedition of Humphrey Clinker*, ed. P. Miles (1993), p. 209.

The Financial Revolution – Bribery and Corruption

The debate over Luxury to some extent paralleled that provoked by the Financial Revolution. Those who criticised it tended to be critics of the Court, accusing the régime of exploiting demands for luxury goods in order to corrupt the people, while those who accepted it were more inclined to be Court supporters. Country writers blamed a corrupt aristocracy for conniving with the Court but were also suspicious of plutocrats in the City of London, whether they derived their wealth from stocks or overseas trade. Thus Pope castigated Sir Balaam in his *Epistle to Bathurst*. A 'Citizen of sober fame', he is tempted by the Devil first by the theft of a diamond then by investments which yield profits 'in one abundant show'r of Cent per Cent'. He sells himself to the prime minister, Sir Robert Walpole, by accepting a place at Court and his soul to the devil by accepting a bribe. Pope draws a contrast between corrupt merchants like Sir Balaam who sell out to the Court and independent merchants like the patriot Sir John Barnard who deplore the corruption of the times.

> Sir Balaam's final sell out is when he
> Leaves the dull Cits, and joins (to please the fair)
> The well-bred cuckolds in St James's air.

There were two quite distinct Londons in 18th-century literature. One was the City, the centre of business and commercial life, inhabited by tradesmen and merchants. The other was the Court end of town, frequented by the aristocracy and gentry who visited the capital for the season or even built town houses there in the new streets and squares north of Oxford street. These represented two distinct sets of values. The City was generally praised as the habitat of frugal, respectable citizens who added to the nation's wealth and well-being. For there was general agreement that England was a trading nation and that the business community contributed to the nation's prosperity. In this respect it is significant that when John Bull, who became the nation's symbol, made his first appearance he was not the bucolic farmer he later became but 'the richest tradesman in all the country'.[17] By contrast, the aristocrats who could afford town houses in London at the Court end of town were

---

[17] Arbuthnot, *op. cit.*, p. 11.

generally regarded as decadent. The West End was consequently decried as the scene of luxury and debauchery.

There were some critics of the City who represented merchants as being grasping and avaricious, having profit as their only motive and treating people as commodities. The type was a stock character on the stage. Sir Humphrey Staple, a merchant in a play by Leonard Welsted which appeared in 1727, deplored the representation of his kind in drama. He complains that

> 'The wits and poets make it their business in their plays and prologues to abuse their betters, and that they treat persons of good reputation very injuriously, giving them nicknames such as Nikin, Gripe, Scrape-all, Split farthing and the like; Now Sir I must be plain to tell you that this licence is unreasonable, and that persons of substance and credit ought not to be libell'd by your poets and people of that character.' [18]

Yet Staple himself deserves this reputation for his treatment of his daughter as an asset to be marketed on the marriage market. As he puts it: 'my daughter is my merchandise, and I'll not part with her upon credit; something for something and nothing for nothing, as I often say, is our family wisdom.' He is rebuked for treating his offspring as 'a commodity to be disposed of' by another character who tells him 'beauty is not the common merchandise, to be sold by cant and auction, or to be put up by inch of candle. That is for African slaves, not free born British ladies'.

Hogarth depicts another grasping merchant like Staple in the mercantile father who sells his daughter into wedlock with a noble lord's son in *Marriage à la mode*. The merchant's motive is pure greed, for his daughter's marriage to the aristocratic rake is doomed from the start, as the image in the first plate of the two dogs chained together symbolises. His miserliness is also depicted in the final plate as he takes the wedding ring off his dead daughter's finger. The unsuitability of a *nouveau riche* tradesman as a husband for the daughter of a well-established landed family is one of the reasons why the odious Solmes, a 'prosperous upstart, mushroomed into rank', is objectionable to Richardson's *Clarissa*.

Despite these representations of the unacceptable face of business, there are signs that the image of merchants in literature was slowly improving during the early 18th century. Among poets,

---

[18] L. Welsted, *The Dissembled Wanton: or, my son get money* (1727), p. 26.

Edward Young wrote an ode in 1729 on British trade, 'The Merchant'. This was a celebration of the role of commerce.[19]

> *Britain, fair daughter of the seas,*
> *Is born for trade, to plough her field, the wave,*
> *And reap the growth of every coast...*

In drama the more favourable representation of merchants was largely due to the efforts of Whig dramatists like Sir Richard Steele and George Lillo. Sealand in Steele's *The Conscious Lovers* (1723) is often seen as a turning point in the characterisation of the merchant, as he is eminently honest and upright. 'We merchants are a species of gentry that have grown into the world this last century,' he declaims, 'and are as honourable and almost as useful as you landed folks.' Though the disclaimer is ironic there is still a defensive view of commerce in *The Conscious Lovers*. It was not until the appearance of George Lillo's *The London Merchant* in 1731 that a major production extolled the virtues of trade in its principal characters.

Defoe Champions Commerce

Before that Daniel Defoe had championed the commercial community. Defoe was an unflagging advocate of trade throughout his long career as a journalist and a novelist, from his *Essay upon Projects* published in 1698 to his *Compleat English Tradesman* which appeared in the years 1726 and 1727. His *Tour through the whole island of Great Britain* boasted that

> 'this whole kingdom, as well as the people, as the land, and even the sea, in every part of it, are employed to furnish something ... to supply the city of London with provisions'.[20]

He delighted in the forest of masts below London Bridge, whose ships connected the capital not only to the rest of the kingdom but to the most distant parts of the world. The result was to make Britain 'the most flourishing and opulent country in the world'. His fiction

---

[19] David Shields, *Oracles of Empire: Poetry, Politics, and Commerce in British America 1690 - 1750* (1990), pp. 23-25. Shields claims that 'the task of British literature, according to Young, was to recognise trade as the predominant heroic action in the modern era'.

[20] D. Defoe, *A Tour through the whole island of Great Britain*, ed. P. Rogers (1971), p. 54.

was equally enthusiastic about the benefits arising from commerce. He even introduced a real merchant, Sir Robert Clayton, into *Roxana*. Sir Robert lectures the heroine on the advantages of trade over land, telling her 'that an Estate is a pond, but that a Trade was a spring; that if the first is once mortgag'd it seldom gets clear, but embarrass'd the person for ever; but the merchant had his estate continually flowing'.[21]

Robinson Crusoe can be read as a paean of praise to business activity. Crusoe starts out not as a merchant but as a mariner, leaving home at the age of 18 when he was too old to be apprenticed either to a tradesman or as a clerk to an attorney. As a mariner, however, he made a profit on his first voyage to Guinea, exchanging toys worth £40 for gold dust worth nearly £300,which he says 'made me both a sailor and a merchant'. He therefore 'set up for a Guiney trader'. Later he became a planter in Brazil and after four years began to prosper, until he estimated that in another three or four years he would be worth £3,000 or even £4,000. Then he made the fateful decision to enter the slave trade, which led to his shipwreck and his long sojourn on an island. During his stay there Crusoe becomes a basketmaker, a boatbuilder, a carpenter, a miller, a potter, a tailor and an umbrella maker.

From the bare outline of Crusoe's adventures Defoe might not seem to have found much to commend in the merchant's calling. Yet though Crusoe is inclined to blame Fate for his misfortune, Defoe makes him the author of his own misery, partly through his lack of piety but mainly through his want of prudence. It is his impious refusal to obey his father's wishes which leads to his first shipwreck in the Yarmouth roads, but it is his imprudently overreaching himself in business ventures which indirectly causes his solitary confinement on the island. Defoe, who had himself failed in business, blamed such failures not on economic conditions but on moral and personal faults in the businessman. As he put it in *The Compleat English Tradesman*:

'There must be some failure in the tradesman, it can be no where else; either he is less sober and less frugal, less cautious of what he does, who he trusts, how he lives, and how he behaves, than tradesmen used

---

[21] D. Defoe, *Roxana*, ed. John Mullan (1996), p. 170.

22

to be; or he is less industrious, less diligent, and takes less care and pains in his business, or something is the matter.'[22]

Crusoe himself admits that, at a time when his plantation was beginning to flourish, 'for me to think of such a voyage was the most preposterous thing that ever man in such circumstances could be guilty of'. He triumphs over adversity by learning to be both pious and prudent. It is especially in his acquisition of skills for physical survival that Defoe indicates his admiration of the characteristics which enabled men to survive in trade.

Joseph Addison also championed the commercial community in the pages of *The Spectator*. 'There are not more useful members in a commonwealth than merchants', he observed in one essay. 'They knit mankind together in a mutual intercourse of good offices, distribute the gifts of Nature, find work for the poor, add Wealth to the Rich, and magnificence to the Great.' In the archetypal merchant he created with Sir Andrew Freeport, one of the leading members of the Spectator Club, he epitomised these virtues. At his first appearance we are told that he is:

'a merchant of great eminence in the City of London: a person of indefatigable industry, strong reason and great experience. His notions of trade are noble and generous, and (as every rich man has usually some sly way of jesting, which would make no great figure were he not a rich man) he calls the sea the British common.'[23]

And yet in the end Sir Andrew sells out and becomes a country gentleman. When he resigned from the Spectator Club he informed its members that he was leaving business to set up as a landed proprietor:

'as the greatest part of my estate has been hitherto of an unsteady and volatile nature, either tost upon seas or fluctuating in funds; it is now fixed and settled in substantial acres and tenements.'

In this respect Sir Andrew Freeport is the archetype of the successful businessman who acquires a country estate and leaves commerce. Their upwardly mobile ambitions were both satirised

---

[22] D. Defoe, *The Compleat English Tradesman* (2 vols., 1727), Vol. 2, p. vi.

[23] *The Spectator*, Vol. i, pp.10-11; Vol. iv, p. 468.

and sanctioned by contemporary writers. And ultimately the goal of landownership has been criticised for eroding the entrepreneurial spirit in England.

The entrepreneurs who rose by manipulating the fiscal system set up in the Financial Revolution to acquire landed estates and set themselves up as country gentlemen were stock characters in the political satire of the age. The archetype of these was Thomas Double, a character created by Charles Davenant, who started out as a shoemaker's apprentice in London, but left shoemaking to buy a place in the Customs with money bequeathed to him by his grandmother 'who sold barley-broth and furmity by Fleet ditch'. In James II's reign, however, he was convicted of fraud and turned out of the customs service. Where he had previously been a loyal Tory, he now became 'a furious Whig'. When his grandmother's legacy ran out he was 'forced to be a corrector of a private press in a garret, for three shillings a week'. Then the Revolution improved his condition, for he was able by an outrageous confidence trick to pass himself off as an agent of the Prince of Orange and by even more brazen cheating at dice to win money from the man he had conned. He then set out to make his fortune from the new régime, starting with shares in the discovery of concealed Crown lands, and moving into the big time with enormous frauds in the disposal of confiscated Irish estates. Double claimed the credit for the Financial Revolution, which had 'run the nation head over ears in debt by our funds, and new devices'. He confessed that £50,000 had stuck to his fingers when he acted as receiver of taxes, and although it had cost him £20,000 to buy off a parliamentary inquiry by bribing MPs, he still had enough left to live at ease, with his country seat, a town house and a coach and six. [24]

A Gentry of War Profiteers?

Tory satirists built on Davenant's Double to depict a whole new upstart gentry of Whig war profiteers who allegedly upheld the corrupt ministry of Walpole. They were indulging in what has been termed 'the politics of nostalgia', imagining a golden age when the country had been ruled by its hereditary aristocracy and gentry, before access to landed estates had been opened up to parvenus from

---

[24] C. Davenant, *The True Picture of a Modern Whig* (1701), pp. 15-31.

the City of London.[25] That such an era existed largely in their imaginations was irrelevant, as was the fact that entry into the landed classes remained very restricted throughout the 18th century. Most businessmen who aspired to life in the countryside sought a house in the country with a few acres rather than a country house with tenanted farms. Travellers noticed these country homes on the approaches to London in Essex and Surrey. Thus in Stratford, Essex, John Macky observed in 1714:

'above two hundred little country houses for the conveniency of the citizens in summer, where their wives and children generally keep, and their husbands come down on Saturdays and return on Mondays.'[26]

Similarly, Defoe noted on the other side of town, along the road from Richmond to London, 'citizens' country houses whither they retire from the hurries of business, and from getting money, to draw their breath in a clean air'.[27] Most businessmen who had houses in the country were commuters rather than landed gentry. Nevertheless, it only needed a few notorious examples in reality to feed the nostalgic myth. The most outstanding was the acquisition by the goldsmith Sir Charles Duncombe of the Helmsley estate of the second Duke of Buckingham, reputedly for £80,000 in cash, to feed the paranoia of the landed interest. As Pope expressed it:

And Hemsley once proud Buckingham's delight,
Slides to a Scriv'ner or a City knight.[28]

Upstart landowners who were allegedly usurping the place of traditional landlords were accused of introducing inappropriate business methods into estate management. Traditionally, country gentlemen were expected to act as patriarchs presiding over their local communities. The relationship between them and their tenants and neighbours was one of reciprocal rights and duties. Inferiors owed deference to their superiors but these in turn were required to

[25] Isaac Kramnick, *Bolingbroke and his Circle: The Politics of Nostalgia in the Age of Walpole* (1968).

[26] J. Macky, *A Journey through England* (1732), p. 30.

[27] D. Defoe, *A Tour through the whole island of Great Britain*, ed. P. Rogers (1971), p. 171.

[28] *The Poems of Alexander Pope*, ed. J. Butt (1963), p. 624.

treat those below them with sympathy and understanding, not rack-renting them in the interests of profit maximisation. The new breed of landlord was accused of acting more like patricians than patriarchs, reducing the traditional relationship to a crude cash nexus. Pope epitomised these contrary types in the characters of the Man of Ross and Timon. The Man of Ross, who was based on a real character, John Kyrle, who lived at Ross on Wye, was depicted as an exemplary patriarch.

> *Behold the Market - place with poor o'erspread!*
> *The MAN OF ROSS divides the weekly bread:*
> *Behold yon Alms - house, neat, but void of state,*
> *Where Age and Want sit smiling at the gate:*
> *Him portion'd maids, apprentic'd orphans blest,*
> *The young who labour, and the old who rest.*
> *Is any sick? The MAN OF ROSS relieves,*
> *Prescribes, attends the med'cine makes, and gives.*
> *Is there a variance? enter but his door,*
> *Balk'd are the Courts, and contest is no more...*[29]

By contrast, Timon exploited his position as a landlord to gratify his own aspirations rather than to satisfy those of his neighbours.

> *At Timon's Villa let us pass a day,*
> *Where all cry out "What sums are thrown away!"*
> *So proud, so grand, of that stupendous air,*
> *Soft and Agreeable come never there.*
> *Greatness with Timon dwells in such a draught*
> *As brings all Brobdignag before your thought.*
> *To compass this his building is a Town,*
> *His pond an Ocean, his parterre a Down:*
> *Who but must laugh, the Master when he sees,*
> *A puny insect, shiv'ring at a breeze!*
> *Lo, what huge heaps of littleness around!*
> *The whole a labour'd Quarry above ground.*[30]

---

[29] *Ibid.*, p. 582.

[30] *Ibid.*, p. 592.

Timon has no sense of serving the community. He uses his wealth only to indulge his own vanity. His dining-room is described as a temple, the object of his worship being himself. Pope had to admit, however, that Mandeville had a point when he claimed that the conspicuous consumption of the aristocracy stimulated economic growth. As he conceded of Timon:

> *Yet hence the Poor are cloath'd, the Hungry fed;*
> *Health to himself, and to his Infants bread*
> *The Lab'rer bears: What his hard Heart denies,*
> *His charitable Vanity supplies.*[31]

Yet such side-effects of luxury and vanity were not as beneficial to society in Pope's view as an economy in harmony with nature. The Man of Ross with his traditional patriarchal ways stimulated economic activity more naturally than did Timon. This is symbolised by their variant uses of water. Thus the Man of Ross conducted water from the dry rock:

> *Not to the skies in useless columns tost,*
> *Or in proud falls magnificently lost,*
> *But clear and artless, pouring thro' the plain*
> *Health to the sick, and solace to the swain.*

At Timon's villa:

> *Two Cupids squirt before; a Lake behind*
> *Improves the keeness of the Northern Wind.*

After Timon's death the estate will be developed more in conformity with nature, so that

> *Another age shall see the golden Ear*
> *Imbrown the Slope,and nod on the Parterre,*
> *Deep Harvests bury all his pride has plann'd,*
> *And laughing Ceres re - assume the land.*[32]

---

[31] *Ibid.*, p. 594.

[32] *Ibid.*, p. 594.

Swift drew a similar contrast between a patriarchal landlord practising traditional methods of estate management and upstart landowners exploiting new techniques in the persons of Lord Munodi and his neighbours whom Gulliver met in Balnibari. Munodi is presented as an archetypal patriarch. 'Everything about him,' Gulliver recorded, 'was magnificent, regular and polite.' He treated the traveller with much kindness and in a most hospitable manner in his town house and then took him to his country seat, where Gulliver did not 'remember to have seen a more delightful prospect'. The estate was divided into neat and prosperous farms, while the house was 'a noble structure, built according to the best rules of ancient architecture'. Gulliver notes that the neighbouring lands are barren in contrast, but Munodi confesses that his old-fashioned methods are derided by his neighbours and that

'he doubted he must throw down his houses in town and country, to rebuild them after the present mode; destroy all his plantations, and cast others into such a form, as modern usage required; and give the same directions to all his tenants'.[33]

The severest condemnation of businesslike methods of estate management found expression in a poem by Oliver Goldsmith, *The Deserted Village*. Goldsmith linked changes in the countryside to the rise of luxury which in his view caused a rise in the standard of living for the privileged classes but not to the mass of the rural population: 'the rich man's joys increase, the poor's decay.' Auburn, an idyllic example of a traditional community, is transformed by a 'tyrant', 'one only master' who 'grasps the whole domain', and 'trade's unfeeling train' into 'The Deserted Village'. 'The man of wealth and pride,' like Timon, 'has robbed the neighbouring fields of half their growth' in order to extend the bounds of his country house. Worse still, he has enclosed 'the fenceless fields' and even the common land. As a result the villagers are forced out to seek a livelihood either in a town or in the colonies.

Thus fares the land by luxury betrayed,
In nature's simplest charms at first arrayed;

---

[33] *Gulliver's Travels, op. cit.*, pp. 175-76.

But verging to decline, its splendours rise,
Its vistas strike, its palaces surprise;
While scourged by famine from the smiling land,
The mournful peasant leads his humble band,
And while he sinks, without one arm to save,
The country blooms - a garden and a grave.[34]

Other writers were more inclined to applaud than to deplore what they saw as the refreshing of the landed classes by new entrants from the business community. Addison made this quite clear by the contrast he drew between the traditional landlord, Sir Roger de Coverley, and the policy which Sir Andrew Freeport intended to adopt towards the estate he acquired through commercial success. Sir Roger is an archetypal patriarch, 'the best master in the world', with 'a mixture of the father and the master of the family'. 'Family' is here used to denote Sir Roger's household as well as his immediate kin. His servants have a particular fondness for him, greeting him with joy when he makes his way from London to his Worcestershire seat in the company of Mr Spectator:

> 'some of them could not refrain from tears at the sight of their old master, and every one of them pressed forward to do something for him, and seemed discouraged if they were not employed.'

The baronet's kindness to his servants extended to their children, so that he paid the premium for his coachman's grandson to become apprenticed. He is kind to his tenants as well as to his servants, so that 'the greatest part of Sir Roger's estate is tenanted by persons who have served himself or his ancestors'. Being a good churchman he has given all his fellow parishioners a hassock and a copy of the Book of Common Prayer. In short, as Sir Roger confides to Mr Spectator, he 'resolved to follow the steps of the most worthy of my ancestors ... in all the methods of hospitality and good neighbourhood'. In return he is 'beloved and esteemed by all about him. He receives a suitable tribute for his universal benevolence to mankind in the returns of affection and goodwill which are paid him by every one that lives within his neighbourhood'. [35]

---

[34] O. Goldsmith, *The Deserted Village*, (1770), pp. 16-17.

[35] *The Spectator*, Vol. i, pp. 439-40, 454-55, 460, 464, 498.

Sir Roger de Coverley's old-fashioned values are not upheld by the merchant Sir Andrew Freeport. There is an explicit rejection of the baronet's ideas in favour of a more business-oriented ideology in a passage wherein the two members of the Spectator Club discuss charity. Sir Andrew objects to Sir Roger's indiscriminate benefaction:

'If to drink so many hogsheads is to be hospitable, we do not contend for the fame of that virtue; but it would be worthwhile to consider whether so many artificers at work ten days together by my appointment, or so many peasants made merry on Sir Roger's charge, are the more obliged? ... Sir Roger gives to his mane; but I place mine above the necessity or obligation of my bounty.'[36]

Sir Andrew's practical rather than sentimental approach to such matters is extolled when he buys an estate and plans to run it along lines very different from the traditional methods employed by Sir Roger:

'This will give me great opportunity of being charitable in my way, that is, in setting my poor neighbours to work, and giving them a considerable subsistence out of their own industry. My gardens, my fishponds, my arable and pasture grounds shall be my several hospitals or rather workhouses, in which I propose to maintain a great many indigent persons who are now starving in my neighbourhood ... As in my mercantile employment I so disposed my affairs, that from whatever corner of the compass the wind blew it was bringing home one or other of my ships; I hope, as a husbandman, to contrive it so, that not a shower of rain, or a glimpse of sunshine shall fall upon my estate without bettering some part of it, and contributing to the products of the season.'[37]

Although Robinson Crusoe extolled the advantages of the middle station of life at the outset of his career, he ended it as a substantial landowner and proprietor of an overseas colony. Walter Shandy, the presumed father of Sterne's Tristram, was a country gentleman established at Shandy Hall at the time of Tristram's birth, but 'was originally a Turkey merchant' who 'had left off business for some years in order to retreat to, and die upon, his paternal estate'.

---

[36] *Ibid.*, Vol. ii, pp. 20-21.

[37] *Ibid.*, Vol. iv, pp. 467-68.

Wealth and Greatness the Cause of Corruption

Adam Smith both commented on and criticised this social aspiration to emulate the great landed proprietors. In *The Theory of Moral Sentiments* he observed the 'disposition of mankind to go along with all the passions of the rich and the powerful'. He went on to deplore it as

> 'the great and most universal cause of the corruption of our moral sentiments. That wealth and greatness are often regarded with the respect and admiration which are due only to wisdom and virtue; and that the contempt, of which vice and folly are the only proper objects, is often most unjustly bestowed upon poverty and weakness, has been the complaint of moralists of all ages.'[38]

The discrepancy between the social and moral hierarchies was also a concern of the 18th-century novel. Although it is often regarded as a bourgeois art form it is much more concerned with the landed classes than with the business world. Eighteenth-century novelists explored the social relationships of the aristocracy and gentry rather than those of the middle classes. Insofar as they dealt with concerns of those below the landed élite they tended to discuss professional men – the clergy, doctors, lawyers and soldiers – rather than merchants and manufacturers.

Until the 1790s novelists did not generally attack the landed élite *per se*. On the contrary, while they castigated landlords who abused their privileged position, they held out the prospect of their heroes and heroines acquiring élite status as a desirable goal. Under the impact of the French Revolution, however, novels began to appear which challenged the desirability of identifying with aristocracy as such. In Gothic novels aristocrats were depicted as exploiters of their position in society in order to exert social and psychological terror over their inferiors. The most notorious of these figures was Montoni, the tyrannical Italian nobleman of Anne Radcliffe's sensational *Mysteries of Udolpho*. He was but the archetype of Gothic villains in this popular genre. Jacobin novels were even more explicit in their condemnation of aristocrats. Godwin's *Caleb Williams* castigated not just individuals who failed to live up to the

---

[38] A. Smith, *The Theory of Moral Sentiments*, ed. D. D. Raphael and A. L. McFie (1976), pp. 61-62.

patriarchal ideals of aristocracy but the very system itself which sustained the landed élite in its position.

Writers in the late 18th century did not, however, espouse bourgeois values to offset those of the aristocracy. On the contrary they deplored the increasing urbanisation of the century's closing decades and advocated a rural rather than an urban way of life. In the incipient class war associated with industrialisation they tended to sympathise with the poor against their new exploiters, the industrial entrepreneurs. The early Romantics thus anticipated the debate on whether or not the social impact of the Industrial Revolution had been more detrimental than beneficial, a debate which still can divide historians into optimists and pessimists. The Romantic view was definitely pessimistic.

William Cowper anticipated the Lake poets in many ways in his poem *The Task*, and not least in deploring the way men had lost sight of Nature in cities which 'breathe darkness all day long'. The celebrated Preface to *Lyrical Ballads* in 1798 criticised 'the increasing accumulation of men in cities'. As for the impact of industry, Blake's condemnation of 'dark satanic mills' is well known, though it can be disputed whether it refers to factories or mental processes. A less equivocal critique of industrialisation came from Robert Southey who, writing about the increase in poverty in his *Letters from England* (1807), claimed that

> 'many causes have contributed to the rapid increase of this evil... But the manufacturing system is the main cause; it is the inevitable tendency of that system to multiply the number of the poor, and to make them vicious, diseased and miserable'.

He illustrated these propositions by getting the fictitious author of the *Letters*, Don Manuel Alvarez Espriella, to visit a Manchester cotton mill. It employed two hundred hands, including small children. The mill owner assured Espriella that they were well treated. 'Here Commerce is the queen witch,' observed the Don, 'and I had no talisman strong enough to disenchant those who were daily drinking of the golden cup of her charms.' For in Southey's view the reality was very different. Debauchery, disease, ignorance and poverty were prevalent. The employees either died of diseases inherent in their environment,

> 'or they live to grow up without decency, without comfort and without

hope, without morals, without religion, and without shame, and bring forth slaves like themselves to tread in the same path of misery.'[39]

Literary Condemnation of the Slave Trade

The comparison of workers with slaves was highly charged in the year 1807, which saw the abolition of the slave trade in the British Empire. That had come about remarkably quickly following a campaign which really got going only 20 years before. Previously there had been isolated condemnation of slavery and the traffick in Africans which had been echoed in literature. Even John Dyer, whose poem *The Fleece* enthused about commerce, drew the line at the slave trade. Lawrence Sterne wrote a critique of the treatment of Africans by Europeans in the last volume of *Tristram Shandy*. While he was working on it he received a letter from Ignatio Sancho, the Duke of Montagu's black butler. Ignatios wrote: 'I am one of those people whom the illiberal and vulgar call a nigger.' He had read and admired *Tristram Shandy* and also Sterne's *Sermons*. One sermon in particular, 'Job's Account of the Shortness and Troubles of Life considered', had impressed him because of what he called a 'truly affecting passage' on slavery. 'Consider slavery — what it is,' Sterne observed in it, 'how bitter a draught! and how many millions have been made to drink of it.' Sancho asked Sterne to write further on the subject, which 'handled in your own manner, would ease the yoke of many, perhaps occasion a reformation throughout our islands'. Sterne obliged by including a passage in the ninth volume of *Tristram Shandy* in which Corporal Trim asks Uncle Toby, doubtingly, if a negro has a soul. Toby replies: 'I suppose God would not leave him without one, any more than thee or me' ... 'Why then an' please your honour, is a black wench to be used worse than a white one?' 'I can give no reason,' said my uncle Toby. 'Only,' cried the Corporal, shaking his head 'because she has no one to stand up for her.' ''Tis that very thing, Trim, quoth my uncle Toby, which recommends her to protection — and her brethren with her; 'tis the fortune of war which has put the whip into our hands now — where it may be hereafter, heaven knows.' [40]

---

[39] R. Southey, *Letters from England*, ed. J. Simmons (1951), pp. 142-47, 207-13.

[40] L. Sterne, *Tristram Shandy*, (Everyman, 1914), p. 447.

'In 1776 Adam Smith wrote the economic death warrant for slavery,' observes David Shields in one of the few investigations of the literary response to the campaign to abolish slavery.

'In a passage that became quasi-scriptural among abolitionists during the 1800s, Smith declared that "the experience of all ages and nations, I believe, demonstrates that the work done by slaves, though it appears to cost only their maintenance, is in the end the dearest of all. A person who can acquire no property, can have no other interest but to eat as much, and to labour as little as possible".' [41]

Shields notes 'the formation in the 1770s of a school of poets whose members included William Cowper, John Marjoribanks and Hannah More' who took up the cause of slaves. He also singles out James Field Stansfield's *The Guinea Voyage* as 'the rhetorical horizon of anti-slavery poetry'.[42] In it Stansfield imagines the African being handed over to a slave ship.

Confin'd with chains, at length the hapless slave,
Plung'd in the darkness of the floating cave,
With horror sees the hatch-way close his sight –
His last hope leaves him with the parting light.

Historians have lately stressed the economic rather than the evangelical causes behind the abolition of the slave trade in 1807.[43] The literary response to the campaign, however, appealed more to the hearts than to the purses of readers in the closing decades of the 18th century.

---

[41] Shields, *op. cit.*, p. 86, citing *The Wealth of Nations*. As Shields notes (p. 241): 'no adequate literary history of the abolitionist poets exists, and to write one would be a worthy effort.'

[42] *Ibid.*, p. 82. To them might be added William Blake, who wrung the withers with his poem the 'Little Black Boy'.

[43] J. Walvin, Slaves and Slavery: *The British Colonial Experience* (1992), pp. 88-100.

3

EARLY NINETEENTH CENTURY:

BIRMINGHAM – 'SOMETHING DIREFUL

IN THE SOUND'

Geoffrey Carnall

University of Edinburgh

Introduction

THE STRIKING EXPANSION OF THE BRITISH ECONOMY in the latter half of the 18th century and after is to some extent a matter of technology – a matter, too, of the industrial organisation needed to exploit that technology. But the technology was only one element in a large social process much more difficult to analyse. What else was going on in the development of a society where commerce was becoming ever more influential? Industrial expansion, and its relation to the economy as a whole, remains a matter of continuing research and debate. One area of inquiry is essentially psychological: How did this phenomenon affect the mental and emotional condition of the people who lived through it? How did they perceive it?

After the lapse of two centuries we have become so inured to an accelerating process of technological development, with all the consequences that flow from it, that the notion of an 'industrial revolution' takes on an air of threadbare commonplace. The raw experience of living in an economy whose productivity has begun to multiply itself many times over must have been profoundly disorientating – the more so when among its side-effects were substantial movements of population, large-scale working-class political activity demanding radical social change, and, just to keep everyone insecure, a recurrent tendency for banks to fail and for the currency they issued to become worthless.

The disorientation is indeed apparent in the poetry and fiction of this period. Gothic horrors, the excitements of power and a morbid fascination with powerlessness, manifest themselves in a bewildering variety of ways, converging in such characteristic texts as Coleridge's *Ancient Mariner* and Shelley's *Ode to the West Wind*. A whole range of solitary figures, from Wordsworth's deserted women to Byron's Childe Harold, testify to a deeply-felt insecurity, a sense of irremediable homelessness.

On the other hand, the sense of power could be a source of reassurance. Wordsworth in *The Prelude* expressed the conviction that a benignant spirit was abroad that might not be withstood. In *Prometheus Unbound*, Shelley prophesied that a subversive Demogorgon would rise up irresistibly and overthrow a tyrannical Jupiter, symbol of the oppressive old régime of aristocrats and churchmen. But neither poet was particularly willing to register the extent to which their millennial hopes were based upon social conditions generated by technological innovation on an unprecedented scale. Indeed, Wordsworth famously deplored in the preface to *Lyrical Ballads* the effects of 'the increasing accumulation of men in cities', and saw society's salvation in the rediscovery of the virtues of humble and *rustic* life.

Walter Scott's Nostalgia for the Old Order

A more balanced response may be found in the novels of Walter Scott. He repeatedly articulates the passing of an old order to a new in a way which evidently appealed to his contemporaries and gained him an unprecedentedly large readership. No previous novelist had ever been as commercially successful as the Great Unknown, 'the Author of *Waverley*'. But his success is linked to his preoccupation with issues that no longer aroused strong passions, the question of the Jacobite claim to the British crown and, to some extent, the relations between England and Scotland. He is aware – how should he not be? – of the contemporary transformation of the economy. In an appendix to *The Monastery* (1820), he refers to James Watt as

> 'the man whose genius discovered the means of multiplying our national resources to a degree perhaps even beyond his own stupendous powers of calculation and combination; bringing the treasures of the abyss to the summit of the earth, ... commanding manufactures to arise, as the rod of the prophet produced water in the desert'.

But what appeals to Scott is Watt's wide culture and manifold interests, and, above all, his addiction to fiction, 'shameless and obstinate peruser of novels' that he was. Similarly with the poet George Crabbe. He was a friend of the inventor of a power loom, Edmund Cartwright, and remarked to Cartwright's son how much he admired the father's 'unwearied and active mind'.

> 'It is a part of the Character of a Poet that he is a kind of Creator, a Maker of new Things. Mr Cartwright therefore is a poet still, only differing from his more visionary Brethren, in giving his works not the mere Forms and Images that verses do, but the substantial realities of tangible Machinery.'[1]

Those 'substantial realities' could be distinctly alarming. Crabbe and his wife once visited Cartwright's factory in Doncaster, and she at least was much distressed.

> 'When she entered the vast building, full of engines thundering with resistless power, yet under the apparent management of children, the bare idea of the inevitable hazard attendant on such stupendous undertakings, quite overcame her feelings, and she burst into tears.'[2]

Such 'stupendous undertakings' evidently overcame the feelings of many of Mrs Crabbe's contemporaries. Some poets of no importance may have celebrated technological progress. There was a certain James Jennings – a life-long earnest believer in the March of Intellect towards the Reign of Mind – who marvelled at the 'SPIRIT OF IMPROVEMENT' that

> *through the land*
> *Strides like a giant, at whose high command*
> *Bridges, Roads, Domes, Canals at once appear*
> *As if by magic.*[3]

But, understandably, Jennings does not figure in the received canon of romantic poetry. Erasmus Darwin is a writer of more consequence, but when he attempts to describe mechanical processes in *The Botanic Garden*, notoriously the effect is ludicrous

---

[1] *Selected Letters and Journals of George Crabbe*, ed. T.C.Faulkner and R.L.Blair, Oxford:Oxford University Press, 1985, p.66 (7 July 1796).

[2] See N.Blackburne, *The Restless Ocean*, Lavenham: Dalton, 1972, p.102.

[3] *Metropolitan Literary Journal*, Vol.1, May 1824, p. 8 (from a lecture on poetry by Jennings).

rather than sublime:

> *Press'd by the ponderous air the Piston falls*
> *Resistless, sliding through its iron walls.*[4]

Again, Robert Southey can rise to the occasion when contemplating his friend Thomas Telford's great engineering work in the construction of the Caledonian Canal:

> *Huge rivers were controll'd, or from their course*
> *Shoulder'd aside; and at the eastern mouth,*
> *Where the salt ooze denied a resting place*
> *There were the deep foundations laid, by weight*
> *On weight immers'd, and pile on pile down-driven,*
> *Till steadfast as the everlasting rocks,*
> *The massive outwork stands.*[5]

But it is significant that the poet's imagination is fired by a setting sublimely picturesque, where human power acts in concert with the powers of nature. As we shall see, Southey found the inside of a factory as disagreeable as did Mrs Crabbe.

The fact is that the literature of the period pays surprisingly little direct attention to Britain's economic transformation, and although, as we shall see, the world of trading and business is not completely ignored, it commonly appears in an unfavourable light.

Wordsworth's Denigration of Industrial Development

We have remarked that Wordsworth looks to rustic life to heal the disorders of an over-urbanised society. If he looks at the developments of his time at all, he does so to lament them. Once in *The Excursion* (1814) he mentions the expansion of industrial towns:

> *From the germ*
> *Of some poor hamlet, rapidly produced*
> *Here a huge town, continuous and compact, ...*
> *O'er which the smoke of unremitting fires*
> *Hangs permanent.*[6]

---

[4] *The Botanic Garden* (1791), Vol. I, p. 27.

[5] R. Southey, 'Inscription for the Caledonian Canal: 2. At Fort Augustus.'

[6] W. Wordsworth, *The Excursion* (1814), Book 8, lines 118-126.

And this leads towards a passage deploring the effects of factory work on the children thus employed: 'Can hope look forward to a manhood raised / On such foundations?'[7] As the years went on, the poet found more and more things to deplore about 'the Thirst of Gold / That rules o'er Britain like a baleful star'. These words occur in a sonnet devoted to a project he found particularly distasteful, the building of a railway between Kendal and Windermere. 'Hear YE that Whistle?' he asks the mountains of Westmorland:

> As her long-linked Train
> Swept onwards, did the vision cross your view?
> Yes, ye were startled.[8]

Still, such laments form only a small part of Wordsworth's huge output. Generally he averts his gaze from the depressing prospect. He has more elevating visions to record.

The 'Thirst of Gold' recurs in a variety of forms and in the work of many writers as a symptom of the sickness inherent in the new order of things. When Wordsworth creates a meritorious tradesman, it is one utterly untouched by that sickness – the Wanderer in *The Excursion*,

> A vagrant Merchant under a heavy load
> Bent as he moves, and needing frequent rest.[9]

He is now retired, but had once serviced rural communities, and acquired a profound wisdom which Wordsworth's poem endeavours to communicate. Significantly, the first readers found this attribution of intellectual dignity to a pedlar peculiarly difficult to accept. A man, said Francis Jeffrey in the *Edinburgh Review*,

> 'who went about selling flannel and pocket-handkerchiefs in this lofty diction, would soon frighten away all his customers; and would infallibly pass either for a madman, or for some learned and affected gentleman, who, in a frolic, had taken up a character which he was peculiarly ill qualified for supporting.'

There is nothing in the poem that relates to the pedlar's 'low

---

[7] *Ibid.*, lines 333-34.

[8] W. Wordsworth, 'Miscellaneous Sonnets', Part 3, No.46 (written in 1844).

[9] *The Excursion, op. cit.*, Book 1, lines 324-25.

occupation'. Higgling about tape, or brass sleeve-buttons, is unlikely to engender philosophical profundity, so that there is a 'revolting incongruity' in Wordsworth's idea, which can only arouse ridicule and disgust in many of his readers.[10]

'Low occupation' is the crucial expression, for it suggests not only the conviction that trade is incompatible with human dignity, but also that it may well exclude common honesty. And this was a common assumption. When Jane Austen tells her sister Cassandra that she has heard from John Murray, who is publishing *Emma*, she adds, as one speaking of a truth universally acknowledged, that 'he is a rogue of course, but a civil one' (17 October 1815). And take the heroine of Fanny Burney's last novel, *The Wanderer*, which appeared in 1814. At one point Juliet helps her friend Gabriella in a haberdasher's shop. She is well aware of the petty frauds and over-reaching tricks of retailers, 'but the difficulties of honest trade she had neither seen nor imagined'.

> 'New to the mighty difference between buying and selling; to the necessity of having at hand more stores than may probably be wanted, for avoiding the risk of losing customers from having fewer; and to the usage of rating at an imaginary value whatever is in vogue, in order to repair the losses incurred from the failure of obtaining the intrinsic worth of what is old-fashioned or faulty; – new to all this, the wary shop-keeper's code, she was perpetually mistaken, or duped.'[11]

George Crabbe provides a further variation on the general theme. Francis Jeffrey warmly admired his poems about lower-class life: 'He delights us by the truth, and vivid and picturesque beauty of his representations, and by the force and pathos of the sensations with which we feel that they are connected.' All this is in striking contrast to Wordsworth and his 'school', who introduce us to 'beings whose existence was not previously suspected by the acutest observers of nature'.[12] One may infer, accordingly, that whatever Crabbe presents in his poetry would have been accepted as authentic by most of Jeffrey's contemporaries. Although his concern is mainly

---

[10] *Edinburgh Review*, November 1814.

[11] F. Burney, *The Wanderer*, ed. M.A. Doody, R.L. Mack and P. Sabor, Oxford: Oxford University Press, 1991, Ch. 67, p. 623.

[12] *Edinburgh Review*, April 1808.

with rural life, and he has little to say directly about trade and industry, there is one section of *The Borough* entitled, emphatically, 'Trades'. In many ways this reinforces a common stereotype. He begins with epigraphs from Latin poets about the folly of avarice. The text itself confirms that tradesmen do not appreciate scholarly pursuits; they are dogged by insecurity; the most successful are those who forget their common humanity. But Crabbe makes one interesting exception. He notes that some tradespeople – not, it seems, the most affluent ones – are devoted to studies like botany and entomology. His friend the weaver is well-informed about moths and butterflies:

> *Eager he looks; and soon, to glad his eyes,*
> *From the sweet bower, by nature form'd, arise*
> *Bright troops of virgin moths and fresh-born butterflies;*
> *Who broke that morning from their half-year's sleep*
> *To fly o'er flowers where they were wont to creep.*[13]

Crabbe presents this as pre-eminently a love of beauty, but references to the microscope and technical terms of botany suggest a more strictly scientific concern, which is fully borne out by the evident interest in 'natural history' in the burgeoning periodical publications of the time. The insignificant James Jennings was a grocer and druggist by trade, and although his poetry was altogether undistinguished, he was a competent ornithologist, and a pioneer in the systematic study of the Somersetshire dialect. But such modest contributions to the scientific culture established earlier by manufacturers like the Wedgwood family and their colleagues in the Lunar Society of Birmingham are barely visible in the received canon of English literature.

Blake's Revolt Against Economic Expansion

Because pessimism about the impact of economic expansion was so widespread, there was evidently great reluctance to allow the literary imagination to contemplate it in any form. One exception is that most proletarian of romantic poets, William Blake. He deplored with prophetic vigour, indeed, the elaboration of machines: 'the sons of Urizen' despised the hour-glass

---

[13] G. Crabbe, *The Borough*, Letter 8, lines 73-77.

> *because its simple workmanship*
> *Was as the workmanship of the plowman, and the water wheel*
> *That raises water into Cisterns, broken and burn'd in fire*
> *Because its workmanship was like the workmanship of the shepherd.*

But then the poet goes on to create a nightmare vision of industrial servitude:

> *And in their stead intricate wheels invented, wheel without wheel,*
> *To perplex youth in their outgoings, and to bind to labours*
> *Of day and night the myriads of Eternity, that they might file*
> *And polish brass and iron hour after hour, laborious workmanship ...*[14]

His poetry is a massive attempt to articulate a revolt against the ethos of a machine-dominated society.

Paradoxically, though, Blake's concerns as an engraver reveal him as a characteristic entrepreneur. In his *Prospectus* (1793) he points out that artists, poets and musicians have been 'proverbially attended by poverty and obscurity'. This was because they had no way of publishing their own works. But Blake has discovered a way of cutting out the middle-man. He has

> 'invented a method of printing both Letter-press and Engraving in a style more ornamental, uniform, and grand, than any before discovered, while it produces works at less than one fourth of the expense.'[15]

His illuminated texts may not have made Blake's fortune, financially speaking, but of course a commercial speculation can never be guaranteed success.

Jane Austen's Approach to Commerce

As a working engraver, Blake was unavoidably caught up in the stresses of a trading life. But people placed in a more favourable financial and social position found it easier to evade what was going

---

[14] W. Blake, *Vala*, Night the Seventh (b), lines 175-182. Cp. *Jerusalem*, Ch. 3, Plate 65, lines 17-24.

[15] W. Blake, *Complete Writings*, ed. Geoffrey Keynes, London: Oxford University Press, 1969, p.207.

on around them. It is a commonplace of criticism to remark the extent to which Jane Austen excludes the great events of her time from her fiction. None the less, in this respect she is rather typical. She is certainly not exceptional in taking for granted the values of country gentlefolk, whose incomes came either from rents or from government securities. Her own family, indeed, fostered clergymen and naval officers, professions which gave scope for some measure of upward social mobility. And her favourite brother, Henry, was certainly involved in the world of commerce, as he was a banker. She paid a number of visits to him in London, and benefited from his business and social contacts. In temperament he seems to have exemplified the entrepreneurial spirit to excess. There is a story of his impatience with the postillion of a postchaise in which he was travelling, considering that it was going too slowly through a rough country lane. 'Get on, boy! get on, will you?' he shouted. – 'I *do* get on, sir, where I can.' – 'You stupid fellow! Any fool can do that. I want you to get on *where you can't*.'[16] While this is not quite the attitude one expects in the director of a bank, it may have served him well enough in times of economic buoyancy. It did not, however, carry him through the depression that blighted Britain after the end of the Napoleonic War, and his bank was one of the casualties. After its failure, he reverted to the family norm and entered into holy orders.

There are few intimations of this new, bustling, anxious world until her last completed novel, *Persuasion*, and even there the adverse effects of an economic depression, apparent in the financial difficulties of Sir Walter Elliot, are attributed to his folly rather than to the state of the country. But in the story on which she was working just before her death, *Sanditon*, business concerns are at last very much in the foreground. The setting is that of a characteristic enterprise of the period, turning a small coastal village into a holiday resort. The entrepreneur is a Mr Parker, obsessed with his investment, 'a complete Enthusiast', as Austen remarks, no doubt mindful of the pejorative overtones that clung to the word throughout the 18th century.

'Sanditon – the success of Sanditon as a small, fashionable Bathing Place – was the object for which he seemed to live. A very few years

---

[16] *Letters of Jane Austen*, ed. Lord Brabourne, London: Bentley, 1884, Vol.1, pp.35-36.

ago, and it had been a quiet Village of no pretensions; but some natural advantages in its position and some accidental circumstances having suggested to himself, and the other principal Land Holder, the probability of its becoming a profitable Speculation, they had engaged in it, and planned and built, and praised and puffed,[17] and raised it to something of young Renown – and Mr Parker could now think of very little besides.'[18]

The story opens with Mr Parker in quest of a medical man to add to the amenities of Sanditon, and he takes pleasure in the collateral effects of his enterprise on the village economy:

> '"Civilization, Civilization indeed!" cried Mr P, delighted. "Look my dear Mary – Look at William Heeley's windows. – Blue Shoes, and nankin Boots! – Who would have expected such a sight at a Shoemaker's in old Sanditon! – This is new within the Month. There was no blue Shoe when we passed this way a month ago. – Glorious indeed! – Well, I think I *have* done something in my Day. ..."'[19]

Austen is clearly unimpressed by the claims of commerce to promote the progress of the human race, and it is not surprising that in general her fiction inhabits a world of gentlefolk, of people who could say, as Elizabeth Bennet said to Lady Catherine de Bourgh, that her father was a gentleman, and she herself a gentleman's daughter. Lady Catherine, of course, retorted that Elizabeth's father might be a gentleman, 'but who was your mother? Who are your uncles and aunts?'[20]   And the answer was that they were involved in *trade*, something one would not care to acknowledge incautiously.

Now it is true that in *Pride and Prejudice*, Austen is concerned to show Elizabeth's uncle Gardiner as a distinctly gentlemanlike man. While his income comes from some unspecified business in the City of London, he is able to spend a month away from it in a tour of the north, and is treated as an equal by Mr Darcy, whose ancestors, as Austen may well have learned from David Hume's *History of England*, came over with William the Conqueror in 1066. Mr and Mrs Gardiner had qualified for gentry status. That was sufficient for

---

[17] 'Puffed' = advertised.

[18] *Sanditon*, Ch.2.

[19] *Ibid.*, Ch.4.

[20] *Emma*, Vol.2, Ch. 4.

the enlightened Mr Darcy, if not for his aunt. It is clear that Austen is not in the least concerned with Mr Gardiner's conduct of his business, any more than she is with the nature of Sir Thomas Bertram's estate in Antigua. An office in the City is beyond the horizon as much as a ship bound for the West Indies. What she is aware of is how people performed in Austen's own world, and Mr Gardiner did better than most.

It is to be feared that Austen saw the egregious Mrs Elton in *Emma* as more representative than the Gardiners. We hear of her first as a Miss Augusta Hawkins, younger daughter 'of a Bristol – merchant, of course, he must be called'. The word suppressed is 'tradesman', connecting her with the 'rude mechanicals' of *A Midsummer Night's Dream* rather than with merchants of Venice. And though Mrs Elton was a good deal more at home in Highbury society than Bottom the Weaver was at the court of Theseus, she showed almost as little familiarity with the manners of gentlefolk as he had done, though her lapses are more subtle. She fails to realise, for example, that while it is allowable for one gentleman to refer to another by his surname alone, it is not at all the done thing for a wife to do the same.

> 'Never seen him in her life before [exclaims Emma] and call him Knightley! and discover him to be a gentleman! A little upstart, vulgar being, with her Mr E., and her *caro sposo*, and her resources, and all her airs of pert pretension and under-bred finery. Actually to discover that Mr Knightley is a gentleman! I doubt whether he will return the compliment, and discover her to be a lady.'[21]

But there are depths of social impropriety beneath even the families of questionable merchants of Bristol. Mrs Elton's sister Selina Suckling, who has married a moderately wealthy Bristolian, is disturbed by some upstart people called Tupman, who have settled in the neighbourhood.

> 'How they got their fortune nobody knows. They came from Birmingham, which is not a place to promise much, you know, Mr Weston. One has not great hopes from Birmingham. I always say there is something direful in the sound.'[22]

---

[21] *Ibid.*, Vol.2, Ch.14.

[22] *Ibid.*, Vol.2, Ch.18.

Austen leaves us to guess at the abysses of indecorum indicated here, but as to how the Tupmans gained their fortune in Birmingham, not only does nobody know, but nobody is interested.

Birmingham's sinister reputation can be understood if one turns to the relevant chapter of Robert Southey's *Letters from England*, published in 1807. This is a book supposed to be written by a Spanish traveller, Don Manuel Alvares Espriella, and Southey evidently found the persona liberating, allowing him to view English society with an ingenuous directness which would have been difficult for a native. Don Manuel finds Birmingham the most repulsive city he has ever visited: noisy beyond description, filthy with a dirt that 'penetrates every where, spotting and staining every thing, and getting into the pores and nostrils. I feel as if my throat wanted sweeping like an English chimney'.[23] The goods manufactured are often shoddy, and illegal practices are carried on with impunity, including forging the currencies of every country with whom England carries on trade. But the Spaniard adds that employment in Birmingham is so insecure, so vulnerable to changes in markets, that the pervasive dishonesty is almost excusable. No doubt the Tupmans, Mr Suckling's undesirable neighbours, had been lucky and made their escape while their luck held.

Birmingham is not the only centre of commerce to dismay Don Manuel. Manchester too excites his revulsion, but this is because of the way its cotton mills exploit the labour of children. He looks at the 'unnatural dexterity' with which these young victims do their work, while he himself is half giddy with the noise and the endless motion. The proprietor explains that one shift works from five in the morning until six at night, when the night shift takes over: 'the wheels never stand still.' When, Don Manuel continues,

> 'he told me there was no rest in these walls, day nor night, if Dante had peopled one of his hells with children, here was a scene worthy to have supplied him with new images of torment.'[24]

He is appalled by the degrading effect this life must have on the children, and by the positive cruelty to which it would expose them.

'They are deprived in childhood of all instruction and all enjoyment; of

---

[23] *Letters from England*, ed. J.Simmons, London: Cresset Press, 1951, p.198, letter 36.

[24] *Ibid.*, pp.207-08, letter 38.

the sports in which childhood instinctively indulges, of fresh air by day and of natural sleep by night. Their health physical and moral is alike destroyed; they die of diseases induced by unremitting task work, by confinement in the impure atmosphere of crowded rooms, by the particles of metallic or vegetable dust which they are continually inhaling; or they live to grow up without decency, without comfort, and without hope, without morals, without religion, and without shame, and bring forth slaves like themselves to tread in the same path of misery.'[25]

The proprietor is a humane and kindly man, and does not realise what he is inflicting on this generation. Don Manuel thought of cities in Arabian romance where all the inhabitants were enchanted: 'here Commerce is the queen witch, and I had no talisman strong enough to disenchant those who were daily drinking of the golden cup of her charms.'[26]

In a later letter, this attack on the commercial spirit is generalised to encompass the entire development of English society in the previous half-century. The ethos of business poisons everything: 'literature, arts, religion, government are alike tainted.' Agriculture has become a trading speculation: 'field has been joined to field; a moneyed farmer comes, like Aaron's rod, and swallows up all within his reach.' Agriculture is certainly improved, but at the cost of profound social disruption. Throughout the country there is too much wealth and too much poverty: 'were there less of the one there would be less of the other.' And the solution? 'Taxation might be so directed as to break down the great properties.'[27]

Southey adopts essentially the same stance some two decades later in his *Colloquies of Society* (1829). The liberating persona here is Sir Thomas More, who, as is natural in a Catholic martyr, subjects the protestant reformation to a sharp scrutiny. It has, he says, 'prepared the way for the uncontrolled dominion of that worldly spirit which it is the tendency of the commercial system to produce and foster'.[28] Mammon has acquired an undisputed and acknowledged supremacy, above all in England. Southey, appearing

---

[25] *Ibid.*, pp.209-10.

[26] *Ibid.*

[27] *Ibid.*, p.368, pp.371-72, letter 60.

[28] R. Southey, *Colloquies*, 1829, Vol.I, p.154.

himself in this book as More's partner in dialogue under the name of Montesinos, points out that without the 'manufacturing system', Britain could not have won the last war with France. But More sweeps this objection aside. Evil can produce only evil. Modern manufacturing debases everyone engaged in it. It forces people to work in unwholesome conditions, and 'any result would be dearly purchased at such an expense of human misery and degradation'.[29]

Sir Thomas and Montesinos do indeed go on to make a distinction between 'manufactures' and 'commerce'. The merchants of ancient Tyre, and the medieval Moors, were worthy patrons of the state and of the arts, and such merchants are still to be found. It is not usual to class merchants among the liberal professions, but it should be, as mercantile pursuits require the most general knowledge, and provide good opportunities for acquiring and enlarging it.[30] This emphatic concession to the business community is, as is often the case in Southey's writings, not well defined, but one may guess he is thinking of people like William Roscoe of Liverpool, who was a banker, or possibly the directors of the East India Company. To complicate matters further, Southey sees most hope for the future in the plans of one of the most successful manufacturers of his time, Robert Owen.

Not that it is as a cotton manufacturer that Owen appears in the *Colloquies*. Southey invokes him purely as a philanthropist, author of the famous plan of co-operative associations, which would, he believes, greatly better the condition of the working classes if only it could raise the necessary capital. But alas! the Bible Society has far greater success in stimulating contributions than the eloquent Robert Owen, and it is a pity he is so constrained by the secularism which he insists on proffering to an unappreciative public.[31]

Southey: Robert Owen and the 'Invisibility' of Business in Early 19th-Century Literature

Southey's presentation of Owen is a striking example of the sheer invisibility of serious business activity in the literature of the early 19th century. When Owen came to write his autobiography, the story

---

[29] *Ibid.*, p.170.

[30] *Ibid.*, p.196.

[31] *Ibid.*, pp.132-45.

of his success as a manager is riveting, and his account of the way he foiled his fellow-directors' attempt to oust him from the management of the New Lanark mills is one of the most dramatic narratives to come from the period. But although it is hard to imagine that Owen would not have told his story many times over to sympathetic hearers, the fact remains that it was not published until 1857, when it took its place among the writings of the Victorian prophets, and when business had become an acceptable subject for writers of fiction.

Edmund Burke: Tradesmen Should Not Rule the State

In the early 19th century itself, the business community is repeatedly presented as ill-bred and unimaginative. 'Business community' of course includes a wide social range, with bankers in particular passing easily into the ranks of the gentry. But preoccupation with one's trade and with matters of the market-place continued to incur the judgement pronounced in 1790 by Edmund Burke, in his *Reflections on the Revolution in France*:

> 'The occupation of a hair-dresser, or of a working tallow-chandler, cannot be a matter of honour to any person – to say nothing of a number of more servile employments. Such descriptions of men ought not to suffer oppression from the state; but the state suffers oppression, if such as they ... are permitted to rule.'[32]

Burke clinches his argument with an apposite text from holy writ. 'How', asks the author of *Ecclesiasticus*, 'can he get wisdom that holdeth the plough ... and whose talk is of bullocks?'

One might wonder whether Coleridge had this passage from Burke in mind when he recalled, in *Biographia Literaria* (1817), his attempts in 1796 to secure subscribers for his radical periodical, *The Watchman*. He set off on his quest in a tour of the industrial districts of the English midlands and the north, beginning in Birmingham. His first interview was with a tallow-chandler, tall and lean, with a face to match, giving Coleridge 'a dim notion of some one looking at me through a used grid-iron, all soot, grease and iron!' He listened patiently enough, in spite of its being one of his busy days

---

[32] E. Burke, *Reflections on the Revolution in France* (1790), in *The Writings and Speeches of Edmund Burke*, Vol. 8, ed. L. G. Mitchell and W. B. Todd, Oxford: Clarendon Press, 1989, pp. 100-101.

when he was melting down the tallow from animal carcasses, an industrial process accompanied by a peculiarly penetrating and unpleasant smell. At the end of the poet's harangue he asked the price.

> 'Only four-pence,' – (O! how I felt the anti-climax, the abysmal bathos of that four-pence!) – 'only four-pence, Sir, each number, to be published on every eighth day.' – That comes to a deal of money at the end of a year. And how much, did you say, there was to be for the money?' – 'Thirty-two pages, Sir! large octavo, closely printed.'– 'Thirty and two pages! Bless me! why except what I does in a family way on the Sabbath, that's more than I ever reads, Sir! all the year round. I am as great a one as any man in Brummagem, Sir! for liberty and truth and all them sort of things, but as to this, – no offence, I hope, Sir, – I must beg to be excused.'[33]

An anecdote like that obviously serves to reinforce a common stereotype: tradesmen engage in malodorous activities, are unable to speak grammatically, tend to be close-fisted, and have limited intellectual horizons. They also smoke stupefying tobacco – doubtless suited to their coarse sensibilities – as Coleridge found when he afterwards dined with a more sympathetic tradesman 'and three other *illuminati* of the same rank'. He was pressed to join them in a post-prandial smoke, and almost at once became uncomfortably giddy. Recovering, he went off to an appointment with a unitarian minister, but then sank into a swoon, from which he only recovered after a party of the minister's friends had assembled to meet him. These were not tradesmen but *gentlemen*, and never, Coleridge recalled, had he since heard 'conversation sustained with such animation, enriched with such a variety of information, and enlivened with such a flow of anecdote'. One suspects that, as this was Birmingham, many of these gentlemen were engaged in business – but Coleridge does not say: presumably, the thought never crossed his mind.[34]

He mentions one other interview, this time in Manchester, with 'a stately and opulent wholesale dealer in cottons'. Unlike the tallow-chandler, the dealer did not give Coleridge an opportunity to say his piece, but merely looked at the prospectus and then 'crushed it

---

[33] S. T. Coleridge, *Biographia Literaria*, Ch.10.

[34] *Ibid.*

within his fingers and the palm of his hand'. Saying that he was 'over-run with these articles', he retired to his counting-house. And that, Coleridge claims, was the last time he tried to get a subscriber.

Lewis Patton, who edited *The Watchman* for the standard *Collected Works* of Coleridge, gives a somewhat different account of the subscription tour. He bases this on Coleridge's letters at the time to Josiah Wade, who like Jane Austen's Mr Hawkins, was a Bristol merchant. Coleridge did well in enlisting subscribers, not only in Birmingham but also in Derby, Nottingham, Lichfield, and to some extent in Sheffield, though here he was inhibited by not wishing to encroach on James Montgomery's radical paper, the *Iris*. The letters were written to Wade because of the financial help he was giving Coleridge, and Patton also remarks that another Bristol tradesman, Joseph Cottle the bookseller, gave material assistance in gaining subscribers for *The Watchman* and in seeing to its distribution. None of this assistance is acknowledged in *Biographia Literaria*, an ingratitude that Cottle in particular deeply resented. But the ingratitude is evidently the consequence of a pervasive conviction that tradesmen may be worthy fellows, but are not to be taken seriously.

Charles Lamb: His Archetypal Tradesman Juke Judkins

One of the most carefully finished presentations of the early 19th-century idea of the archetypal tradesman is provided by Charles Lamb in his 'Reminiscences of Juke Judkins, Esq., of Birmingham'. The essay appeared in the *New Monthly Magazine* in 1826, and emphasises the meanness rather than the imperfect education that one would normally expect in a tradesman. Judkin is a brazier, whose familiarity with brass as a material presumably makes his impudence the more brazen. The first thing that we learn is that he pays £93 a year to his widowed mother as a pension, which the prosperity of his business enables him to do with ease. But his mind evidently circles round the possibility of his *not* paying the £93, as the wording of his father's will might be open to an interpretation that would relieve him from the outlay. But, he adds piously, 'the wishes of a dying parent should in some sort have the effect of law'. Even so, the £93 deduction from his profits still rankles: the annual profits might *seem* to total £1,303, but 'the real proceeds in that time have fallen short of that sum to the amount of the aforesaid payment of ninety-three pounds sterling annually.'[35]

He has been close-fisted since childhood. He recalls the occasion when he sold off by pennyworths the surplus gingerbread his mother had given him to take to his boarding school. 'By this honest strategem I put double the prime cost of the gingerbread into my purse,' incidentally making sure that he retained enough to have plenty for himself while it remained good and moist. His father congratulated him on this stroke of business, but his mother burst into tears, saying 'it was a very niggardly action'. Of course, he never shared the food his parents sent him, but neither did he defraud anyone even of a halfpenny, and he was always willing to do anything to serve his fellows in any way that was consistent with his own well-being. Still, unaccountably, he was never much of a favourite with them, and in later life he found it difficult to prosper in love.

Lamb provides a hilarious account of Judkins's courtship, which is dominated by discussions about the choice of a house and associated expenses, and founders on his assiduity in bargaining over the oranges on sale outside the theatre, when he was prevailed upon to take his fiancée and her mother to a play. An enterprising cousin who had joined the party dashed off and got some fine oranges at a nearby fruiterers, and thus insinuated himself into the affections of the lady. Not that Judkins can bring himself to believe that such a trifle could have been the motive of her inconstancy:

> '...for could she suppose that I would sacrifice my dearest hopes in her to the paltry sum of two shillings, when I was going to treat her to the play, and her mother too (an expense of more than four times that amount), if the young man had not interfered to pay for the latter, as I mentioned?'[36]

We leave him wondering.

Fifteen years earlier, Lamb had depicted the ethos of the world of business in terms equally mordant. 'The Good Clerk' in the essay with that title has lost almost every vestige of human spontaneity, although Lamb is so directly imitating the 17th-century

---

[35] *The Works of Charles and Mary Lamb*, ed. T.Hutchinson, London: Oxford University Press, 1909, Vol.1, pp.369-70.

[36] *Ibid.*, p.376.

Theophrastan 'character' that the reader instinctively perceives that what is being presented is an ideal to which no one, happily, could quite attain. The good clerk is clean and neat, temperate, either celibate or married – all on strictly commercial principles. He is honest:

> 'not for fear of the laws, but because he hath observed how unseemly an article it maketh in the Day Book, or Ledger, when a sum is set down lost or missing; it being his pride to make these books to agree, and to tally, the one side with the other, with a sort of architectural symmetry and correspondence.'[37]

Lamb informs us that this 'character' was sketched during intervals in his employment as a clerk, and was inspired by 'those frugal and economical maxims' put about a century earlier by writers like Daniel Defoe. He then enters into a searing analysis of Defoe's *Complete English Tradesman* as a guide to 'every little mean art, every sneaking address, every trick and subterfuge (short of larceny) that is necessary to the tradesman's occupation', all tending to one purpose, 'the sacrificing of every honest emotion of the soul to what he calls the main chance', narrowing and degrading the heart. He illustrates this charge out of a chapter on the government of the temper. Tradesmen must discipline themselves to be patient under the most extreme provocation: behind the counter they must have no flesh and blood about them – there must be no passion, no resentment. Even customers who obviously have no intention to buy, but yet rummage through five hundred pounds' worth of goods, must be borne with: ''tis his business to be ill used and resent nothing.' Even if his real temper is fiery and hot, it must not show in his shop. Of course, nature will out, but it must be upstairs, with his family.

> 'I heard once of a shop-keeper [Defoe continues] that behaved himself thus to such an extreme, that when he was provoked by the impertinence of the customers, beyond what his temper could bear, he would go up stairs and beat his wife, kick his children about like dogs, and be as furious for two or three minutes, as a man chained down in Bedlam; and again, when that heat was over, would sit down and cry faster than the children he had abused; and after the fit, he would go

---

[37] *Ibid.*, p.162. (*The Reflector*, No. 4, Oct.-Dec.1811.)

down into the shop again, and be as humble, courteous, and as calm as any man whatever; so absolute a government of the passions had he in the shop and so little out of it: in the shop, a soul-less animal that would resent nothing; and in the family a madman.'[38]

Clearly what fascinated Lamb in this passage was the dichotomy between being soul-less and being mad: a dichotomy that would have had a painful resonance in his own family, with the homicidal mania of his own sister a constant anxiety. In the context of the present inquiry, it throws a strong light on the shortcomings – to put it mildly – of commercial life as perceived in the early 19th century.

Neither of the essays considered here was collected in *The Essays of Elia*, and so have remained little known. They provide a helpful context, though, for the incident that closes the essay on 'Imperfect Sympathies'. Lamb has been admitting that, although he loves Quaker ways and Quaker worship, he could not actually live the Quaker life. 'I must have books, pictures, theatres, chit-chat, scandal, jokes, ambiguities, and a thousand whim-whams, which their simpler taste can do without.' Although he does not actually say so, he would evidently find the emphasis on complete veracity difficult to sustain, but he admires the presence of mind which is the evident result of this self-imposed watchfulness on words. He illustrates 'the astonishing composure of this people' by an incident that occurred while he was travelling on a stage-coach with three Quaker merchants. They halted for refreshment in Andover, where both tea and a supper were provided. Lamb had the supper, the Quakers confined themselves to tea. When the landlady proceeded to charge them all for both meals, the Quakers objected. They offered to pay for the tea; Lamb offered to pay for his supper. The offers were refused, and the Quakers put away their money and marched out. Lamb followed their example.

'The coach drove off. The murmurs of mine hostess, not very indistinctly or ambiguously pronounced, became after a time inaudible – and now my conscience, which the whimsical scene had for a while suspended, beginning to give some twitches, I waited in the hope that some justification would be offered by these serious persons for the seeming injustice of their conduct. To my great surprise, not a syllable was dropped on the subject. They sate as mute as at a meeting. At

---

[38] *Ibid.*, pp.164-66.

length the eldest of them broke silence, by inquiring of his next neighbour, 'Hast thee heard how indigos go at the India House?' and the question operated as a soporific on my moral feeling as far as Exeter.'[39]

But not, perhaps, much beyond Exeter. It would be absurd to apply a heavy moral judgement to this 'whimsical scene', but there is a family resemblance between the 'good clerk' and these Quaker men of business, not to mention a quiet ruthlessness which no doubt assisted greatly in the successful conduct of affairs.

Walter Scott: The Quaker Entrepreneur – A Dedicated 'Improver' – and the Decline of the 'Old Order'

Another Quaker entrepreneur who figures in an early 19th-century text is Joshua Geddes, in Walter Scott's *Redgauntlet*. Although clearly seen as a landowner, Scott being at pains to emphasise the continuity between the Quaker and his wild Border ancestors, he is a dedicated improver, and the plot of the novel partly turns on his 'improved' method of fishing. He uses tide-nets instead of the traditional methods of spear and line. The result, says Redgauntlet, is that 'you will destroy the salmon which makes the livelihood of fifty poor families'. In due course a crowd of 'damned smuggling wreckers' armed with guns, fish-spears, iron crowbars, spades and bludgeons comes to destroy the nets. Published in 1824, this episode would inevitably remind readers of the Luddite machine-breaking of the previous decade. The riot serves to facilitate the capture of Darsie Latimer, and so leads on to issues more romantic than the enterprises of Joshua Geddes. But the implications of this element in the narrative reinforce the theme of the novel as a whole – that the old order cannot sustain itself, whether as a nation ruled by the Stuart dynasty, or in communities wringing a subsistence from the land and from the rivers in the way they have done for centuries. Although much is made of Joshua's courageous non-violence, it is clear that he is willing to invoke the law against the disturbers of his property, and the rioters are doubtless correct in thinking that the overseer of his fisheries has gone to Dumfries to fetch down redcoats and dragoons. But Redgauntlet himself is probably unduly jaundiced in warning Darsie that Joshua 'will himself shear thee like

---

[39] *Ibid.*, pp.550-52.

a sheep, if you come to buying and selling with him'.[40]   But while discounting a natural prejudice, the reader may well take the hint that it is as well to be on one's guard in any dealings with a man of business, Quaker or not.

In *Redgauntlet*, Joshua is a marginal figure, but in *Rob Roy*, published in 1817, the world of commerce takes centre stage, juxtaposed with that lusty survival of a pre-commercial society, the Scottish Highlands before Bonnie Prince Charlie and the disaster of 1745. The hero's father, the elder Osbaldistone, is a merchant in the most respectable sense, a man whom even Jane Austen's Emma would hesitate to call a tradesman. Scott, indeed, endows him with all the narrowness of outlook that forms part of the early 19th-century stereotype of the businessman. For him, the depreciation of the French currency was the most remarkable national occurrence of the time, and of course he regarded all merely literary pursuits with contempt.[41] When Di Vernon chides Frank for his ignorance of the figures of heraldry, she wonders at the upbringing that allowed him to remain in such a benighted state: 'Of what could your father be thinking?' – 'Of the figures of arithmetic,' Frank replies, 'the most insignificant unit of which he holds more highly than all the blazonry of chivalry.'[42] Scott evidently wants the reader to think of Edmund Burke's celebrated lament over Marie Antoinette: the age of chivalry is gone; that of sophisters, economists and calculators has succeeded. And if the elder Osbaldistone is no sophister, he is certainly a calculator and economist in the 18th-century senses of the words, which focus on the sparing and effective use of resources. Although his son magnanimously pays tribute to the estimable functions of commerce, it is as part of a tactful attempt to free himself from the obligation to devote his life to the family firm.

> 'It is impossible, sir, for me to have higher respect for any character than I have for the commercial, even were it not yours. ... It connects nation with nation, relieves the wants, and contributes to the wealth of all; and is to the general commonwealth of the civilised world what the daily intercourse of ordinary life is to private society, or rather, what air

---

[40] W. Scott, *Redgauntlet*, Letter 6, and Chs. 3 and 4.

[41] W. Scott, *Rob Roy*, Ch. 2.

[42] *Ibid.*, Ch. 10.

and food are to our bodies.'[43]

That may be the theory, but it leaves on one side the question of what kind of character is most successful in commerce. The elder Osbaldistone's self-command is not ludicrous, as Defoe's much-tried shopkeeper's is, but it is integral to his insensitively dominating personality. He behaves with arbitrary authority, dismissing the son of his French associate for no good reason, and displacing Frank in favour of an unknown cousin, who, as it turns out, almost brings ruin on the firm. He had something of the temperament of a political adventurer. He seemed driven by a need

> 'to push on from achievement to achievement, without stopping to secure, far less to enjoy, the acquisitions which he made. Accustomed to see his whole fortune trembling in the scales of chance, and dexterous at adopting expedients for casting the balance in his favour, his health and spirits and activity seemed ever to increase with the animating hazards on which he staked his wealth.'[44]

The insecurity of trade was foremost in the minds of many people at this time of bank failures and ill-comprehended movements in the trade cycle. Scott himself was to suffer personally from this instability, and the horror of bankruptcy was an important element in the emotional power of *Rob Roy* for its first readers. For Frank's father, bankruptcy was 'an utter and irretrievable disgrace, to which life would afford no comfort, and death the speediest and sole relief'.[45]

But financial failure was not merely a personal disaster. It could entail social cataclysms, revolutions. Bailie Nicol Jarvie explains to Frank how English firms have bought woods in the Highlands, and paid for them with bills that find credit in Glasgow and Edinburgh – 'I might amaist say in Glasgow wholly, for it's little the pridefu' Edinburgh folk do in real business.' If the Osbaldistone firm could not support these bills, the Highland economy would be crippled, and social unrest would necessarily follow, probably in a desperate rising. Frank thinks it singular that the mercantile transactions of

---

43 *Ibid.*, Ch. 2.

44 *Ibid.*, Ch. 1.

45 *Ibid.*, Ch. 18.

London citizens should become involved with revolutions and rebellions.

> 'Not at a', man – not at a',' returned Mr Jarvie, 'that's a' your silly prejudications. I read whiles in the lang dark nights, and I hae read in Baker's Chronicle that the merchants o' London could gar the Bank of Genoa break their promise to advance a mighty sum to the King of Spain, whereby the sailing of the Grand Spanish Armada was put off for a haill year.'[46]

The attempt to ruin Osbaldistone is, of course, foiled, but then Frank and his father have to join with other mercantile houses to support the credit of government when the 1715 Jacobite rising threatens financial stability.[47]

Tradesmen and Men of Commerce: Arithmetic Their Common Currency

If Osbaldistone represents commerce at its most socially elevated, Jarvie is emphatically a tradesman. But the two men, antithetical in so many ways, have something in common. As Frank remarks, they both considered 'commercial transactions' the main object of human life, and they shared a profound faith in arithmetic: for Jarvie, one of the most appalling disabilities of his Highland relatives is that 'they dinna ken the very multiplication-table itself, whilk [which] is the root of a' usefu' knowledge.'[48] Tradesman as he is, though, he has moved upwards in society. He has progressed from being a working weaver to trading only as a wholesaler, and, as we have seen, he is a man of reading, during the winter months anyhow. Frank notices that his conversation 'showed tokens of a shrewd, observing, liberal, and, to the extent of its opportunities, a well-improved mind'.[49] These qualities are obscured by his 'oddity and vulgarity of manner', and Frank thinks him ridiculously vain – but then he has something to be vain about. He is a magistrate of some consequence, at least in Glasgow. He still has to lament the fact that great men in the state will not profit from the advice of one

---

[46] *Ibid.*, Ch. 26.

[47] *Ibid.*, Ch. 37.

[48] *Ibid.*, Ch. 34.

[49] *Ibid.*, Ch. 27.

whom they would dismiss as a 'Glasgow weaver-body', while Osbaldistone's head clerk, Mr Owen, thinks of him as 'a petulant, conceited Scotch pedlar' – until the progress of events changes his mind. But within certain limits, Jarvie is clearly a man of considerable intellectual pretension. In Chapter 26 he treats Frank and Mr Owen to an elaborate statistical analysis of unemployment in the Highlands:

> "'Ye maun understand I found my remarks on figures, whilk, as Mr Owen here weel kens, is the only true demonstrable root of human knowledge."
> Owen readily assented to a proposition so much in his own way, and our orator proceeded.'

And proceed he does, remorselessly estimating, multiplying, subtracting, and reaching the conclusion that half the population have no access to honest work.

> "'Aweel, sir, this moiety of unemployed bodies, amounting to" –
> "To one hundred and fifteen thousand souls," said Owen, "being the half of the above product."
> "Ye hae't, Maister Owen – ye hae't – whereof there may be twenty-eight thousand seven hundred able-bodied gillies fit to bear arms, and that do bear arms, and will touch or look at nae honest means of livelihood even if they could get it – which, lack-a-day! they cannot.'"

Jarvie benevolently offers to help Rob Roy's sons to honest employment, but the offer is not appreciated. Rob Roy strides furiously about, cursing in a peculiarly expressive Gaelic. His sons weavers, indeed! – 'but I wad see every loom in Glasgow, beam, traddles and shuttles, burnt in hell-fire sooner!' He calms himself, though, appreciating that Jarvie meant well, and concedes that if he should ever think of apprenticing his sons, he would give Jarvie the first refusal.[50]

Jarvie's deficiencies in gentlemanly qualities are summed up in his pointed unconcern with the idea of honour. When Frank speaks of acting in a way that will be to his father's advantage and to his own honour, Jarvie remarks that he will attend to nothing about honour:

---

[50] *Ibid.*, Ch. 34.

'We ken naething here but about credit. Honour is a homicide and a blood-spiller, that gangs about making frays in the street; but Credit is a decent honest man, that sits at hame and makes the pat play.'[51]

Not that Jarvie does sit at home, but goodnaturedly ventures into the Highlands to assist Frank and his father, and encounters considerable perils on the way. But when rust prevents him from drawing his sword at the beginning of the fight in the inn at the Clachan of Aberfoil, he has no hesitation in seizing a red-hot poker from the fire and setting his adversary's plaid on fire. It is hardly sporting – no gentleman would have demeaned himself thus – but it is highly effective.[52]

Jarvie's liberality of mind does not extend to the picturesque. He is entirely unmoved by the scenery surrounding Loch Lomond, so magnificent that it inspires Frank to thoughts of retiring as a hermit 'in one of the romantic and beautiful islands amongst which our boat glided'. Jarvie, however, enters into a series of calculations which enable him to prove the practicability of draining the loch, and 'giving to plough and harrow many hundred, ay, many a thousand acres, from whilk no man could get earthly good e'enow'. He would have retained just enough of the loch to form a canal, greatly facilitating the transport of coal north of Glasgow.[53]

Although Scott's satirical intention here is unmistakable, an engineering project on this scale would not have seemed out of the question to a generation which was seeing the ambitious and varied enterprises of men like Thomas Telford. 'Never before in history,' wrote one of Telford's biographers, 'had man created works of such magnitude as the mighty aqueducts that Telford flung across the valleys of the Ceirog and the Dee'; and while he may not have drained Loch Lomond, the same writer claims that 'no man in his century performed a greater service for Scotland', turning the Highlands from an almost trackless country of dispirited people into one served by his harbours, his roads, his great Caledonian Canal and his many bridges.[54] Although outrageously unromantic, Jarvie's

---

[51] *Ibid.*, Ch. 26.

[52] *Ibid.*, Ch. 28.

[53] *Ibid.*, Ch. 36.

[54] L.T.C.Rolt, *Thomas Telford*, London: Longmans, Green, 1958, pp.xii-xiii.

project was in tune with that diffuse sense of power which informs a good deal of English romantic poetry.

John Galt's Mr Cayenne – Entrepreneur and Benefactor

It has to be admitted that Scott's attitude to Jarvie is patronising. There is, however, at least one fairly respectful presentation of the manufacturing tradesman in the received canon of early 19th-century literature, and that is John Galt's Mr Cayenne, in *Annals of the Parish* (1821). Galt was well aware of the conventional view of the mean-minded tradesman, and has in fact left a fine example of the type in *A Rich Man*, his fictional autobiography of a self-made man, Archibald Plack, a poor Glasgow lad who became Lord Mayor of London. His skill at pursuing the 'main chance' resembles the relentless close-fistedness of Lamb's Juke Judkins, but he is better at dealing with people, and has greater intelligence. It may be more than a coincidence that Galt's people, like Bailie Nichol Jarvie, belong to the west of Scotland, away from 'the pridefu' Edinburgh folk' and the rest of the literary establishment.[55] Not that Mr Cayenne himself is presented as a typical inhabitant. He is a loyalist exile from the newly independent American colonies, with a hot temper and an aggressively secular outlook that horrifies Galt's narrator, the Rev. Micah Balwhidder. But he sets up a successful cotton mill in the parish of Dalmailing and gives employment to large numbers (some imported from Manchester), housing them, too, in handsome dwellings. The necessary investment is supplied with an unstinted hand by Cayenne and his partners in London. The factory village is, alas, a source of corruption, and Balwhidder is particularly distressed by the way it nourishes dissenting sects. But Cayenne is a strong supporter of the established order, even though he on occasion manifests his support in a blasphemous manner. Two youths who are brought before him as subversive reformers plead that Jesus Christ too was a reformer. Like the notorious Lord Braxfield on a similar occasion, Cayenne did not allow this as a plea. '"And what the devil did he make of it?" cried Mr Cayenne, bursting with passion; "Was he not crucified?"' Balwhidder was shattered: it was for him as if "the pillars of the earth sunk beneath me", and the roof carried away in a whirlwind. But the Lord failed

---

[55] John Galt, *A Rich Man and other stories*, ed. W.Roughead, London: Foulis, 1925.

to show His displeasure, and the lads were acquitted also.[56]

Cayenne, however, has his philanthropic side. It was due to his humane foresight that the parish was supported through a period of dearth, he having organised corn imports from the Baltic and America. He was also generous in his support of refugees from the troubles in Ireland in 1798, making no distinction between rebels and loyalists:

> 'He said he carried his political principles only to the camp and the council. "To the hospital and the prison," said he, "I take those of a man" – which was almost a Christian doctrine, and from that declaration Mr Cayenne and me began again to draw a little more cordially together; although he had still a very imperfect sense of religion, which I attributed to his being born in America, where even as yet, I am told, they have but a scanty sprinkling of grace.'[57]

This last observation by Balwhidder is a reminder that Cayenne unites a number of stereotypes, and is not just an example of the manufacturer. He is a coarse-speaking colonial, and something of an irascible humourist like Matthew Bramble in Smollett's *Humphry Clinker*. But the combination exempts him from the patronage or contempt which the literary world commonly felt to be appropriate on the rare occasions when its attention was turned to trade. At one point, he acts in precisely the way one would expect of the lord of the manor. This was during the alarm about an imminent French invasion in 1803, when Dalmailing raised a fine troop of volunteers to defend the nation in its hour of peril. After the inaugural parade and demonstration of fighting skill, everyone

> 'marched to the cotton-mill, where, in one of the warehouses, a vast table was spread, and a dinner, prepared at Mr Cayenne's own expence, sent in from the Cross-keys, and the whole corps with many of the gentry of the neighbourhood, dined with great jollity, the band of music playing beautiful airs all the time.'[58]

Admittedly, this is an event which Balwhidder sees as an exceptional testimony to the unity of all classes, but the fact remains

---

[56] John Galt, *Annals of the Parish*, Ch. 34.

[57] *Ibid.*, Ch. 39.

[58] *Ibid.*, Ch. 44.

that Cayenne rises to the occasion with the ease of an accomplished gentleman.

Cayenne's colonial roots and his growing integration into the Dalmailing community also help to set him apart from the malpractice associated with the world of business. In Chapter 43 we see him seeking Balwhidder's advice about how to respond to an unreasonable demand from his partners that he should give up part of his share in the business for the benefit of one of their relatives. Balwhidder advises him to accept the admission of a new partner, but at the same time to suggest that his own shareholding should be *increased*, in view of his undoubted services to the firm.

> 'I thought Mr Cayenne would have louped out of his skin with mirth at this notion, and being a prompt man, he sat down at my scrutoire, and answered the letter which gave him so much uneasiness.'

The partners withdrew their proposal, and wrote to him that it was not considered expedient to make any change 'at that time'. As soon as he received this letter, he came straight over to Balwhidder, 'and swore an oath, by some dreadful name, that I was a Solomon'. By thus juxtaposing Balwhidder's unworldly discernment and Cayenne's rough good nature, and making them triumph over metropolitan business interests, Galt prepares the way for a more sympathetic portrayal of trade and industry. Cayenne's partners, of course, reinforce the stereotype of rascally tradesmen: Cayenne himself emerges as a Captain of Industry, a resourceful benefactor of his local community. We are almost in the world of Disraeli's *Coningsby* and Charlotte Bronte's *Shirley*. But not quite.[59]

Keats and Hazlitt: Merchants/Business Men Condemned – 'Ethically Ambiguous...Intellectually and Emotionally Stunting'

In John Keats's poem *Isabella*, there are some stanzas in which he denounces the heroine's brothers, who are merchants, 'ledger-men', for whom 'many a weary hand did swelt / In torched mines and noisy factories'. 'Why', he asks five times in stanza 16, 'Why were they proud? ... Why in the name of glory were they proud?' Well might the poet ask the question, as it was the almost unanimous

---

[59] I am indebted to Ivan Melada's *The Captain of Industry*, Albuquerque: University of New Mexico Press, 1970, for some of the suggestions made here about Mr Cayenne.

conviction of the literary establishment of his day that business was at best ethically ambiguous, and intellectually and emotionally stunting. It is significant that when the politically radical essayist William Hazlitt was attempting to define the *Zeitgeist* in the pen-portraits of *The Spirit of the Age* (1825), he included no one whose primary concern was with trade or industry. Nor does business figure in his writings, unless one excepts his mockery of Robert Owen and his philanthropic plans. There is, however, one direct consideration of the business world. It is a series of 'Hints to Persons in Business and Men of the World', never published until P. P. Howe included them in his Centenary Edition of Hazlitt in 1934. Hazlitt insists that the 'spirit of gambling ... is the soul of commerce', and that when men of business 'think they are consulting their own interest ... they are in fact governed by pride, caprice, obstinacy, and fancy'.

> 'They are in love with money – and, like other lovers, are capricious and headstrong, mad at disappointment, the slaves of suspicion and idle rumours, let go the substance to catch at the shadow, live in a dream (as much as the poet or alchemist), and in their anxious desires and feverish expectations, lose all judgment and common sense, though they suppose these qualities to be confined to themselves.'[60]

Bailie Nichol Jarvie and Mr Cayenne might point to better things, but to the literary world of Hazlitt's contemporaries his indictment would have seemed an extreme formulation of an unquestionable commonplace.

---

[60] *The Complete Works of William Hazlitt*, ed. P.P.Howe, London: J. M. Dent, Vol. 20, 1934, pp.350-52.

4

THE HIGH VICTORIAN

PERIOD (1850-1900):

'THE WORSHIP OF MAMMON'

Angus Easson

Salford University

'Perhaps a clever man would find it worth his while to write a book on the romance of trade.'
[Henry Morley], 'Patent Wrongs', *Household Words*, VII (7 May 1853), p. 229.

Introduction

THIS ESSAY DEALS WITH THE HIGH VICTORIAN AGE. Even when authors of this period set their work back in time, as Dickens (1812-1870), for example, commonly does, his *Little Dorrit* of 1857 being set 30 years before, they yet continuously write about the present. Dickens's financier Merdle is not a businessman of the 1820s but one for the 1850s, modelled on a swindling suicide of 1855. The chronological parameters are basically 1850 to 1900, though I draw in Thomas Carlyle from earlier, while George Bernard Shaw's *Heartbreak House* of 1919 offers a summation of the period, when the Great War, 'a tremendous jolt', might be the culmination and (hopefully) the apocalyptic close of the Industrial and Victorian ages. Faced with so vast a field, in business and in literature, I am only too conscious how necessarily limited this survey must be.

Nineteeth-Century Financial Institutions: Buildings and Appearance

Perhaps we should begin with the 19th-century financial institutions. What goes on in banks? How do insurance companies work? They impress by their buildings, even if many have suffered change of use: banking halls have now become café bars and the great Manchester Refuge Assurance building (1891-1912) is the Palace Hotel. Such evidence of conspicuous consumption was meant to proclaim in bricks and mortar, and in marble and mahogany, the solidity of these institutions and the profits generated by them. To read the Victorian writers is often to find representations of banks and of the outer display, not so often information in detail of financial processes. The display and the consequences of both success and failure are of greater interest. In Charles Dickens's *Little Dorrit* (1857), Merdle, the great financier and yet greater swindler, the man whose name is the name of the age, has married a stately widow, with a splendid bosom which has vied with the snows of Canada and not come off worse in point of comparison of either whiteness or cold. Mrs Merdle, the Bosom, does very well to display the jewels, to host the dinner parties and salons, that assure people of Merdle's security, just as he and his bank in the City become an object of veneration:

> 'the carriage, and the ride into the City; and the people who looked at them; and the hats that flew off grey heads; and the general bowing and crouching before this wonderful mortal, the like of which prostration of spirit was not to be seen...in Westminster Abbey and Saint Paul's Cathedral put together, on any Sunday...' [II.xvi.591][1]

The worship of Merdle, a worship of Mammon in the modern age, is all part of Dickens's satirical purpose, just as the obscurity of Merdle's financial activities is deliberate too. Dickens based Merdle upon a real-life figure, John Sadleir, the Irish banker and railway promoter, who committed suicide on Hampstead Heath in 1855. But Merdle is given none of the particularity of Sadleir's earlier career, because Dickens's purpose is to show not a swindler's progress, but Merdle as a kind of black hole which sucks money in, only for it to vanish like anti-matter. Merdle has no enjoyment from his scheming – no appetite for food, drink, horses, clothes, sensuality: he is a darkly inane figure, part of a mysterious process of acquiring and dissipating money, that Dickens deliberately shows

---

[1] All references are by book or volume (where appropriate); chapter; and page to the edition given in the Bibliography.

as mysterious.[2]

Yet such representations by Dickens and others do not necessarily spring from ignorance. Dickens himself in the 1840s had struggled to secure the financial backing to launch a newspaper, *The Daily News*, while in Manchester, Elizabeth Gaskell (1810-1865) knew many mill-owners, not only as members of her husband's Unitarian congregation but as manufacturers to whose premises she regularly took visitors, just as she knew and conducted visitors to see James Nasmyth's engineering works at Patricroft. Yet in reading Elizabeth Gaskell's *Ruth* (1853), it is difficult to identify the business of Mr Bradshaw, the most influential member of a Nonconformist congregation. He seems to have a factory or mill, and his partner is necessarily absent on the Continent, especially Germany, for weeks and even months at a time. More important to the novel than the Bradshaw product is the fact of the business, conducted with rigour but justice by Bradshaw, and his willingness to undertake financial business for others: he has invested money for the chapel minister, Mr Benson, holds the certificates, and pays out the interest. It is upon Bradshaw's business and religious principles and upon the criminal opportunities given his son by shares the firm holds that a crucial plot element turns, rather than upon the need to know whether he produces yarn or cloth and what the production process is.

That commercial and financial processes could indeed be the stuff of romance, giving pleasure through the imaginative faculty, Thomas Macaulay shows in his *History of England* (1848-61), describing the founding of the Bank of England (Ch.XX), the origin and nature of the National Debt (Ch.XIX), and the restoration of the currency (Chs. XXI and XXII). The misery resulting from the corrupt coinage, Macaulay declared to be worse than bad Kings, bad Ministers, bad Parliaments, for bad currency produced 'wrangling from morning to night...Even men of business were often bewildered by the confusion into which all pecuniary transactions were thrown', while under bad government still

> 'the grocer weighed out his currants: the draper measured out his broadcloth: the hum of buyers and sellers was as loud as ever in the

---

[2] For information about banking or financial procedures see Bagehot or (with reference to the literature) Russell.

towns: the harvest home was celebrated as joyously as ever in the hamlets: the cream overflowed the pails of Cheshire: the apple juice foamed in the presses of Herefordshire...' [III.xxi.392]

Yet if the authors do not set out to inform us in detail, they were well aware of the transactions of an industrial and a business age, more aware of business *per se*, indeed, than were writers in the first half of the century. People, authors among them, had money and looked for ways to invest it, not in land (though urban – often meaning slum – housing became an important investment) but in business, with railways at home and abroad an obvious opportunity from the 1830s onward. Trade recessions and losses of business confidence alternated with periods of boom and are often reflected in fictional plot turns and crises: the 1840s railway frenzy and the busts associated with George Hudson and John Sadleir; the trade stagnation of the 1830s and 1850s; the Bank Charter Act suspended in 1847, 1857, and 1866.[3] The sense of industrial power actual and latent had long been recognised and was stressed still. Thomas Carlyle (1795-1881), a Romantic by date of birth, whose main work and influence was on the Victorian period, lauded work as heroic. To Carlyle, the Industrial Age was an achievement as great as a force of Nature and greater because it was man-made and man-controlled. The trample of boots and clogs on a Manchester Monday morning was the sound of a staggering power:

> 'Hast thou heard, with sound ears, the awakening of a Manchester, on Monday morning, at half-past five by the clock; the rushing-off of its thousand mills, like the boom of an Atlantic tide, ten-thousand times ten-thousand spools and spindles all set humming there, – it is perhaps if thou knew it well, sublime as a Niagara, or more so.' [*Chartism* (1840); p.211]

Manchester – a 'Shock' City

Manchester had been a key city in the earlier stages of the Industrial Revolution, a 'shock' city,[4] receiving the brunt of industrialisation's onset and a shock to the world, a place to be visited, the place of the new. Benjamin Disraeli (1804-1881), later Prime Minister, set

---

[3] See Horsman, p.150; Russell, pp.140-41.

[4] Briggs, p.56 and Ch.3, 'Manchester: Symbol of an Age'.

Manchester up in his novels as the successor to Rome and Athens. In *Coningsby* (1844), Disraeli's hero, wishing to complete his education, proposes to go to Italy and Greece. But a mystic figure, Sidonia (Disraeli's novels, often funny and theatrically effective, are full of such mysterious strangers, who, combining wisdom with all knowledge, are curiously like their author would wish himself to be), counsels him otherwise:

> 'I never was in the Mediterranean,' said Coningsby. 'There is nothing I should like so much as to travel.'
> 'You are travelling,' rejoined his companion. 'Every moment is travel, if understood!'
> 'Ah! but the Mediterranean!' exclaimed Coningsby. 'What would I not give to see Athens!'
> 'I have seen it,' said the stranger, slightly shrugging his shoulders; 'and more wonderful things. Phantoms and spectres! The Age of Ruins is past. Have you seen Manchester?' [III.i.141][5]

Industry, trade, transport transformed the age: London was finance and commerce; Manchester, as the Cook and Watts Warehouse (1851; now the Britannia Hotel), with its great staircase and display floors proclaimed, was making and selling. The age was a business age and the writers were well aware of this transformation: it was the material of their fiction and they saw themselves increasingly as part of it. The processes of printing and publication were transformed by steam printing and by stereotyping, by linotype and railway distribution, by increased population and wider education. More and more authors in the later Victorian period saw themselves as professionals and became increasingly concerned about the value of their product. Professionalisation did not necessarily mean writing full time, any more than now. So Anthony Trollope (1815-1882) never gave up his day job with the Post Office, while the Brontë sisters always had the certainty of a roof over their heads at Haworth, so long as their father survived (though they had no reason to think that he would – as he did – outlive them all). The Haworth Parsonage, in turn, benefitted considerably from Charlotte Brontë's income, with new furniture,

---

[5] See also the opening of Bk IV: 'rightly understood, Manchester is as great a human exploit as Athens'; and Disraeli's less happy claims for Birkenhead's superiority over Damascus: *Tancred* (1847), V.v.378-9.

wallpaper, carpets, and curtains from the success of *Jane Eyre* (1847). Again and again, authors show an awareness of the need to deal and to know how to deal in the market-place. Dickens was a shrewd businessman, his determination and acumen sharpened by disadvantageous contracts, signed in the first flush of his success, from which he escaped only with some difficulty. Once free, Dickens controlled his own work and copyright, became in the 1850s his own publisher, and effectively paid Bradbury and Evans as printers rather than publishers. He worked his copyrights in a series of editions and invested time and energy as well as money in a weekly magazine. He died in 1870 worth £93,000, so his executor and biographer John Forster estimated, and surely underestimated, since this included only two years' purchase on the magazine and probably nothing on the copyrights.[6] George Eliot (1819-1880) was equally successful, building on her experience as *de facto* editor of *The Westminster Review*, with all its hurly-burly of journalism and editorial work. In the fiction market, apart from the excellence of the product, she had her partner, George Henry Lewes, to negotiate the best price and conditions. By 1873, George Eliot had enough money invested, with other income, to enjoy £5,000 a year, and could afford to have her underwear made for her.[7] In common with other Victorians, Elizabeth Gaskell had shares in Liverpool's Catherine Dock and in the Manchester, Sheffield and Lincolnshire Railway,[8] while Charlotte Brontë, even before her literary earnings, had railway shares (which caused her some anxiety): later, Charlotte's publisher, George Smith, put money for her into Government funds. Charlotte's marriage settlement (1854), by which she shrewdly alienated all her money from her husband, shows £1,678 in trust.[9] These dealings and earnings came out of a shrewd knowledge of the market. George Eliot raised her price (her success made this possible) from £800 for *Adam Bede* (1859) to

---

[6] Forster, p.860 (Appendix: Dickens's Will). What £93,000 would be worth in today's terms is of course highly problematical: see Patten, particularly the Introduction (p.3), and the whole work for an excellent account of Dickens as businessman.

[7] Haight, pp.458-59; investments included 'stocks and bonds of railways and public utilities, many of them American' (p.455).

[8] *The Letters of Mrs Gaskell*, p.690.

[9] E. Gaskell, *The Life of Charlotte Brontë*, pp.232, 567 (note to p.448).

£2,000 for *The Mill on the Floss* (1860) to £7,000 for *Romola* (1863); *Middlemarch* (1872) brought in £9,000 over seven years.[10] If George Eliot was a star, even Elizabeth Gaskell, who did not turn the screw so tightly, could eventually expect £600 and £1,000 for a novel.[11] These facts and figures, however briefly given, stress the business awareness of writers of the period, their hard-headedness eliciting admiration. There was some shock when Anthony Trollope in his *Autobiography* (1875-76; published 1883) set out his mechanical production of a set number of words a day, regardless, plus a table of his earnings,[12] but knowledge of business deals and operations never adversely affected the sense of Charles Dickens's or George Eliot's genius.

English Literature and the Age of Business

When writers came to represent business in their work, why did they do so? The first and most obvious answer, though it has to be tied in with a strong literary convention of realism, is that these writers sought to validate their work, to make it convincing to their readers, by representing their age. There were business transactions, trade deals, manufacturing contracts, and these spoke of the reality of the world when embodied in literary form. In George Eliot's *Middlemarch* (1872), its heroine, Dorothea Brooke, is constrained by things which need not have bothered an heroic spirit like St Theresa of Avila in 16th-century Spain. Dorothea's aspirations are as high as the Spanish saint's, but she must painfully recognise the constrictions of the world against which she beats her wings in vain, just as the idealistic doctor, Lydgate, is in some measure defeated by setting up home with furniture he cannot afford and which must yet be paid for. Economics are not the sole consideration, but the realities of a world of buying and selling, of goods against cash, are part of the world that these Victorians seek to recreate within their fiction.

---

[10] Figures from Haight; they take no account of the particular arrangements that brought the rights back to the author after a fixed term: for example with *Adam Bede* it was a copyright sold for four years, with *Romola* for 10. Further money came from American publication, translations, and Continental publication in English.

[11] For details of Gaskell's payments, see *Elizabeth Gaskell: The Critical Heritage*, pp.4-13.

[12] XX.316-7; he reckoned just under £69,000 between 1847 and 1879.

But the novels (and later the plays) of the period are not mere photographic reproductions of society, tempted though the novelist Harold Biffen is, in George Gissing's *New Grub Street* (1891), by the idea of a novel which would be exactly true to life:

> '...What I really aim at is an absolute realism in the sphere of the ignobly decent...I don't know any writer who has treated ordinary vulgar-life with fidelity and seriousness. Zola writes deliberate tragedies; his vilest figures become heroic from the place they fill in a strongly imagined drama...' [I.10.173]

The result, Biffen admits, would be 'something unutterably tedious', and the Victorians were not into that. Again and again these writers seek to dwell on what Dickens called 'the romantic side of familiar things' – not simply the London fog or the money bill or the twist of thread, represented though each was in its reality, but the fog realised and then transformed to a metaphor for legal obfuscation, for pervasive disease, the money bill a trap for the usurer's victim, the twist of thread a clue to tie together people who knew nothing of each other's existence. Business provides opportunities of setting, plot, character, satire, analysis, prediction. Society is again and again represented as an interconnective structure, 'this great web' as George Eliot called it in *Middlemarch*, and the transactions of business interweave and lead on. Society is seen as multi-layered and its analysis as a means to understand something immensely complex. Plot may show the interconnections: a financier who breaks or who peculates ruins not just himself and his family (paradoxically, may not ruin his family at all), ruins not just large investors, but whole swathes of individuals who have contributed their mite to his enterprises. In Elizabeth Gaskell's *Cranford* (1853) it is (correctly) rumoured that the Town and County Bank will break. The elderly heroine, Miss Matty, shows her faith in the Bank by exchanging coins for the bewildered countryman's worthless banknote, and then, her own money lost in the crash, sets herself up to sell tea and sweets. She is a comic conception (in the larger sense of 'comedy') of those at all levels of society who suffer when the financial dam bursts and its waters sweep away investor, depositor, tradesman, and the genteel middle-class. The fall-out is through the depths as well as the breadth of society. And that sense of layers and of the reactions to different kinds of business and business people leads into a major preoccupation, which is class. Business throws up questions of where a man comes from, on what sufferance he may do his business, what lines (if any) he may cross. Can a financier be a gentleman? Can a tailor? 'But,' Dora Milvain asks in *New Grub Street*, 'is an advertising agent a gentleman?' (II.22.330). If these writers analyse class, can a way be found to represent England's social and political history and begin to construct a future?[13]

As already suggested, writers do not necessarily go into detail of process: that fascination is more obviously a French one, with Balzac's financial intrigues in *César Birotteau* (1837) or Zola's worlds of business that explore the traffic of laundering or prostitution or department stores (*L'assomoir* (1877); *Nana* (1880); *The Ladies' Paradise* (1883)). Yet significant detail can be 'read' and understood. In Elizabeth Gaskell's *Ruth* (1853), a dressmaker's workshop at the opening is detailed and our understanding of its organisation and economics essential to Ruth's subsequent history. This is not a novel about sweated labour, yet the harsh conditions that govern a trade where the business is controlled, not by steady production, but by demand, are vividly established:

> '...more than a dozen girls still sat in the room into which Ruth entered, stitching away as if for very life, not daring to gape, or show any outward manifestation of sleepiness. They only sighed a little when Ruth told Mrs Mason the hour of the night [two o'clock]...for they knew that, stay up late as they might, the work-hours of the next day must begin at eight, and their young limbs were very weary.
> Mrs Mason worked away as hard as any of them; but she was older and tougher; and, besides, the gains were hers.' [I.1.7]

The girls eat standing in their breaks, so as not to spoil the materials, and Ruth finds little consolation in the thought that it will not always be as bad as tonight: 'We often get to bed by ten o'clock' (I.1.11) is scarcely reassuring. Mrs Mason herself as a business woman is not cruel, but she needs in her own financial straitness (a widow, she has six or seven children dependent on her) to be ignorant of what her apprentices do on a Sunday, otherwise fire and a meal might be expected. Ruth, who has no relatives or friends, stays in the house, but without warmth or food beyond a bun or

---

[13] And not just England: class is a key issue in America too. See, for example, Edith Wharton (1862-1937) in *The House of Mirth* (1905) and *The Age of Innocence* (1920).

biscuit in the workroom, separated by her status from the servant in the kitchen. With such toil and friendlessness, so carefully established, it is no surprise that Ruth responds to the companionship, then passion, of the dashing Mr Bellingham, which leads to the crisis of 'discovery' by Mrs Mason, of dismissal, and of Bellingham taking Ruth to London and then Wales, where she is abandoned, pregnant. Details of stitching, Persian silks, matching of colours and materials, are the validation of a business that explains Ruth's conduct and develops her story.

Dickens's Little Dorrit: *English Social Hierarchy and Business*

I have referred to examples of business: finance, manufactures, dress-making, and to the conception of society as layered by class and socially interconnected. It may be useful to consider a novel that serves to illustrate both what 'business' means and how society is represented. Dickens's *Little Dorrit* peculiarly exemplifies the hierarchical nature of English society, as Dickens came to conceive it. And it is intensely concerned with business that involves economic transactions, exchanges of labour and goods for other goods or services or cash. Business constantly goes on in *Little Dorrit*'s world. Seamstresses, dressmakers, dancing masters, horse-dealers, keepers of inns, pieshops, and lodgings, bankers, theatre directors, tobacconists, wine merchants: the novel weaves these and financial and commercial dealers into all the traffic of society. This essay is not concerned with political or social business, Parliament, for example, or the Civil Service, or the family, though causal connection or metaphor may link such activities to business, as Dickens does in *Little Dorrit*, representing a network of political corruption and influence; of jobbery; and of posts under government seized upon greedily for the salary and for reciprocal favours. When Merdle the financier is bought into the Government interest, part of the 'dowery' is a job for life for his gormless step-son, Sparkler, in the Circumlocution Office. The satire of *Little Dorrit* on the failure of government to do its business, to get things done, sets the word 'business' resonating against 'jobs' and 'jobbery', just as that satire echoed, at the time of the novel's publication during the criminally mismanaged Crimean War, the demand of the Administrative Reform Association, constituted largely of men active in finance, shipping, and industry, for efficiency in public affairs and for the 'right man in the right place'.

The greatest businessman in *Little Dorrit* is Merdle, the master spirit of the age, into everything good, and without whose name no one will consider a project or an enterprise. He is an MP and has a bank, among many other things. He has a wife to run the Society side, though for all his vast schemes, his excellent health (he has 'the concentration of an oyster'), his display of wealth, he is yet browbeaten by his own butler, while his lips are powdered black as though with a trail of gunpowder and he seems constantly, in his nervous gesture of grasping one wrist with a hand, to be taking himself into custody. While Society woos him, cadges money, urges him to throw his political weight behind them, he is not a gentleman. His wife and stepson complain that Merdle carries his business affairs about with him, that (in his stepson Sparkler's irreverent phrase) he 'carries the Shop about, on his back rather – like Jew clothesman with too much business' (I.xxxiii.386). Goaded by his wife's demands that he accommodate himself to Society, Merdle retorts:

> '...in the name of all the infernal powers...who does more for Society than I do? Do you see these premises, Mrs Merdle? Do you see this furniture, Mrs Merdle? Do you look in the glass and see yourself, Mrs Merdle? Do you know the cost of all this, and who it's all provided for? And yet will you tell me that I oughtn't to go into Society? I, who shower money upon it in this way? I, who might be almost said–to–to– to harness myself to a watering-cart full of money, and go about, saturating Society, every day of my life?' [I.xxxiii.384]

At this stage, the semitic slur suggested by Sparkler's comparison to the Jew clothesman is hardly directed more than subliminally at Merdle by either Sparkler or Dickens. The canard, though, is commonly enough associated with finance and is later made quite shockingly explicit in Anthony Trollope's *The Way We Live Now* (1875).

Merdle is a man from nowhere, a monstrous mushroom growth, but the old-fashioned financial House of Clennam goes back into the 18th century, so old-fashioned indeed that it avoids being swept up into Merdle speculation fever (an abstention that is also a plot requirement). If Merdle's business is deliberately obscured by Dickens, to enforce the combination of the financier's criminal swindling and his dupes' eagerness to be cut into a 'share of the action', the House of Clennam's business is merely obscure. It has dealt in goods, but now uses a commission-merchant for all such business. Clennam and his father have been 20 years in China, but to what end by way of trade or transaction is unknown. The House offers money facilities to those recommended by its foreign correspondents; and one of its partners goes about the institutions and coffee-houses where business is done – the Custom's House, the Exchange, Garraway's – but we are little the wiser about what goes on to make its meagre profit. Against Merdle, it is respectable but hardly thriving, running down and haunted by some secret, the very fabric of the building loosening, shifting, and in the end falling, as the business house, and the family home, and the personal structure of the Clennam family all collapse when the guilty secret of its chief partner comes out. For Mrs Clennam, that chief partner, has a dark secret, hidden beneath the darker threatenings of a perverse Calvinism. And yet, we note, in business she is an equal partner. She may assert that as a woman she has no power, but she is partner in the firm and with her son's withdrawal, senior partner, a reminder of the presence of women at all levels of business in the 19th century, even if her guilty secret reveals among other things that she has had no legal right to be a partner. Her marriage was invalid and the man known as her son is not hers at all. That supposed son, Arthur Clennam, fearful that a wrong has been perpetrated by the firm, resigns his share in the House of Clennam and seeks the means of livelihoood elsewhere, investing his money with Doyce the engineer, an inventor, whose workshop produces (unspecified) engineering goods. Doyce is chaffed by his friend Meagles as a genius but no man of business, a common stereotype. Yet Doyce proves to be shrewdly business-like, and welcomes Arthur to provide the office expertise in correspondence and book-keeping that allows him to work at the mechanical side, eventually to be summoned by a 'certain barbaric Power', which

> 'had occasion for the services of one or two engineers, quick in invention and determined in execution: practical men, who could make the men and means their ingenuity perceived to be wanted, out of the best materials they could find at hand...' [II.xxii.643]

This barbaric Power, probably Russia in the context of the 1850s, seeks to have things done, a smart hit by Dickens at England's great discovery of How Not To Do It. Against Doyce, the engineer, the mechanical artist, Dickens places Henry Gowan, a painter, a man with a grievance, who believes his order, the nobs, owes him a living (and has failed to give him one) and resents alike its neglect and its patronage. He claims to be a businessman. Dickens was sure that the artist should be fully professional and asserted the claims of the dignity of literature. But Gowan claims that all business is a matter of selling dear what is produced cheap, and that he is no greater an imposter than anyone else; they all do it:

> 'Painters, writers, patriots, all the rest who have stands in the market. Give almost any man I know, ten pounds, and he will impose upon you to a corresponding extent; a thousand pounds – to a corresponding extent; ten thousand pounds – to a corresponding extent.' [I.xxvi.303]

There is nothing wrong in an artist having a head for business; what grates is Gowan's 'slight, careless, amateur way' (I.xvii.206).

Below these is a range of small financial agents. The biggest fish in this pool is Casby, 'the patriarch', his white locks and benevolent appearance disguising a voracious rack-renter. Formerly Lord Barnacle's town-agent, Casby has bought houses as a speculation and employs his own agent, Pancks, to screw rents out of his tenants. Pancks, seen as the tyrant, not merely Casby's tool, is one of those ambiguous figures in Dickens, who, essentially benevolent in his eccentricity, seems yet inexplicably bound to work for his dark master, to take the blame, and unable (until driven beyond all bearing) to take revenge or even simply go elsewhere. Pancks lodges at the house of Rugg, a general agent, debt collector, and money advisor. Rugg's daughter has been shrewd enough in business to bring an action for breach of promise against the local baker and invested the damages awarded in government stock. Rugg is not averse to lending money at high interest, even when entering into a friendly conspiracy with his lodger, charging Pancks 20 per cent (5 per cent was a fairly standard 19th-century rate). Below these again come the self-employed artisans, notably Plornish the Plasterer of Bleeding Heart Yard, who finds work scarce, and whose wife is set up in business as a grocer, her neighbours determined to help the shop by patronising it:

> 'Influenced by these noble sentiments, they had even gone out of their way to purchase little luxuries in the grocery and butter line to which they were unaccustomed; saying to one another, that if they did stretch a point, was it not for a neighbour and a friend, and for whom ought a

point to be stretched if not for such? So stimulated, the business was extremely brisk, and the articles in stock went off with the greatest celerity. In short, if the Bleeding Hearts had but paid, the undertaking would have been a complete success...' [II.xiii.551-2]

Social Distinctions Among the Professions

Separate from trade, yet still in some sense business, are the professions. An interestingly anomalous example in Dickens's novel is Mrs General, employed by Mr Dorrit to form his daughters, to teach them correct polite behaviour. She again raises class distinctions. She insists she is not a governess, that often miserable and certainly ambiguous creature, suspended between family and servants. Mrs General refuses to talk about contracts and salary, while making it clear that she received £300 for forming the single daughter of her previous employer and must therefore have one-third more in a family where there are two daughters: by contrast, a governess might have expected between £20 and £50 at this time. Mrs General thus avoids losing the gentility she claims through birth and marriage (her father a clergyman, her husband military). While the daughters of gentlefolk became governesses, their status in the families where they worked was rarely that of gentility.

More clearly professional than Mrs General, their depiction exploring the subtle shadings of class distinction and boundaries that entwine and hedge 19th-century business, are the barrister, known simply as Bar, and the physician, again simply so called. Dickens is entertained by Bar, as well as suspicious of him, as Dickens usually is of lawyers. Bar exploits language and gesture, playing to his audience, using facial expression to collude with or intimidate jurymen, yet he works hard, has a sense of purpose. He is admitted to Society, dines with Merdle, and is instrumental in getting Merdle and Lord Decimus Tite Barnacle (literally) together, so that a political bargain may be struck. Bar is a barrister, not an attorney or solicitor. In the law, a barrister is a gentleman, but the distinctions grow more uneasy below that level. In medicine, a surgeon might be regarded as little more than a descendant of the barber-surgeons, blood-letters, tooth-drawers, 'saw-bones', mechanicians.   A physician, who does not work with his hands, who directs the pharmacist,[14] but does not himself dispense, is a gentleman. But the Victorians generally also admire the physician for his healing powers and a knowledge of humanity, held confidentially and acquired when, reduced by illness to helpless and pitiful individuals, people are stripped of their pretentions to honour or wealth or power. Yet the physician does not mock people in their nakedness, but seeks to cure or helps to die.

Dickens, like other writers, draws on the image of Jesus as the healer, who cured without distinction of race or position, and in *Little Dorrit*, a novel where Merdle is seen as the anti-Christ, people standing so the shadow of that great man may fall upon them, the character Physician becomes a shadowing counterpart of the Divine Healer, set against Merdle. Physician attends Merdle, but does not judge him. His knowledge, no matter of fact alone, allows him a survey of humanity that would be terrifying if revealed, yet is never put to improper use:

> 'Few ways of life were hidden from Physician, and he was oftener in its darkest places than even Bishop. There were brilliant ladies about London who perfectly doted on him, my dear, as the most charming creature and the most delightful person, who would have been shocked to find themselves so close to him if they could have known on what sights those thoughtful eyes of his had rested within an hour or two, and near to whose beds, and under what roofs, his composed figure had stood...Many wonderful things did he see and hear, and much irreconcileable moral contradictions did he pass his life among; yet his equality of compassion was no more disturbed than the Divine Master's of all healing was.' [II.xxv.672-3]

A doctor is but one way, though an important one, in which parallels may be drawn between the world of business and the world of the gospels, parallels prompted not only by Satan's temptation of Christ and by Matthew being summoned from the collection of taxes and by the cleansing of the Temple, but also by the constant business traffic of the parables: of talents, and vineyards, and silver

---

[14] The dispensing of drugs was an issue through much of the 19th century (it plays a key part in Lydgate's eventual disaster in George Eliot's *Middlemarch*), as was the status of the surgeon. Pharmacists rose as a distinct trading class, while surgeons, with the development of medical research and teaching, could increasingly claim to be gentlemen.

pence, and stewards, and debtors, and rich men entering the kingdom of heaven.

In *Little Dorrit*, people's business affairs become entangled or involved. The novel's great metaphors are of imprisonment and of debt, combined literally in the Marshalsea Debtors' Prison. Debt can slide into bankruptcy; the novel's concern is to represent an insolvent society, politically, morally, and financially. Yet here too important distinctions drawn from business reality are made. Mr Dorrit has been imprisoned for debt (probably over some government contract) for nearly a quarter of a century. His affairs are entangled, he has no idea how, and he is clearly unfitted for business, yet he was not criminal in his financial dealings. On the other hand, Merdle's spectacular fall reveals his 'complaint' as not physical illness nor 'pressure', but, quite simply, 'Forgery and Robbery' (II.xxv.680). Yet Merdle is not even declared bankrupt, while his fall involves many others in his ruin. Clennam, partner to Doyce, who has invested the firm's money with Merdle, unable to satisfy his creditors, is arrested and chooses to go also to the Marshalsea Debtors' Prison. All seems lost. He becomes a scapegoat, a living object of execration now death has placed Merdle beyond reach of his victims. Yet since arrest for debt meant also that no seizure could be made of the debtor's goods or assets, the firm and Clennam can eventually be saved by payment of the debts (Doyce the engineer returns financially successful from the barbaric Power) and the business be set running, more firmly established than ever. In a business situation, known to Dickens and accurately represented by him, to be imprisoned and one's assets thus secured, proves an advantage.

Questions of Status and Class

The hierarchical organisation of *Little Dorrit* and the questions of status with regard to Merdle and to Bar and Physician touch very clearly on questions of class. But first, after this exemplification of the range and niches of business activity represented by Dickens, I want to consider more generally the way that business marks people and how writers represent and exploit those stigmata. Business, and more particularly trade, has its marks, sometimes physical and permanent, sometimes only in dress, sometimes in necessary restrictions of time: in business, dinner, the main meal of the day, is eaten at one o'clock or two, while the gentry eat at six or eight (as will financiers moving in or into society). The businessman must be in his office, while the gentry ride for airing and social intercourse in Hyde Park between two and four. Plornish the plasterer in *Little Dorrit* is marked by his trade, his clothes lime-whitened, and he fills a gap in the conversation by picking 'a bit of lime out of his whisker, [putting] it between his lips, [and turning] it with his tongue like a sugar-plum' (I.xii.143). Even trades less manual entail marks, though some are in the eye of the beholder. At the end of George Gissing's *New Grub Street* the 'hero', Jasper Milvain, recalls Marian, the woman who lives by writing and whom he has *not* married: 'Do you know, I never could help imagining that she had ink-stains on her fingers. Heaven forbid that I should say it unkindly!' (though clearly, he does). 'It was touching to me at the time, for I knew how fearfully hard she worked' (III.37.550). The facts of trade are that it takes time to master, that it is difficult to be master of more than one, and that the training and occupation have their signs, not least the very physical conformation of the body. Ruth in Elizabeth Gaskell's novel has the numbing experience of dress-making, while in George Meredith's *Evan Harrington* (1861), Evan, as someone who would master the trade of tailor, is confronted by the grim prospect 'that at the root of the tree of tailoring the novitiate must sit no less than six hours a day with his legs crossed and doubled under him, cheerfully plying needle and thread' (XXXVIII.397). Trade takes your time and physically alters you. H.G.Wells followed through the evolutionary implications of such physical deformity in *The Time Machine* (1895) with his Eloi and Morlocks, the human race splitting into the light effete race of the surface, the dark bestial race of underground.

If trade so marks a man or woman and is inseparable from the business, at what point do these signs, if not plaster splashes or ink stains or feeble physique or sallow complexion, yet the witnesses of business, fade and allow someone to pass as a gentleman, whether in appearance or in the acceptance of society? Dress may do this, markedly distinct spheres of work and leisure, or one's habitation. In Elizabeth Gaskell's *Ruth*, the manufacturer Bradshaw determines to buy a country house, Eagle's Crag, provoked by a casual remark. The town's prospective MP, far from being impressed by Bradshaw's production of pineapples on his table, pities those who cannot afford their own hothouse, 'as if to be without a pinery were indeed a depth of pitiable destitution' (II.xxii.218). Bradshaw purchases Eagle's Crag, exorbitantly dear though it is, first and foremost as a means of exhibiting his wealth. He also begins that progress, though, so characteristic of the increasingly well-to-do businessman, who has two houses (one for weekdays, one for weekends) and, in due course, only one from which he commutes, proof that he no longer carries the Shop with him. A progress through houses is also traced in H.G.Wells's *Tono-Bungay* (1909), as Uncle Ponderevo's growing wealth takes him from a dead-and-alive Kentish town to London digs, through small house and large Home Counties house, to the buying up of an old family's home and the eventual building of his own. Not one house, in fact, successfully transfers Ponderevo to the inner circle of gentility, even though these later moves mark 'those magnificent years that followed his passage from trade to finance' (III.1(i).187).

Again and again, authors are interested in the degrees that mark out tradesmen from financier from gentleman. When does 'shop' or business become removable like a suit, to be left behind in the office? Such a question lies behind the complaint of Mrs Merdle and the observation of her son, that Merdle carries the business about with him: he might leave it behind and yet will not. Finance of course is not associated with articles produced for sale – such articles themselves usually being judged on a sliding scale: in Meredith's *Evan Harrington* a distinction is made between tailoring and brewing, partly a matter of the physical constraint (the tailor stitches *and* keeps a shop), partly of the money generated. But finance itself may have its own brand. It is not landed property, nor is it unearned income. The financier is in all the hurly-burly of money and market transactions. The old resentments of the poor (including the impoverished gentry) and the unsuccessful may surface against the financier, especially if he falls from grace. Where do financiers come from? And what is their nature? In fiction, many of them come from nowhere, rootless men, and some at least are tainted with usury and the Jew. A comparison of Dickens's Merdle and Trollope's Melmotte from *The Way We Live Now* is instructive both in the concept of the financier as an unknown man and in the contrast of treatment.

Merdle and Melmotte: Dickens's and Trollope's 'Financiers'
Merdle comes from nowhere. He is established in his position of affluence and influence when we meet him, accepted by Society:

'Mr Merdle was immensely rich; a man of prodigious enterprise; a Midas without the ears, who turned all he touched to gold. He was in everything good, from banking to building. He was in Parliament, of course. He was in the City, necessarily. He was Chairman of this, Trustee of that, President of the other. The weightiest of men had said to projectors, "Now, what name have you got? Have you got Merdle?" And, the reply being in the negative, had said, "Then I won't look at you".' [I.xxi.244]

Though Dickens based Merdle on an original, John Sadleir, 'that precious rascality', as Dickens called him,[15] he does not trace Merdle's earlier career and indeed we never learn anything about his origins, any more than we ever see him at work. He carries the 'shop' about with him, but his whole reputation is built up by others, so far as the action of the novel is concerned. At Merdle's dinner party, the guests accumulate by hundreds of thousands of pounds, one from another, the rumour of the value of his latest coup, and all the time the reader has the evidence of Merdle before him, a man without energy, of sluggish blood, overshadowed by his magnificent butler (who looking out of the window is mistaken by admiring passers-by for his master).

Anyone might see through him: as of course people do in retrospect, for that is part of Dickens's point. A man so situated does not need delicacy or intelligence, once people believe in him. He becomes an object of worship, a figure of gold, Mammon himself or the anti-Christ in an age where signs and wonders herald the end of all things. He is a religion, whose worshippers, abject believers, are seized by a devout desire to be both cured and trampled by him, and he is a disease, which must and will run its course. London becomes, with Merdle's death and the revelation that he is 'Forgery and Robbery', a pullulating body possessed by a putrid fever. The talk

'swelled into such a roar when night came, as might have brought one to believe that a solitary watcher on the gallery above the Dome of St Paul's would have perceived the night air to be laden with a heavy muttering of the name of Merdle, coupled with every form of execration.' [II.xxv.680]

---

[15] Russell discusses Dickens's and Trollope's use of originals for Merdle and Melmotte.

What the reader has suspected all along becomes clear in Merdle's sordid end. He lies in a public bath where he has cut his throat, a man who went to do the deed dancing as though possessed by devils, and now revealed with 'an obtuse head, and coarse, mean, common features' (II.xxv.676). The financial Messiah is incarnate as this grossness and his dupes do not take kindly to having to say with Shakespeare's Caliban, 'what an ass I was to take this drunkard for a god'.

Merdle may be no gentleman (the butler, in resigning, makes it clear he has never taken Merdle to be such), but that he is English, native born, though never stated, is never in doubt. Trollope's Melmotte is not only a financier who deals in dubious schemes and finally breaks, but he is also a foreigner and indeed a Jew – though just as Dickens works through what other characters say and believe about Merdle, so also Trollope uses rumour rather than authorial statement. While we can never be exactly sure about Melmotte, we can be sure enough about his background and activities, be sure enough that the rumours derive from a core truth about the man, however much each detail is falsified in repetition or highly coloured. Like Merdle, Melmotte is a great financier, though one from the first called in question by some. Like Merdle, after reaching a high point – election as MP for Westminster and the entertaining of the Emperor of China to dinner, a highly comic episode, yet memorably and irretrievably damaging to all his schemes – Melmotte commits suicide, though not suddenly, for the process is set against a financial deadline in which Trollope and the reader pursue the quarry's twists and turnings.

Melmotte claims to be British born, but has arrived in London from France and we piece together a career that has taken in Frankfort (where the family was Jewish) and Paris (where they all became Christian), while later he is associated with a failed assurance company now located in Vienna (I.iv.30-31; I.xi.106-07; II.liv.32-3). Where Merdle's frauds are never suspected until the revelations sprung by his death, Melmotte is constantly shadowed by his past. Each stage of his London career is fought against an increasingly tight threat of failure to meet payment deadlines and so the imminence of ruin and flight. His greatest scheme is the South Central Pacific and Mexico Railway, an entire fiction (so far as we can grasp), but a highly profitable one. Melmotte runs his course, returned for Westminster, entertaining the Emperor of China, yet entangled in deferred payment for an estate, itself remortgaged to buy slum property in the East End. Faced with a charge of forgery and unable to get his daughter Marie to sign back the money he has, as future security, put into trust in her name, Melmotte reflects that 'men would at any rate remember him' (II.lxii.113).

Trollope largely presents Melmotte externally, through his actions at the office or the Railway board meetings and through the dense web of rumours. Yet his fraudulent purpose is never in doubt, even if, as Melmotte's end approaches, we are told the most remarkable circumstance of his career 'was the fact that he came almost to believe in himself' (II.lvi.57). In distinct contrast, Merdle remains and deliberately remains always occluded, a dark mystery upon which others project their fantasies and desires. As Melmotte, overtaken by events and defied by his daughter, who resists not only threats but beatings, he is both fraud and hero, a man who dares like Zola's heroes, especially in contrast to the jackals that accompany him and to the contemptible gentleman of good society. Yet for all his greatness (a dark greatness, true), Melmotte seems denigrated. On his last night, Melmotte goes down to the Commons, defiantly eats alone in the Members' dining room, and then, having drunk too much, disgraces himself in the Chamber, toppling forwards onto the MP in front of him, though able still with some difficulty to walk unaided out. True, he is allowed a death effective in its shocking quietness. He goes to his sitting room with a bottle of brandy:

> 'Neither of the ladies of the family came to him, nor did he speak of them. Nor was he so drunk then as to give rise to any suspicion in the mind of the servant. He was habitually left there at night, and the servant as usual went to his bed. But at nine o'clock on the following morning the maid-servant found him dead upon the floor. Drunk as he had been, – more drunk as he probably became during the night, – still he was able to deliver himself from the indignities and penalties to which the law might have subjected him by a dose of prussic acid.' [II.lxxxiii.319]

Melmotte is a man who lives with danger, yet Trollope makes him guilty of an extraordinarily clumsy forgery and leaves him without expedients or ruses to defy his opponents. Trollope seems to fear making Melmotte too heroic in a world of the greedy, the feeble, and the dull, though he makes a nice point in Marylebone's desire to erect a posthumous monument to him and there are hints that, with a pinch more luck, Melmotte might have survived and even thriven.

Melmotte was a Jew in Frankfort and while that is not particularly dwelt upon even by his enemies, the smear of 'Jew' bursts shockingly into Trollope's narrative. Dickens's references to Jews in *Little Dorrit* are observational: a minor law officer is a Jew; Sparkler compares Merdle in carrying the 'shop' around with him to a Jewish second-hand clothesman. When Georgiana Longstaffe in Trollope's novel, desperate for a husband, proposes to accept Mr Brehgert, the objections are not only that he is in his fifties, a widower with two children, and a tradesman ('a banker', Brehgert mildly observes), but and above all that he is a Jew. In her father's objections, we may wonder how far we hear the objection of caste or of the age or even of Trollope himself: "'A Jew! an old fat Jew! Heavens and earth! that it should be possible that you should think of it!...It will kill [your mother]. It will simply kill her...'" (II.lxv.143). Mrs Longstaffe's comment that there is surely something in the Bible against it, is some assurance on Trollope's own view, and Mr Brehgert's sensible letter to Georgiana and her foolish reply by which she effectively breaks off the engagement (II.lxxix.269-73, 276-7), sufficient to make clear that the marriage would have failed on her side. But the energy of execration disturbs not merely because of our reading *now* of such hatred: its vehemence lies too with a hatred that surfaces later in Sir Clifford Chatterley's hysterical denunciation of Mellors as working class and, more relevantly here, with the vivid contempt for trade and for tailoring in particular of Meredith's *Evan Harrington*.

Money, Race, Class and Morality

Brehgert, answering Mr Longstaffe's objections to his marrying Georgiana, stresses how Longstaffe has hardly kept pace with the movements of the age on Jews, while as for the idea that being in trade is an objection, 'my business is that of a banker; and I can hardly conceive it to be possible that any gentleman in England should object to his daughter marrying a banker, simply because the man is a banker' (II.lxxix.270). There is a perspective here on money: a banker is respectable, equal to the daughter of a gentleman, and again and again these writers offer us perspectives on money. Dickens's Paul Dombey in *Dombey and Son* (1848) had asked: What is money? What can it do? And told it can do anything, asks why, then, it did not save his mother? The challenge to money is perhaps naturally a common response, deriving from the Christian tradition of it as the root of all evil. It did not need R.H.Tawney, though, to point to *Religion and the Rise of Capitalism* (1926) for a strong link between the Protestant ethic and commercial success to be noted and (sometimes) approved. Still, the sense in the earlier part of the period is strong that money may be bad as well as good, according to its source, and that it can be put to base use as well as virtuous. Money in any quantity, indeed, is seen as unnecessary. The wealth which Mr Dorrit inherits in *Little Dorrit* vanishes (through Merdle) as though it had been fairy gold, leaving nothing achieved by its means, and the codicil of a will, that would benefit Amy, Little Dorrit herself, is burnt at her request by Arthur Clennam, without him knowing what it is, lest it be a barrier between them in happiness. They marry and pass down into the crowded street, blessed and happy in each other. Dickens is not such a fool as to think they can live literally without money – Clennam's partnership with Doyce is being remarkably successful – but the business of this world (to twist the word 'business' a little) is not with inherited money or money unearned.

In contrast, Trollope's *The Way We Live Now* offers, though without approving, an American perspective on money. Hamilton K.Fisker is the moving force behind the South Central Pacific and Mexico Railway. Far from being downhearted at Melmotte's suicide, he seeks to buy up every share he can, coming to England specially for the purpose:

> '...These shares are at a'most nothing now in London. I'll buy every share in the market. I wired for as many as I dar'd, so as not to spoil our own game, and I'll make a clean sweep of every one of them. Bu'st up! I'm sorry for [Melmotte] because I thought him a biggish man; – but what he's done'll just be the making of us over there.' [II.xcii.394]

Fisker is true to his business philosophy, early expressed, that 'there's more to be got out of the smash up of such an affair as this [the railway], if it should smash up, than could be made by years of hard work out of such fortunes as yours and mine in the regular way of trade' (I.x.85). Even so, Trollope allows there to be more weight in one word of Melmotte than a whole speech by Fisker. Merdle's railway would have crashed with everything else; Melmotte's, or rather America's, survives in what Trollope identifies as a new 'money age' – where financial trading is not to promote a product but to promote the generation of money that sticks to those who know a good thing and how to manipulate it; fortunes are to be made, not by the railway, but by floating railway shares (I.x.89-90). This new age is enforced by Mrs Hurtle, who comes to England hoping to marry the novel's romantic hero, Paul Montague. She is a new kind of woman in England: she has killed a man and is divorced from her husband (in one State at least). She believes in dollars and success, not tradition. To her, it would be better to see Melmotte than 'your Queen': what grandeur, what power. Yes, answers Paul, if Melmotte came by it honestly. Such a man, Mrs Hurtle insists, rises above honesty; this man with a scratch of the pen can send out or call in millions of dollars (I.xxvi.245-6). Trollope clearly delights in shocking his readers about business and morality, and in some degree challenges their assumptions, though Melmotte's situation is somewhat rockier than Mrs Hurtle believes. Still, Mrs Hurtle's is the voice of new ways, however unwelcome, and indeed Mrs Hurtle comes out well in her dealings with most people. In the end, though, she packs back to America, in the company significantly of Melmotte's widow and daughter: the widow marries Melmotte's confidential clerk and the daughter marries Fisker – once she is clear about married women's property in California. All these ladies are determined never to revisit England (II.xcviii.457), yet the Americanisation of business has been deferred rather than defeated.

If money is not tied in with Christian morality, nor to be legitimately gained by manipulating shares (both views are strongly represented within the period), then money may be a force for political and class transformations, once outdated and sentimental principles are jettisoned. The obvious advocate of this position is George Bernard Shaw. To him, money is powerful; without it, in society as presently constituted, there can be no reform or change. Here is a new master-worker relationship, where the benevolent employer provides first for the body, not the soul. In *Major Barbara* (1905), Andrew Undershaft, the munitions manufacturer, is set against his daughter Barbara, a major in the Salvation Army. The struggle that half a century before would have been between Barbara and Andrew for her father's soul, now is a struggle, often apparently effortless on the part of the witty Undershaft, for Barbara's enlightenment. She must understand that the Salvation Army (to which Shaw is not, as such, hostile) only patches over symptoms, cannot reach the root problem. Bread and tea exchanged for a confession and fake conversion is not transforming the world, as Barbara herself recognises when she rejoices that 'we have got rid of the bribe of bread'. Barbara experiences a crisis when the Army accepts a donation from Bodger's Whiskey, and again when she visits her father's factory, where there are fair wages and welfare provision: it is Utopian, even millennial, in its rational organisation and future prospects. Shaw is well aware of the paradoxes of his presentation. Undershaft is a dealer in death, yet his money goes to the welfare of his workers – Shaw could easily have made the proposal more palatable and less interesting, if Undershaft were a spinner or weaver or an ironfounder. For Undershaft the body, not the soul nor Carlyle's divine spark, must be provided for first.

'Captains of Industry': The Modern Heroes

Undershaft is a modern hero and in 1905 still recognisable as the hero redefined in the 1830s and 1840s by Thomas Carlyle, for whom the true benefactor was not a king or warrior, but he 'who first hammered out for himself an iron spade' (Carlyle, p.53). Carlyle coined the term 'Captains of Industry' to establish a new kind of warrior class.[16] Business itself became an heroic endeavour, though in a different key from that struck by Mrs Hurtle. In Dickens's *Bleak House* (1853), the ironmaster Rouncewell (whose mother is housekeeper at Chesney Wold, the home of the old landed interests) has great power in transforming society. He names his son Watt, after James Watt, the heroic engineer, though the ear of reaction hears it as an ominous repetition of the rebel Wat Tyler. Dickens sees Rouncewell as symptomatic of the new age, and a welcome symptom. Sir Leicester Dedlock is a gentleman in the best sense, but he is the best of an older way that, seized by paralysis, must now pass with all the stifling relics of a worn-out age. The horror at the idea that Rouncewell will stand for Parliament was manifestly ridiculous in 1853, but underlines the emergence of a new class that sought to challenge an older landowning caste.

Rouncewell, to the astonishment of some, has the manners of a gentleman, and while fun could be made of the rudeness of northern magnates, the figure of John Thornton in Elizabeth Gaskell's *North and South* (1855) exemplifies Carlyle's new industrial captain and

---

[16] See further Melada (1970).

new hero who seeks to cultivate himself and provide for his workforce. Thornton's father failed in business and Thornton, supported by his indomitable mother, paid off his father's debts and established himself as a millowner in Milton Northern (a lightly disguised Manchester). Thornton lives on the premises: his house is part of the mill complex and he is proud of that fact. He is not a wealthy man, as Milton men go, though well-to-do. Others have realised their wealth and turned it into land, while 'his was all floating capital, engaged in his trade' (II.ii.212). This is one reason he needs to bring in scab labour ('blacklegs') when the men go on strike, since otherwise he will break. It is only the financial aid given him by Margaret Hale, a southerner settled in Milton, that preserves him at a time of recession. Thornton is the north to Margaret's south, his world observed shrewdly by Margaret. These northern men are powerful through wealth and not afraid. Margaret likes that, though she urges Thornton, who is more thoughtful and more cultivated than most, that such power demands responsibility as well as ostentation, social acceptance as well as individualism. Thornton, while highly critical of some millowners, speaks for this new strength of the industrial north, in ways that echo Carlyle on racial characteristics and echo too those businessmen who believed they should not be put to unnecessary expense by law to curb their smoke or fence their machinery:

> '...I belong to Teutonic blood...we do not look upon life as a time for enjoyment, but as a time for action and exertion. Our glory and our beauty arise out of our inward strength, which makes us victorious over material resistance, and over greater difficulties still. We are Teutonic up here...in another way. We hate to have laws made for us at a distance. We wish people would allow us to right ourselves, instead of continually meddling...We stand up for self-government, and oppose centralisation.' [II.xv.334]

At the end of the period, Shaw's Undershaft is a very different figure: a southerner, established in the manufacturing process, with (apparently) no labour problems. But he too is a benevolent paternalist in the workplace, providing housing and welfare, a 'superman' still recognisably Carlyle's heroic Captain of Industry, though Shaw has very different purposes from Gaskell's conciliatory politics. Like Thornton, Undershaft is a new man, a point stressed by the firm of Undershaft never passing by inheritance but only to an orphan (as its founder had been), who must make his own way, from obscurity, without ancestors. If certain likenesses link Thornton and Undershaft, both are in marked distinction to H.G.Wells's Uncle Ponderevo in *Tono-Bungay*, though he too is a man without origins or ancestry. But Ponderevo is not a Captain of Industry, in any sense understood by Carlyle. He is an exploiter of advertising, of 'American' methods in business, in a field, patent medicines, that prompted the detailed and scathing report of the Patent Medicines Committee in August 1914. What Ponderevo's nephew, the narrator of *Tono-Bungay*, celebrates is this new emphasis on selling, even while he is charting a history of England and of class. Young Ponderevo exposes the sham of the huckster and the sham of the gentleman.

Social Climbing, Money, Commerce and Trade

The 'old proverb' says, 'It takes three generations to make a gentleman',[17] and most of these writers are keenly aware of social movement, usually though not invariably upward, and aware too of the commercial origins in fact (which they transfer to fiction) of many upper-class families. In Meredith's *Evan Harrington*, the Beckley estate, owned by Mrs Bonner, was bought by her father, a grocer (XV.158); the Jocelyns are noble, but they are Bonners on their mother's side and look eagerly to the Bonner inheritance. Yet this very fact, of money buying its way, becoming respectable in the third or even second generation, meant that people were acutely alive to distinctions and niceties, which sometimes astonish us and undoubtedly astonished some of their contemporaries.

Evan Harrington is about attitudes to business rather than about business itself. Evan himself determines, on the death of his father Melchisedec Harrington, the 'Magnificent Mel', a tailor who liked mixing with the gentry, going riding, and the rest, that he must become a tailor himself to pay off his father's debts. The novel's course shows how Evan avoids that fate, not by his own default, but by the machinations of his sister, the Countess, married to a Portugese nobleman, who fights a series of 'campaigns' designed to conceal the trade origins of herself and her two sisters, and to secure the hand of Rose Jocelyn for Evan. Much of the action takes place

---

[17] Melada (1970), p.13, quoting James Fennimore Cooper.

at Beckley, to which the Countess has contrived invitations for herself and Evan.

The comic possibilities of embarrassment and eventual discovery are fully exploited by Meredith, if the premise is accepted that being a tailor is so awful (part of this springs from the exaggerated notions of the Countess) and that exposure could be so long avoided. As 'Jew' was the fatal word in *The Way We Live Now* when Brehgert offered marriage to Georgiana, so 'snips' is the ignominious slur here. The disgust generated by the brand, not just of trade but of physical degradation (sitting cross-legged to work), is akin to that produced by 'Jew' in Trollope, and extraordinary for the sense of shame it generates. It is true that the Jocelyn family may rightly feel a deception is being practised upon them, but even before Evan's origins are known, 'snips' is a topic of ridicule and contempt. Rose herself, told the truth by Evan (despite his sister purloining from a servant Evan's letter of revelation), still is sickened by the idea and has to gaze on her beloved for reassurance. Even to herself, she cannot name what Evan is:

> '[S]he thought she had completely conquered whatever could rise against him. But when Juliana Bonner told her that day that Evan was not only the son of the thing, but the thing himself, and that his name could be seen any day in Lymport, and that he had come from the shop to Beckley, poor Rosey had a sick feeling that almost sank her. ...Her eyes had to feed on Evan, she had to taste some of the luxury of love, before she could gain composure...' [XXVII.286]

Meredith himself, ready to laugh at the English readiness to toady to those who are above trade (evidence, he notes, of how wrong Napoleon was to call us a nation of shopkeepers [II.10]), ready to laugh at the Countess (while admiring her campaigning skills), and to laugh at gentry whose wealth is from trade, seems in the end to denigrate business. The 'Great Mel' is laughed at but his adventures admired; the Countess if defeated retires in reasonable order to Italy; Evan inherits Buckley, even if he gives it away again. Meredith, in this comedy of embarrassment, insists that Evan should end, not stitching at his bench nor even running his shop, but married to Rose and in the first stages of the diplomatic service.

H.G. Wells on Class in English Society

More instructive on class, though equally convinced of its being deeply (and perniciously) embedded in the history and structure of

English society, is H.G.Wells's *Tono-Bungay*. Tono-Bungay itself, the business project, is a patent medicine, a cocktail of Uncle Ponderevo's contriving, containing two tonics (one with a marked effect on the kidneys), alcohol, and a secret ingredient (II.2(i).115). Ponderevo's nephew, George, is clear about this concoction, when invited to come into the business: it's 'a damned swindle'. Ponderevo enters his protest:

> 'I'd like to know what sort of trading isn't a swindle in its way. Everyone who does a large advertised trade is selling something common on the strength of saying it's uncommon. Look at Chickson – they made him a baronet. Look at Lord Radmore, who did it on lying about the alkali in soap!...It's the modern way!...[If not, among] other things, all our people would be out of work. Unemployed! I grant you Tono-Bungay *may* be – not *quite* so good a find for the world as Peruvian bark, but the point is, George – it *makes trade!*' [II.2(ii).118-19]

This is Mrs Hurtle's 'American' world of business, though some Americans felt they could learn from the British example.[18] Once George agrees to join his Uncle in the project, already started, with its assembly line and its advertising, he manages the mechanics of production and sales: 'It sounds wild, I know, but I believe I was the first man in the city of London to pack patent medicines through the side of the packing case, to discover there was a better way in than by the lid' (II.3(i).138). Ponderevo's advertisements, successful and unsuccessful, are laid out delightfully by Wells, including three 'preliminary sketches' by this 'Napoleon of domestic conveniences' (I.1(i).4). The company flotation produces a subscription of £150,000; soon Ponderevo has £2 million of property and a controlling influence near £30 million. The iridescent bubble expands and inevitably, with unrealisable securities in hand, bursts (though Tono-Bungay itself continues to 'this day' to sell regularly). Ponderevo flees with George to France (by flying machine), where he dies: he cannot outlive the enterprise that intoxicated him.

---

[18] In Henry James's *The Ambassadors* (1903), Chad, the scion of a successful manufacturer of a never-identified product, is struck by advertising in London: 'Advertising scientifically worked presented itself thus as the great new force: "It really does the thing, you know"' (12.iv.363).

Wells's Analysis of the History and Class System of England

But when he invokes 'this old British system' (III.2(viii).236), so stable and yet able to accommodate new men, Ponderevo touched on Wells's own analysis not only of business methods and speculative finance, but also, as Ponderevo's collapse leaves the building of his last home, Crest Hill, abandoned and already crumbling in its gerry-built splendour, on his analysis of the history of England. This began with Bladesover House, where George lived 'below stairs', his mother being the housekeeper, representative of that old world of landed gentry being taken over by the Chicksons and the Radmores, being taken over by the Ponderevos. The houses in which the Ponderevos live mark their social rise and aspirations. Yet, just as the baize door at Bladesover marked the boundary of below stairs and above stairs (through which George made secret raids upon the treasures hidden in the library), so also these houses again and again show Ponderevo up against the impermeable membrane of a rigid class system. For Wells this barrier must be broken, not for Ponderevo especially but for everyone, and the system itself destroyed.

Yet his regard for what England means also gives us the novel's closing bravura run down the Thames from Hammersmith to the open sea: 'To run down the Thames so is to run one's hand over the pages in the book of England from end to end' (IV.3(ii).348). Business in *Tono-Bungay* leads to a vision that suggests, from the Socialist Wells, an end to England, even though Wells, like other great Socialists, like George Orwell, for example, is intensely bound up with Englishness.[19]

> 'Out to the open we go, to windy freedom and trackless ways. Light after light goes down. England and the Kingdom, Britain and the Empire, the old pride and the old devotions, glide abeam, astern, sink down upon the horizon, pass – pass. The river passes – London passes, England passes...' [IV.3(ii).352]

It is an elegy and an epitaph for the old world. For the Utopian Wells there is an unknown yet vibrant future ahead, an old world to be discarded, a new world to be found. The novel does not end on

---

[19] That Vaughan Williams based a movement of his London Symphony on Wells's passage reinforces the Englishness.

'England passes', though its saying is deeply felt. It ends, rather, on a vision of the future, challenging yet optimistic:

> 'I have come to see myself from the outside, my country from the outside – without illusions. We make and pass.
> We are all things that make and pass, striving upon a hidden mission, out to the open sea.' [IV.3(iv).353]

That was a vision of 1909. By 1919 some had grown wiser or wearier. Wells's vision is essentially apocalyptic, as so much of his writing is. It sees that revelation of the end or intimations of it, whether in Wars of the Worlds or in the Time Machine's dying sun low over a dark sea where crab-like creatures scuttle. Such apocalyptic ideas had played already in Dickens's world of *Little Dorrit*, with Merdle as Anti-Christ and the collapse of the House of Clennam in rubble an image of the end of all things. George Bernard Shaw, in *Heartbreak House*, a work that attempted, foolhardily but with a failure that outdoes success, to encapsulate the meaning of the past century and to view its end, envisaged a world drifting, frivolous, that invites destruction and yet escapes it, perhaps because there is the future hope of new love and new life, perhaps just because it is England. At the end of *Heartbreak House*, 'A Fantasia in the Russian Manner on English Themes', its inhabitants frenziedly turn on all the lights and tear down the curtains as the Zeppelins pass overhead on their night raid. There is a frantic desire for excitement, for an epic immolation. The bomb, though, hits the cave with the dynamite and blows up Boss Mangan and the burglar, the play's only two 'practical men of business'. The war, the culmination of a century's capitalism and national competition, of blind power and mechanical ingenuity, the end of political idealism, has promised the end of all things. Yet these people (except the 'practical men of business') survive; the raid passes on. The play sums up a whole era of business and its representation by a conclusion in which nothing quite is concluded. England survives; perhaps tomorrow (as always) it will perish:

MRS HUSHABYE: But what a glorious experience! I hope theyll come again tomorrow night.

ELLIE [*radiant at the prospect*]: Oh, I hope so. [p.160]

BIBLIOGRAPHY

Primary

Carlyle, Thomas, *Selected Writings* (ed. Alan Shelston, Penguin Classics, 1971).

Dickens, Charles, *Bleak House*, 1853 (ed. Stephen Gill, World's Classics, 1996).

—: *Little Dorrit*, 1857 (ed. Stephen Wall and Helen Small, Penguin Classics, 1998).

Disraeli, Benjamin, *Coningsby*, 1844 (ed. Thom Braun, Penguin Classics, 1983).

—: *Tancred*, 1847 (Longmans, Green, 1894).

Eliot, George, *Middlemarch*, 1872 (ed. David Carroll, World's Classics, 1998).

Gaskell, Elizabeth, *Cranford*, 1853 (ed. Elizabeth Porges Watson, World's Classics, 1980).

—: *The Life of Charlotte Brontë*, 1857 (ed. Angus Easson, World's Classics, 1996).

—:*Ruth*, 1853 (ed. Angus Easson, Penguin Classics, 1982).

Gissing, George, *New Grub Street*, 1891 (ed. Bernard Bergonzi, Penguin Classics, 1968).

James, Henry, *The Ambassadors*, 1903 (Everyman Library, 1959).

Macaulay, Thomas, *The History of England from the Accession of James II*, 1848-61 (Everyman Library, 3 vols., 1906).

Meredith, George, *Evan Harrington*, 1861 (Constable, 1907).

Shaw, George Bernard, *Heartbreak House*, 1919 (Penguin, 1964).

—: *Major Barbara*, 1905 (Penguin, 1961).

Trollope, Anthony, *An Autobiography*, 1883 (Williams & Norgate, 1946).

—: *The Way We Live Now*, 1875 (ed. John Sutherland, World's Classics, 1982).

Wells, H. G., *The Time Machine* (William Heinemann, 1895).

—: *Tono-Bungay*, 1909 (ed. John Hammond, Everyman Library, 1994).

Wharton, Edith, *The Age of Innocence*, 1920 (Penguin, 1974).

—: *The House of Mirth*, 1905 (ed. Martha Banta, World's Classics, 1994).

Secondary

Bagehot, Walter, *Lombard Street: A Description of the Money Market*, (H.S. King, 1873).

Briggs, Asa, *Victorian Cities*, 1963 (Pelican, 1968).

Cameron, Rondo, *Banking in the Early Stages of Industrialization*, (Oxford University Press, 1967).

Forster, John, *Life of Charles Dickens*, 1872-74 (ed. J.W.T. Ley, Cecil Palmer, 1928).

Easson, Angus (ed.), *Elizabeth Gaskell: The Critical Heritage* (Routledge, 1991).

Gaskell, Elizabeth, *The Letters of Mrs Gaskell*, ed. Arthur Pollard and J.A.V.Chapple (Manchester University Press, 1966).

Gilmour, Robin, *The Idea of the Gentleman in the Victorian Novel*, (Allen & Unwin, 1981).

Haight, Gordon S., *George Eliot: A Biography* (Clarendon Press, 1968).

Horsman, Alan, *The Victorian Novel* (Oxford History of English Literature), (Clarendon Press, 1990).

Malchow, H.L., *Gentlemen Capitalists: The Social and Political World of the Victorian Businessman* (Stanford University Press, 1992).

Melada, Ivan, *The Captain of British Industry in English Fiction 1821-1871* (University of New Mexico Press, 1970).

Patten, Robert, *Charles Dickens and His Publishers* (Clarendon Press, 1978).

Russell, Norman, *The Novelist and Mammon: Literary Responses to the World of Commerce in the Nineteenth Century* (Clarendon Press, 1986).

Tawney, R. H., *Religion and the Rise of Capitalism* (Pelican, 1926).

Turner, Paul, *English Literature 1832-1890* (Oxford History of English Literature) (Clarendon Press, 1989).

5

THE EARLY TWENTIETH CENTURY: UNIFORMITY, DRUDGERY AND ECONOMICS

Allan Simmons

St Mary's College, University of Surrey

Introduction

> *Unreal City,*
> *Under the brown fog of a winter dawn,*
> *A crowd flowed over London Bridge, so many,*
> *I had not thought death had undone so many.*
> *Sighs, short and infrequent, were exhaled,*
> *And each man fixed his eyes before his feet.*[1]

T.S. ELIOT'S DAMNING PORTRAYAL OF THE POWER OF ECONOMIC FORCES, in the opening section of *The Waste Land*, is illustrative of how business is represented in the literature of the early 20th century. The dehumanising daily routine, that drains these workers of life and renders them anonymous, is reinforced by a host of poetic devices ranging from simple repetition ('*Un*-real', '*Un*-der', '*un*-done'; 'so many'), through half-rhyme ('brown', 'dawn'; 'crowd,' 'flowed'), alliteration ('death', 'undone'; 'fixed', 'feet'), and sibilance ('Sighs', 'short', 'exhaled'), to passive constructions ('were exhaled'). The effect of these literary techniques is to underscore the sense of drudgery in the lives of workers, caught up in the homogenising rituals of labour. For this is the age of the faceless multitudes of office-bound clerical-workers whose entrapment within a dehumanising and impenetrable 'system' is captured in the novels of Franz Kafka. Thus, in his description of

---

[1] T. S. Eliot, *The Waste Land* (ll.60-65), in *The Complete Poems and Plays of T. S. Eliot*, London: Faber, 1969, p. 62.

99

workers, which associates them, by allusion, with the dead in Dante's *Inferno*, Eliot might be said to be responding to a key feature of the age: this is the age of Modernism, the age of the masses, and the age of the 'anonymous' worker. As John Carey observes in *The Intellectuals and the Masses*:

> 'Between 1860 and 1910 the section of the middle and lower-middle class employed in commerce, banks, insurance and real estate increased markedly in all Western European countries, as a result of the emergence of the imperialist and international economy of the late nineteenth century. In England by 1911 the clerical profession, including 124,000 women, was one of the most rapidly expanding occupational groups.'[2]

Whilst attempts to date literary movements are notoriously imprecise, it is helpful to think of the movement we call 'Modernism' as extending, roughly, from 1880 to 1930. If art reflects and passes comment upon the prevailing philosophies and mores of the moment in which it is written, then Modernism captures the vulnerabilities and scepticism associated with the abandonment of comforting certainties of the Victorian period in the wake of the combined impact of thinkers such as Freud, Marx, and Darwin. The challenges their theories posed for man's settled sense of self, his place within a social order, and his place within a divinely arranged scheme, inform all the arts in this period. The formal experiments in such literary works as *Ulysses* and *The Waste Land* are of a piece with those in, say, the paintings of Picasso and Braque, or the music of Stravinsky. In each case, the artist's experiments with technique reveal a quest for new ways in which to communicate with an audience, whilst simultaneously suggesting a new uncertainty about the power to communicate unambiguous, objective truth.

---

[2] John Carey, *The Intellectuals and the Masses*, London: Faber, 1992, p.58. In *The Soul of London*, London: Alston Rivers, 1910, Ford Madox Hueffer notes: 'Workers in London divide themselves, roughly, into those who sell the labour of their bodies and those who sell their attentions. You see men in the streets digging trenches, pulling stout wires out of square holes in pavements, pecking away among greasy vapours at layers of asphalte, scattering shovelfuls of crushed gravel under the hoofs of slipping horses and under the crunching tyres of wheels. If walls would fall out of offices you would see paler men and women adding up the records of money paid to these others. That, with infinite variations, is work in London.' (p. 68)

Essentially, Modern literature is a literature of doubt. It questions the ideas by which Victorian man oriented himself with respect to the world and, through this, the very ideas that sustain Western civilisation. The anxieties of the age are reflected in the stylistic features which typify the literature of the period: Henry James's labyrinthine sentences enact the problems of communication, Joseph Conrad's time-shifts serve to place the reader in the disorientated predicament of his characters, and James Joyce's attempts to present the inner life of his characters trace both the randomness of thought associations and the infinite complexity of other minds. Unsurprisingly, the vulnerability and lack of surety that typifies this age – whose central historical event, the First World War, provides the ultimate example of mankind's loss of confidence in itself and its systems – finds some of its most profound expression in the presentation of man within the context of economic forces. Thus, whilst the literature of the period confronts the unavoidable economic plight of the individual with realism – as H. G. Wells's young draper's shopman, Artie Kipps, is informed: 'we're in a blessed drain-pipe, and we've got to crawl along it till we die'[3] – its presentation of the individual as disorientated and victimised by forces beyond his or her control reflects the scepticism and vulnerability that characterise the age of Modernism.

To consider the representation of business in the literature of the period, this chapter will commence with a brief survey of prevailing attitudes towards business in the literature of the period, across the genres of poetry, drama, and prose. Then, I shall turn to the work of four novelists, whose representations of business are at once more thorough and more realistic than those of their contemporaries: H. G. Wells, Thomas Hardy, D. H. Lawrence, and Joseph Conrad.

Survey of the Literature of the Age

Virginia Woolf voices her economic awareness of the age when she advocates for the aspirant female novelist, hoping to compare with her male counterpart, 'a room of her own and five hundred a year'.[4] This balance between art and life is not always reflected in the literature of the time, though, and some writers seem almost wilfully

---

[3] H. G. Wells, *Kipps: The Story of a Simple Soul*, London: Everyman, 1993, p. 34.

[4] Virginia Woolf, *A Room of One's Own*, London: Hogarth, 1929, p.142.

detached from economic necessity. W. B. Yeats, for instance, seems wholly oblivious at times of the economic plight of the Dublin shop-keepers who he berates in his poetry for their failure to respond to his call to art as the way to find a sense of Irishness rooted in the collective memory of Celtic myths and legends. Yeats's name for the petty huckster is 'paudeen', who he characterises as having 'fumbling wits' and 'obscure spite' (*Paudeen*). There is little redemptive in Yeats's portrait of the paudeen who 'fumble in a greasy till / And add the halfpence to the pence,' oblivious of any finer motive for life than 'to pray and save' (*September 1913*). The usual interpretation of Yeats's sneering tone and his portrait of the small trader as mindless, material, and money grubbing, is that he is behaving like the stereotypical 'other-worldly' poet, who transforms everything he touches into symbol. From this angle, Yeats might be said to voice the rather simplistic view of the romantic generally: that material gain necessarily involves spiritual loss. As we shall see, much Modern literature concerns itself with the spiritual loss rather than the material gain. Looked at from another angle, however, Yeats's view is wilfully escapist and blinkered. Whilst promoting art and culture as the means by which the fragmented elements of Ireland could be reunited, he seems to be consistently oblivious of the economic plight of his countrymen: at the time, Dublin's slums were among the worst in Europe.

Shaw

Initially, Yeats's countryman, George Bernard Shaw, seems to offer a more realistic treatment of the economic plight of his characters. Shaw makes no secret of his Ibsenite leanings. For example, he says in his Dedicatory Letter to *Man and Superman*: 'it annoys me to see people comfortable when they ought to be uncomfortable; and I insist on making them think in order to bring them to conviction of sin.'[5] Thus, Shaw's first play, *Widower's Houses* (1892), deals with tainted money and slum landlords. More pertinent for our purposes, though, is his third play, *Mrs Warren's Profession*, which was written in 1894 but banned by the British censor until 1926. Mrs Warren's 'profession' is, of course, prostitution: she is a brothel-keeper. In his Preface to the play, Shaw lays the blame for her plight squarely at the door of economics:

---

[5] George Bernard Shaw, *Collected Plays*, Vol. 2, London: Bodley Head, 1971, p. 495.

'*Mrs Warren's Profession* was written in 1894 to draw attention to the truth that prostitution is caused not by female depravity and male licentiousness, but simply by underpaying, undervaluing, and overworking women so shamefully that the poorest of them are forced to resort to prostitution to keep body and soul together.'[6]

Much of the economic and social criticism in the play emerges in Mrs Warren's justification of her profession to her daughter, Vivie, who she asks, rhetorically: 'Do you think I did what I did because I liked it, or thought it right, or wouldn't rather have gone to college and been a lady if I'd had the chance?' (p. 309) But the force of the social message in such presentations of the individual determined by the crude reality of financial forces beyond her control is occasionally blunted by the sheer vitality and hyperbole of Shaw's comic irreverence. This happens in *Major Barbara* (1905), for example, where Shaw reverses the expectation that an armaments manufacturer will be morally inferior to a Salvation Army officer.

The role of money in *Major Barbara* assumes prominence immediately: the play opens with Lady Britomart wishing to provide financially for the future of her grown-up children and, without the resources to do this herself, sends for her estranged husband, the children's father, Andrew Undershaft, a millionaire who has made his fortune out of the manufacture of armaments. Undershaft's visit initiates a trial of strength between himself, as arms' merchant, and his daughter Barbara, a major in the Salvation Army. In essence, the play contrasts idealism and realism: Barbara and her fiancé, Adolphus Cusins, are 'converted' to Undershaft's 'religion' and come to see money and power as the weapons by which evil can best be defeated:

> Cusins: 'Excuse me: is there any place in your religion for honour, justice, truth, love, mercy and so forth?'
> Undershaft: 'Yes: they are the graces and luxuries of a rich, strong, and safe life.'
> Cusins: 'Suppose one is forced to choose between them and money or gunpowder?'
> Undershaft: 'Choose money and gunpowder; for without enough of both you cannot afford the others.'
> Cusins: 'That is your religion?'

---

[6] George Bernard Shaw, *Collected Plays*, Vol. 1, London: Bodley Head, 1970, p. 231.

Undershaft: 'Yes.'[7]

In other words, Undershaft's 'religion' is the social dream of satisfying the material needs of his workers. In the play, it is Mammon, and not God, who triumphs, as the Salvation Army is shown to be dependent upon Undershaft's funds to keep its shelters open during the winter and Barbara is made to realise that, in order to help the poor, charities have to rely upon the tainted money of Undershaft and Bodger, a liquor manufacturer.

The play contrasts the two 'kingdoms' (and, as Undershaft's very name suggests, the religious allegory is intentional): first, Undershaft visits the Salvation Army shelter, where he witnesses his daughter dealing with the bully, Bill Walker, then the whole family visit the Undershaft factory and the workers' town in Perivale. By contrast with the tawdriness of the Salvation Army shelter, the kingdom over which Undershaft presides is a workers' paradise. However, given the starkness of such a contrast, one wonders whether the Shavian approach to business is any more satisfactory than Yeats's. Implicit in *Major Barbara*'s suggestion that the struggle to save souls from evil must begin by saving bodies from poverty is the claim that the Salvation Army, in particular, and religion, in general, have missed the point about the business of salvation. At crucial points in the play, the sheer exaggeration of Undershaft's outbursts serve to make the audience wary of this message. Here, for instance, is his description of poverty: '...the worst of crimes. All the others are virtues beside it: all the others are chivalry itself by comparison. Poverty blights whole cities' (p. 172). Whilst such a tide of rhetoric may make Shaw's social points through hyperbole, we need to look elsewhere for a realistic portrayal of business.

Bennett

The social criticism of George Bernard Shaw's plays finds an echo in the many novels of the period which address the changing face of British society through tales of small businessmen. In Arnold Bennett's *The Old Wives' Tale* (1908), for instance, the histories of Constance and Sophia Baines unfold against the backdrop of irrevocably economic forces which transform the life of St Luke's

---

[7]   George Bernard Shaw, *Collected Plays*, Vol. 3, London: Bodley Head, 1971, p.116.

Square. The steady erosion of traditional crafts and small independent businesses in the Five Towns, by mass production and chain-stores, occurs with a remorseless and inevitable logic, in which even the central characters are implicated. In his funeral eulogy for John Baines, Charles Critchlow praises his friend's conservative regard for 'the wise old English maxims of commerce and the avoidance of dangerous modern methods'.[8] But part of the novel's point is that commerce is a dynamic rather than a static force. Thus, we see John Baines's own daughter, Constance, and her future husband, Samuel Povey, designing advertisements to drum up trade:

> 'Those two, without knowing or guessing it, were making history – the history of commerce. They had no suspicion that they were the forces of the future insidiously at work to destroy what the forces of the past had created, but such was the case.' (p. 119)

For his part, it is Critchlow himself who will purchase the draper's business when the Baines's lease expires and, in his turn, will sell it to the Midland Clothiers Company 'which was establishing branches throughout Staffordshire, Warwickshire, Leicestershire, and adjacent counties' (p. 601).

A criticism levelled at Bennett's portrayal of the economic realities of the Staffordshire Potteries in this novel, that spans the period from 1860 to 1906, is that his picture of the rise of economic monopoly is historically incomplete as it omits the rise of the Labour movement.[9] One might argue, however, that this limitation is a deliberate consequence of restricting us to Constance's view of the changing face of Bursley. Significantly, Bennett's clearest comment upon the changing face of business comes in the form of a lament as Sophia, having finally returned to her birthplace from Paris, looks out at the Square again:

---

[8] Arnold Bennett, *The Old Wives' Tale*, Harmondsworth: Penguin Books, 1990, p.114. *Cf.* 'firms remained small and privately owned, antiquated plant was not modernised' in Boris Ford (ed.), *The Cambridge Cultural History of Britain: Early Twentieth-Century Britain*, Cambridge: CUP, 1992, p. 5.

[9] See Arnold Kettle, *An Introduction to the English Novel*, Vol. II, London: Hutchinson University Library, 1953, pp. 85-89.

'The heaven of thick smoke over the Square, the black deposit on painted woodwork, the intermittent hooting of the steam sirens, showed that the wholesale trade of Bursley still flourished. But Sophia had no memories of the wholesale trade of Bursley; it meant nothing to the youth of her heart; she was attached by intimate links to the retail traffic of Bursley, and as a mart old Bursley was done for.' (p. 511)

In this shift from retail to wholesale trade, the scale of problem is presented: mass production has brought with it the end of the small trader, and, with his demise, business has lost its human face. Bennett's narrow concentration upon the sisters, rather than upon the broader picture of social life, in this novel might be read as the sincerest expression of lament for this lost age.

In her essay entitled 'Modern Fiction', Virginia Woolf links Arnold Bennett with John Galsworthy and H. G. Wells, disparagingly calling them 'materialists', by which she means that 'they write of unimportant things ... they spend immense skill and immense industry making the trivial and the transitory appear the true and the enduring'.[10] But, whilst it is true that these novelists have not endured to form part of the 'canon' of Modern literature in the way that, say, Hardy or Conrad have, their attention to the 'unimportant things' does at least ensure a context of economic realism in their novels through the practical concerns of business. There are a number of reasons why these novelists failed to create works of enduring importance: at one extreme, one may identify their inability to convince the reader that the plight of an individual character, like Constance Baines, is representative of the plight of human beings generally; at the other, characters, particularly those of H. G. Wells, are often little more than mouthpieces for his points of view about politics, history, and society, as well as economics. If Bennett's presentation of economic development in the Five Towns through the eyes of a few characters proves to be a limitation in *The Old Wives' Tale*, obscuring the broader picture, Wells's novels suffer from the opposite defect: their emphasis upon ideas rather than character as the mainspring of plot means that the characters are so easily forgettable. What R. C. Churchill says of *Ann Veronica* (1909) can be adapted, *mutatis mutandis*, to much of Wells's writing: 'We remember *Ann Veronica* as a novel about the condition-of-woman

---

[10] Virginia Woolf, *The Common Reader*, First Series, London: Hogarth Press, 1929, p. 187.

question; it is difficult to recall anything about Ann Veronica Stanley as an individual woman.'[11] Allowing for this criticism, though, H. G. Wells synthesises and develops the attitudes towards business that have emerged in the work of writers we have been considering. Given their concentration upon ideas, where Wells's novels do impinge upon the world of business, they might be thought of as economic parables about business in the early 20th century.

Wells

At the age of 14, H. G. Wells (1866-1946) was apprenticed to Rodgers and Benyer, Drapers, of Windsor, and, a year later, to Southsea Drapery Emporium. He draws on these early experiences for the social comedies, *Kipps* (1905) and *The History of Mr Polly* (1910). In both novels, the protagonists, themselves assistant drapers, are shown to transcend the drudgery of their 'clipped and limited lives',[12] but only through legacies. As such, the novels appear to offer escapist fantasies in the manner of the Victorian novel of 'expectations', and yet Wells succeeds in tempering this escapism with a degree of realism: money, *per se*, brings happiness to neither Kipps nor Polly. Rather than freeing the protagonists from the need to work, their legacies offer them the chance to choose their form of occupation. Thus, through a large, unexpected legacy from his grandfather, Kipps is able to progress from the Folkestone Drapery Bazaar of Mr Shalford, at the beginning of the novel, to owning his own small bookshop, at the end. A much smaller legacy, from his father, enables Mr Polly to set up as a small outfitter at Fishbourne, from which he escapes, by means of an insurance scam after a botched suicide attempt, to become the resident handyman at the Potwell Inn. These are novels of self-development rather than escapist fantasies: neither of Wells's heroes ends up outside the system of work. Instead, Wells uses the forum of retail business to demonstrate the degree to which individual choice is a product of social institutions. Thus, beneath the social comedy, his message

---

[11] R. C. Churchill, 'The Comedy of Ideas: Cross-currents in Fiction and Drama', in Boris Ford (ed.), *The New Pelican Guide to English Literature: From James to Eliot*, Vol. 7, Harmondsworth: Penguin Books, 1983, p. 295.

[12] *Kipps, op. cit.*, p. 279.

would seem to be that reconstituting the individual depends, ultimately, upon restructuring these institutions themselves.

In the social commentary they provide, Wells's parables of liberation are founded on his own escape from life as a draper's assistant, by winning a scholarship to study science at Imperial College in Kensington. Here Wells came under the influence of T. E. Huxley whose Darwinist beliefs would profoundly influence his own thinking about social evolution. Both *Kipps* and *The History of Mr Polly* might be said to reflect this influence in the refusal of their central characters to accept the limitations of their comparable social stations, together with the idea (implicit in their attempts to better themselves) that people are capable of progressing beyond these limits. In these novels, the essential entrapment of the individual – and the quashing of individual effort – is traced, by and large, to business, the 'system', that, according to one of Kipps's fellow-apprentices, Minton, is 'a blessed drain-pipe, and we've got to crawl along it till we die' (p. 34). Of course, it is not only their apprenticeships that enslave Kipps and Polly: in *Kipps*, for instance, Wells traces the limitations imposed upon individual potential to such causes as social class, too. In fact, nowhere is the image of stifled and frustrated potential better expressed than in the gift the young Kipps receives from his aunt: 'Once his aunt gave him a trumpet if he would *promise* faithfully not to blow it, and afterwards took it away again' (p. 5). More usually – and more perversely – it is business itself that checks individual effort, as Parsons demonstrates in *The History of Mr Polly* when his attempts to advertise the store's wares more imaginatively lead to a fracas with his employer, which culminates in his arrest and dismissal.

Both *Kipps* and *The History of Mr Polly* present the drive towards business efficiency as somehow excluding the eponymous young apprentices. In this, Wells suggests an inverse relationship between financial gain and spiritual loss. Tied to Mr Shalford by means of 'antique and complex' indentures, and, more particularly, to Mr Shalford's credo of 'System. System everywhere. Fishency', the young Kipps comes to the conclusion that 'save for a miracle, the brief tragedy of his life was over' (pp. 28,27,36). Of course, the legacy that rescues Kipps from this plight is little short of 'a miracle' and it is Wells's point that this financial miracle, by means of the comic topsy-turveydom it suggests, should subvert the very system that has thus far entrapped Kipps. As Sid Pornick says:

'Who's going to work and case in a muddle like this? Here, first you do – something anyhow – of the world's work and it pays you hardly anything, and then it invites you to do nothing, nothing whatever, and pays you twelve hundred pounds a year. Who's going to respect laws and customs when they come to damn silliness like that? ... It's not you I'm thinking of, o' man; it's the system. Better you than most people. Still —' (p. 161).

That Kipps's fortune is subsequently embezzled by Walshingham and then partially restored by the improbable success of Chitterlow's play, '*Pestered Butterfly*', further confirms the subversion of the system by forces alien to but dependent upon it. Even more subversive in this respect is the manner in which Polly secures his release from the drudgery of 'zealacious commerciality':[13] saddled with a wife and business he doesn't want, and having reached the end of his tether, he decides upon suicide as a way out both for himself and for Miriam, who will benefit from his insurance policies. Although Polly botches his suicide attempt, he succeeds in starting 'the great Fishbourne fire' in which his own shop and those of neighbouring retailers are destroyed. One of the great comic moments in the novel ensues when Polly's fellow traders hail him as a hero, ostensibly because of his daring rescue of his neighbour's mother-in-law, but actually because of their chance to claim damages from their respective insurance companies and so escape their collective plight:

'Not one of those excellent men but was already realising that a great door had opened, as it were, in the opaque fabric of destiny, that they were to get their money again that had seemed sunken for ever beyond any hope in the deeps of retail trade. Life was already in their imagination rising like a Phoenix from the flames.' (pp. 133-34)

The fact that one business – insurance – thus provides a hitherto unimaginable escape from the drudgery of another – the retail trade – seems designed to suggest the comic futility of the economic system as a whole.

The indigestion from which Polly suffers until his escape functions as a comic indicator of the 'pathology of business': as Wells sees it, business threatens the very well-being of the

---

[13] H. G. Wells, *The History of Mr Polly*, London: Everyman, 1993, p. 100.

individual. Initially, the desire of both Polly and Kipps to escape from the routine of business is expressed in such activities as Polly's reading about (rather than living out) 'the wonder of life' (p. 101) and Kipps's introduction to 'old Methusaleh' whisky under Chitterlow's influence. When escape comes, in the form of Polly's insurance money and Kipps's legacy, it transforms the static lives of the heroes: Polly's picaresque wanderings, with the sense of freedom these connote, provide a literal counterpart to the abstract mobility of Kipps through the class system. Such transformation suggests that, in Wells's view, the stability necessary for business is limiting to, or at odds with, the desire and growth of the individual spirit.

In *Tono-Bungay* (1909), Wells's focus broadens from the comedies of self-improvement offered in *Kipps* and *The History of Mr Polly* to a consideration of the state of England, as reflected in its business and commerce. In the novel, Wells questions where the relentless pursuit of wealth leads and reveals how, left unchecked through English history, this pursuit has had degenerate effects upon individuals, communities and environments alike. For an example of the breadth of vision in *Tono-Bungay*, this is how the narrator, George Ponderevo, describes the London docks:

> 'One goes down the widening reaches through a monstrous variety of shipping, great steamers, great sailing-ships, trailing the flags of all the world, a monstrous confusion of lighters, witches' conferences of brown-sailed barges, wallowing tugs, a tumultuous crowding and jostling of cranes and spars, and wharves and stores, and assertive inscriptions. Huge vistas of dock open right and left of one, and here and there beyond and amidst it all are church towers, little patches of indescribably old-fashioned and worn-out houses, riverside pubs and the like, vestiges of townships that were long since torn to fragments and submerged in these new growths. And amidst it all no plan appears, no intention, no comprehensive desire.'[14]

Here, the implied critique of the current state of England – and of the forces of commercialism which drive English society – extends to the imperial impulse behind the British Empire itself. The description of London in the novel also provides a fitting correlative for the unplanned chaos of George Ponderevo's path through life

---

[14] H. G. Wells, *Tono-Bungay*, London: Everyman, 1994, pp. 350-51.

and love. His utter disillusionment with the state of England by the end of the novel is fittingly reflected in his eventual profession: he is a military engineer, building naval destroyers.

Tono-Bungay is another of Wells's parables about the place of the individual within the world of business, only here, Wells's focus turns from the plight of the individual to the flawed mechanics of the commercial system. The novel charts the financial rise and collapse of the business empire of the narrator's uncle, Edward Ponderevo, a failed pharmacist, who makes a fortune overnight when he foists his quack patent medicine, the 'Tono-Bungay' of the title, upon the gullible public through skilful marketing. Reviewing the affair, the narrator comes to view his uncle and himself as 'no more than specimens of a modern species of brigand, wasting the savings of the public out of the sheer wantonness of enterprise' (p. 335). As a comment upon 20th-century Britain, this notion that business success depends upon advertising rather than upon the product advertised, that it is an idea without substance, is damning. Granted his 'near view of the machinery by which our astounding Empire is run', the narrator sees England as 'the most unpremeditated, subtle, successful and aimless plutocracy that ever encumbered the destinies of mankind', where the establishment actually encourages his uncle's 'almost naked dishonesty of method' (p. 231-32). This image of the prevailing economic condition as one of unchecked, opportunist profiteering reaches its comic climax in the episode of the, appropriately-named, 'quap,' which George Ponderevo steals from a West African republic to stave off financial ruin. The quap, however, is a radioactive substance and, having first harmed the workers involved in its retrieval, it then destroys the ship in which it is being transported back to England. To the narrator, the analogy between quap and the diseased state of England is obvious: radioactivity, he says, 'is in matter exactly what the decay of our old culture is in society, a loss of traditions and distinctions and assured reactions' (p. 297).

Business and Trade in Hardy, Lawrence and Conrad

Whilst the idea of business-as-decay lies behind the comedy in Wells's novels, the fact that these are *comedies*, and the fact that they propose no real alternative to the economic system they satirise, suggests that, for all its degenerative side-effects, there is no better model of the economic system than that portrayed. But if even

111

a social critic like Wells merely uses business as a convenient structure on which to hang his ideas, are there any early 20th-century authors who approach business and commerce in a manner which foregrounds business and its concerns? I suggest that the work of Hardy, Lawrence, and Conrad offers such an approach and I shall now discuss the work of each of them in turn. I shall argue that the sense of work as an imprisoning routine in Modern Literature commences with the disorientation caused by the migration from *rus* to *urbs*, as reflected in the novels of Thomas Hardy, and continues through the entrapment and victimisation of the individual through industrialism in D. H. Lawrence's presentation of the Nottingham-shire colliers, and into the clear-eyed view of the unglamorous necessity of trade in the work of Joseph Conrad.

Hardy

All ages are 'ages of change' and it is, thus, facile to attribute the character of an age to a single cause. Yet, were one seeking to identify the single element that best characterises British culture in the Modern age, this element would undoubtedly be the transformation of a predominantly rural society into a predominantly urban society. In the middle of the 19th century, only half of the population was urban; at the beginning of the 20th century the modern city was home to most of the population: 'Of the forty-five million inhabitants of the United Kingdom in 1911 (an increase of fourteen million in forty years), nearly 80 per cent lived in England and Wales; and, of these, again, roughly 80 per cent came to live in urban districts.'[15] The social consequences of this shift in population in the second half of the 19th century cannot be overstated. With the loss of rural traditions was lost a way of life, at once individuating and definitive in its communal values, and a major consequence of the urbanisation that followed was to define the workforce in purely financial terms as the self-supporting cottager was transformed into a consumer:

> '…what emerged was a new ethic, familiar enough by then in the towns but less known in the country, the ethic of competition. The effect of this was to reduce man to the level of economic man, one whose community relationships were at the mercy of the cash nexus and

---

[15] G. H. Bantock, 'The Social and Intellectual Background', in B. Ford (ed.), *op.cit.*, p. 15.

whose psychological motivations were thought of largely in terms of self interest.'[16]

The age of the masses had arrived and, in the face of the complexities of urbanised society, writers like Thomas Hardy, D. H. Lawrence, and Joseph Conrad evoked simpler, organic communities – the pastoral community in Hardy's novels and the ship's crew in Conrad's novels, for instance. However, there is nothing escapist in this evocation: each author addresses the role of the individual in relation to the cash nexus with a refreshing dry-eyed realism.

The novels of Thomas Hardy (1840-1928) provide a record of a vanishing way of life as the invention of Wessex enables the contrast between *rus* and *urbs*. Indeed, the use of Wessex across the novels themselves reflects the inescapable influence of urbanisation upon rural society: from its invention in *Under the Greenwood Tree* (1872), the rhythms and pastoral traditions of the Wessex landscape come to dominate novels like *Far from the Madding Crowd* (1874); place itself comes to assume the importance of a central character in *The Return of the Native* (1878) and *The Woodlanders* (1887), through the evocation of Egdon Heath and the Hintock Woods as respective presiding spirits; *The Mayor of Casterbridge* (1886), with its predominantly urban setting, and *Tess of the d'Urbervilles* (1892), through its contrasted rural settings, dramatise the presence of unsettling, and mainly economic, new forces at work in the countryside; until, finally, in *Jude the Obscure* (1896), the Wessex landscape itself is present only in muted form. Hardy's chief interest for us in this study lies in his representation of agriculture as a business and, for Hardy, the business of farming is ultimately dependent upon the relationship between the worker and his or her environment.

Hardy uses landscape and region to promote human values, and, generally speaking, the *genius loci*, which reveals the degree to which an individual comes to be defined by his way of life and environment, is revealed to be hopelessly at odds with the prevailing spirit of social change. Hardy's novels endorse values that Modern man is in danger of forgetting; the implication is that man obtains civilisation at the expense of his organic contacts. In this organically composed world, the life of Old John South can be determined by

---

[16] Ford (ed.), *ibid.*, p. 17.

that of an elm tree, in *The Woodlanders*. The permanence of nature and of traditional working methods, as embodied in such characters as Gabriel Oak, Diggory Venn, Giles Winterborne and Marty South, is reflected in the very landscapes which define them. Thus we learn in the opening chapter of *The Return of the Native* that 'The sea changed, the fields changed, the rivers, the villages and the people changed, but Egdon remained'.[17] This sense of the immutability of nature is further emphasised by its extension to the lives of those 'in tune' with it:

> 'The citizen's *Then* is the rustic's *Now*. In London, twenty or thirty years ago are old times; in Paris ten years, or five; in Weatherbury three or four score years were included in the mere present, and nothing less than half a century set a mark on its face or tone.'[18]

Such sharp distinction encourages the reader to contrast those characters who work 'in tune' with their natural surroundings with those interlopers who bring subversive new attitudes and values. Thus, for instance, we are led to contrast Diggory Venn with Damon Wildeve, Gabriel Oak with Sergeant Troy, the Stokes with the Durbeyfields, and Giles Winterborne and Marty South with Edred Fitzpiers and Felice Charmond. In each case, the organic stoicism of the former throws into stark relief the dislocation of the latter.

The structure of *Far from the Madding Crowd*, like the pace of life of its characters, is governed by the pastoral rhythms of lambing and shearing: the progress of the novel derives not from the usual demands of plot but from the rhythms of the seasons and the farming year. Within this structure, individuals seem to lose their separate identities as they work, suggesting that they form a logical extension of their (natural) activity. In the great shearing scene, for instance, not only do the shearers 'not require definition by name' (p. 137), but the barn itself is compared to a church to suggest that the needs of the body and the needs of the soul cannot be differentiated. In this organic unity 'the barn was natural to the shearers and the shearers were in harmony with the barn' (p. 139). The innate wisdom associated with a life lived in harmony with nature is present in the sixth sense of Gabriel Oak, whose very name

---

[17] Thomas Hardy, *The Return of the Native*, London: Macmillan, 1975, p. 36.

[18] Thomas Hardy, *Far From the Madding Crowd*, London: Macmillan, 1985, p. 189.

combines the connotations of watchfulness and stolidity on which Bathsheba Everdene will come to depend. Thus, Oak is able to predict the impending storm by 'reading' the behaviour of rooks, sheep, horses, toads, and slugs, as messages 'from the Great Mother' (p. 216). The simple juxtaposition of Troy, who has sunk into a drunken stupor at this point, and Oak is felt most keenly in the latter's estimated value of Bathsheba's wheat and barley that needs covering to protect it from the storm:

> '5x30 = 150 quarters = 500*l*.
>
> 3x40 = 120 quarters = 250*l*.
>
> Seven hundred and fifty pounds in the divinest form that money can wear – that of necessary food for man and beast.' (pp. 217-18)

This simple formulation not only distinguishes between Troy and Oak in terms of their attitudes to money – Troy is a consumer and Oak a producer – it also carries a significant endorsement of a definitive feature of rural 'business': here the workers are not separated from the end product of their labours. This point is repeated during the Talbothays Dairy sequence, in *Tess of the d'Urbervilles*, in the discussion between Tess and Angel about who will drink the milk they have just loaded onto the train:

> 'Londoners will drink it at their breakfasts to-morrow, won't they?' she asked. 'Strange people that we have never seen.'
>
> 'Yes – I suppose they will. Though not as we send it. When its strength has been lowered, so that it may not get up into their heads.'
>
> 'Noble men and noble women, ambassadors and centurions, ladies and tradeswomen, and babies who have never seen a cow.'
>
> 'Well, yes; perhaps; particularly centurions.'
>
> 'Who don't know anything of us, and where it comes from; or think how we two drove miles across the moor to-night in the rain that it might reach 'em in time.'[19]

Such emphasis upon the organic, communal nature of rural work, however, might lead one to suspect that Hardy's novels present the

---

[19] Thomas Hardy, *Tess of the d'Urbervilles*, London: Macmillan, 1985, p.189.

rural environment as a time capsule, immune from the demands of the real, changing world. So, can one defend Hardy from the charge of escapism that this suspicion raises?

Hardy writes novels that endorse values that modern man is forgetting, yet, in the natural world of which he writes, both the man-trap, in *The Woodlanders*, and the pastoral tragedy that determines Gabriel Oak's fate in *Far From the Madding Crowd*, have their place. In keeping with this, Hardy's presentation of the business that constitutes the rural economy is anything but escapist. As the eponymous hero, Jude, learns to his cost, there is little room for sentiment in a world where 'Pigs must be killed' because 'Poor folks must live'.[20] Increasingly in Hardy's novels, the nature of rural work is shown to be arduous, physical, and, often, exploitative. The nature of farming as a business, and of labour as a commodity to be bought, is graphically demonstrated in Chapter 6 of *Far from the Madding Crowd* where Gabriel Oak, now unemployed, joins the throng of would-be labourers hoping to be selected at the annual hiring fair at Casterbridge. Hardy expressed his views on the subject of hiring fairs more fully in an essay entitled 'The Dorsetshire Labourer', published 10 years after *Far from the Madding Crowd*.[21] His sympathy and admiration for the labourers are quickly in evidence:

> 'To see the Dorset labourer at his worst and saddest time, he should be viewed when attending a wet hiring-fair at Candlemas, in search of a new master. His natural cheerfulness bravely struggles against the weather and the incertitude; but as the day passes on, and his clothes get wet through, and he is still unhired, there does appear a factitiousness in the smile which, with a self-repressing mannerliness hardly to be found among any other class, he yet has ready when he encounters and talks with friends who have been more fortunate.' (p. 257)

Even though the life-style of people working close to nature is sometimes idealised, 'The Dorsetshire Labourer' makes clear Hardy's unease with this system of securing labour. Interestingly, though, he is not advocating its abolition. Rather, what seems to

---

[20] Thomas Hardy, *Jude the Obscure*, London: Macmillan, 1990, pp. 50, 51.

[21] Thomas Hardy, 'The Dorsetshire Labourer', in *Longman's Magazine*, Vol. 2, 1883, pp. 252-69.

exercise Hardy is that, in the market-place, individuality gives way to uniformity, as evidenced in the loss of the traditional dress which once individuated the shepherds, carters, thatchers, and so on, from each other:

'Formerly they came in smock-frocks and gaiters, the shepherds with their crooks, the carters with a zone of whipcord round their hats, thatchers with a straw tucked into the brim, and so on. Now, with the exception of the crook in the hands of an occasional shepherd, there is no mark of speciality in the groups, who might be tailors or undertakers' men, for what they exhibit externally.' (p. 258)

Developing this idea, Hardy's novels reflect a transitional period on the land that might be thought of in terms of a transformation in agriculture from an occupation that individuates to an occupation that renders its workers anonymous. We should note here that, unlike, say, Wells, Hardy does not fight shy of the need for agriculture to be run as a business; his concern is with the passing of 'natural' values. Hardy is dry-eyed in his observation of farming as a business and the work-force as a commodity. He bemoans the lost sense of contact with the land consequent upon the 'increasing nomadic habit of the labourer' (p. 263), yet recognises that the rural work-force must follow the demand for labour. As Hardy dramatises in the plight of the Durbeyfield family after John's death, his sympathies are with the labouring families, rendered increasingly vulnerable as their cottages are leased to them for the duration of their employment and can be just as easily reclaimed from them on Lady Day. Nevertheless, he is alive, too, both to the inevitability of change and to the fact that change 'is also a sort of education':

'Many advantages accrue to the labourers from the varied experience it brings, apart from the best market for their abilities. ... It is only the old story that progress and picturesqueness do not harmonise. They are losing their individuality, but they are widening the range of their ideas, and gaining in freedom.' (p. 262)

This capacity to present rural life and work as it is and not as he would like it to be, makes Hardy a realist, and it is his realism that enables him to see both the comforting and the malignant side of rural work, and this nowhere better than in *Tess of the d'Urbervilles*.

Her locale provides an index to the emotional state of Tess Durbeyfield: at Talbothays Dairy, her relationship with Angel Clare burgeons 'at a season when the rush of juices could almost be heard below the hiss of fertilisation' (p. 155), whilst the description of the swede-field at Flintcomb-Ash Farm as 'a complexion without features' (p. 273) perfectly reflects the bleakness of her prospects after Angel has abandoned her. But work is a function of locale in Hardy's novels and is, thus, also used to reflect in miniature an important transitional stage in the countryside: the increasing mechanisation. In the harvesting scene, in Chapter 14 of *Tess of the d'Urbervilles*, the mechanical reaper, whose noise resembles 'the love-making of a grasshopper', is followed by women whose movements gathering and binding draw them together 'like dancers in a quadrille' (pp. 102,104). How different this is from the threshing-machine, in Chapter 47, which is described in terms which emphasise dominance and subservience:

> 'Close under the eaves of the stack, and as yet barely visible, was the red tyrant that the women had come to serve – a timber-framed construction, with straps and wheels appertaining – the threshing machine which, whilst it was going, kept up a despotic demand upon the endurance of their muscles and nerves.' (p. 309)

With its emphasis on women serving the machine, this embodiment of new forces on the land is couched in sexual terms. Tess is thus representative of woman's lot in the face of 19th-century patriarchy both as woman and as woman-worker. In 'The Dorsetshire Labourer', Hardy observes that women's labour 'is highly in request, for a woman who, like a boy, fills the place of a man at half the wages, can be better depended on for steadiness' (p. 267). Hardy's presentation of Wessex across his novels is, thus, simultaneously a representation of the changing face of farming as a business, run for profit, and his greatness as a novelist may well lie in his courageous recognition that, despite his own personal sympathies, this business like any other needs to move with the times.

Lawrence

Like Hardy, D. H. Lawrence (1885-1930) addresses the de-humanising effects of new working practices, but his concern is predominantly with industrialism, for which the mining country of Nottinghamshire and Derbyshire where he grew up provides the perfect setting. In his essay, part-autobiography, part-polemic,

'Nottingham and the Mining Countryside', Lawrence, at once more angry and impassioned than Hardy, presents an emotional rather than an intellectual case against the loss of the countryside in the face of industry-led urban expansion:

> 'The Englishman still likes to think of himself as a "cottager" – "my home, my garden". But it is puerile. Even the farm-labourer today is psychologically a town-bird. The English are town-birds through and through, today, as the inevitable result of their complete industrialisation. ... England is a mean and petty scrabble of paltry dwellings called "homes". I believe in their heart of hearts all Englishmen loathe their little homes ... And the promoter of industry, a hundred years ago, dared to perpetrate the ugliness of my native village. And still more monstrous, promoters of industry today are scrabbling over the face of England with miles and miles of red-brick "homes", like horrible scabs.'[22]

In this essay, Lawrence rages against what he sees as the ugliness of England and of English life, an ugliness that, once again, he lays at the door of industry:

> 'The great crime which the moneyed classes and promoters of industry committed in the palmy Victorian days was the condemning of the workers to ugliness, ugliness, ugliness: meanness and formless and ugly surroundings, ugly ideals, ugly religion, ugly hope, ugly love, ugly surroundings, ugly ideals, ugly relationship between workers and employers. The human soul needs actual beauty even more than bread.' (p. 138)

But whilst the mining industry provides Lawrence with an easy target for his attack on materialism generally in this essay, it is employed in his fiction more subtly than this. His short story, 'Odour of Chrysanthemums', provides a good illustration. The tale commences with a brief description of the ineffectuality of mechanisation as a colt out-distances a passing locomotive engine 'at a canter'.[23] But the blight of industry is present in the countryside:

---

[22] D. H. Lawrence, 'Nottingham and the Mining Countryside', in *Phoenix*, Geneva: Edito-Service, S.A., n.d., pp. 139-40.

[23] D. H. Lawrence, *The Complete Short Stories*, Vol. 2, London: Heinemann, 1955, p. 283.

'In the open, the smoke from the engine sank and cleaved to the rough grass. The fields were dreary and forsaken, and in the marshy strip that led to the whimsey, a reedy pit-pond, the fowls had already abandoned their run among the alders, to roost in the tarred fowl-house. The pit-bank loomed up beyond the pond, flames like red sores licking its ash sides, in the afternoon's stagnant light.' (p. 283)

Nature itself seems unable to compete with the forces of industry. This sterility announces the corrosive potential of industry, that spreads from the pit to the countryside and, ultimately, into the Bates's marriage itself. To complete this picture, an unidentified woman stands, 'insignificantly trapped between the jolting black waggons and the hedge,' as the locomotive passes by (p. 283). Through this detail, designed to suggest that industry hems in the lives of those associated with it, Lawrence adumbrates the death of Walter Bates, significantly, by asphyxiation, in a mining accident. At this point, it is tempting to see Lawrence's portrayal of the mining industry as simply reductive. But, however prevalent in his work are the related themes of Nature, including human nature, tainted by mechanisation, and the constrictions of the material world upon instinctual life, Lawrence is attracted, too, to the fellowship and community fostered by the colliers' work. In 'Nottingham and the Mining Countryside' he claims that

'the miners worked underground as a sort of intimate community, they knew each other practically naked, and with curious close intimacy, and the darkness and the underground remoteness of the pit "stall", and the continual presence of danger, made the physical instinctive, and intuitional contact between men very highly developed, a contact almost as close as touch, very real and very powerful' (pp. 135-36).

This curious fascination with what repels him is of a piece with some of the lingering, almost loving, descriptions of, say, Dickens in the presentation of 'Tom-all-Alone's' in *Bleak House*, and it hints at the complexities and contradictions within Lawrence's own approach to industrialism. Interestingly, this same mixture of attraction and revulsion defines the attitude of Gudrun Brangwen towards the Beldover colliers in *Women in Love*:

'It was the same every evening when she came home, she seemed to move through a wave of disruptive force, that was given off from the presence of thousands of vigorous, under-world, half-automatised colliers, and which went to the brain and the heart, awaking a fatal desire, and a fatal callousness.'[24]

Similarly, in *The Rainbow*, the feelings of Winifred Inger for Ursula's uncle, Tom Brangwen, are contradictory: 'She was afraid of him, repelled by him, and yet attracted.'[25] Such contradiction extends to the couple's perverse fascination and acceptance of the plight of the Wiggiston colliers: Winifred and Tom are described as 'cynically reviling the monstrous state and yet adhering to it, like a man who reviles his mistress, yet who is in love with her' (p. 349). Lawrence seems to suggest that it is only through such emotional confusion that the system can be perpetuated, believing that civilisation had corrupted the natural behaviour of men and women. As he said in a letter to Ernest Collings, dated 17 January 1913:

> 'My great religion is a belief in the blood, the flesh, as being wiser than the intellect. We can go wrong in our minds. But what our blood feels and believes and says, is always true. The intellect is only a bit and bridle. What do I care about knowledge. All I want is to answer to my blood, direct.'[26]

It is in the light of such claims that we read such works as *Lady Chatterley's Lover*, with their emphasis upon the re-discovery of a passionate, impulsive life that has been suppressed by the evasions and pretence of the Modern world. The degree to which D. H. Lawrence believed that this instinctual life of mankind had been suppressed by industry is apparent in his presentation of business in the two novels, *The Rainbow* and *Women in Love*, that evolved out of the projected single novel, *The Sisters*, begun in 1913.

The Rainbow (published in 1915 and immediately suppressed on sexual and political grounds) is a family chronicle that charts the history of three generations of the Brangwen family and culminates in the successful struggle of Ursula Brangwen to make her way in a male-dominated world. By contrast, *Women in Love* (written in 1916-17 and published in 1922) is an apocalyptic novel: written

---

[24] D. H. Lawrence, *Women in Love*, London: Heinemann, 1954, p. 108.

[25] D. H. Lawrence, *The Rainbow*, London: Heinemann, 1955, p. 346.

[26] Diana Trilling, *The Selected Letters of D. H. Lawrence*, New York: Farrar, Straus and Cudahy, 1958, p. 46.

under the spirit of the First World War, it charts the fortunes of two couples against the backdrop of an increasing pessimism in the social world. Not unnaturally, given British participation in the First World War, the novels of this period reflect a national self-consciousness of the idea and state of British society. Such novels belong to a genre known as 'condition of England' novels and include such examples as Wells's *Tono-Bungay* (1909) and E. M. Forster's *Howards End* (1910). Lawrence's survey of English life, *Women in Love*, belongs to this tradition.

The pastoral rhythms of the world of the Brangwens are inscribed in the very tissue of the prose at the beginning of *The Rainbow*, where the lyricism and repetitions combine to suggest the continuity of this world:

> 'The young corn waved and was silken, and the lustre slid along the limbs of the men who saw it. They took the udder of the cows, the cows yielded milk and pulse against the hands of the men, the pulse of the blood of the teats of the cows beat into the pulse of the hands of the men.' (p. 2)

Across the two novels, the destruction of this pastoral world is registered in the stylistic transformation from rhythmical prose like this, that reinforces the sense of organic unity between man and his environment, to the fragmentary style of *Women in Love*, whose chapters read like a series of discrete short stories, mirroring the discontinuities of the age. Nowhere is the progressively bleak note that is sounded about the fate of society in these two novels heard to more effect than in Lawrence's presentation of the mines and the miners: industry might be said to provide the index to the state of English society.

Chronologically, the sweep of *The Rainbow* is significant: the novel begins in the late-Victorian period and ends in the Boer War. In other words, *The Rainbow* commences in semi-rural England and, through its presentation of the mining industry in particular, examines the influence of the large-scale industrialisation which characterised this period. Even before the birth of Ursula's grandfather, Tom Brangwen, whose marriage to Lydia Lensky occupies the first third of the novel, new forces are gaining purchase around Marsh Farm:

'About 1840, a canal was constructed across the meadows of the Marsh Farm, connecting the newly-opened collieries of the Erewash Valley. A high embankment travelled along the fields to carry the canal, which passed close to the homestead, and, reaching the road, went over in a heavy bridge.

'So the Marsh was shut off from Ilkeston, and enclosed in the small valley bed, which ended in a bushy hill and the village spire of Cossethay. ... looking from the garden gate down the road to the right, there, through the dark archway of the canal's square aqueduct, was a colliery spinning away in the near distance, and further, red, crude houses plastered on the valley in masses, and beyond all, the dim smoking hill of the town.

'The homestead was just on the safe side of civilisation, outside the gate.' (p. 6)

Symbolically, the canal that supplies the mines also both hems in the lives of the Brangwens and separates their old rural way of life from the new mechanised way of life. Further, in a novel where the past is important, as each generation inherits traits from its predecessors, this 'new' force on the land will itself have a consequence: many years later, Tom Brangwen will be drowned when this same canal bursts its (man-made) banks. Tom is the last of the Brangwen farmers so his death carries the suggestion that industry has now succeeded in replacing agriculture as the local business. Further, his physical death can be seen, in part at least, as an embodiment of the spiritual deaths of the miners, who are identified as the real victims of the forces of social and economic change in the novel.

Another way of saying that the Modern age reflects the migration from *rus* to *urbs*, is to say simply that this is 'the age of the masses'. Indeed, M. D. Biddiss's book on the period has this phrase as its title (1977). But, within the mass production, mass culture, and mass communication, that characterise the age, lie the cause of much of Lawrence's disquiet: the loss of individualism. His novels in general, and *The Rainbow*, in particular, contrast the uniqueness of the individual with the sameness of the mechanical world. In the reduction of the individual to something mechanical lies the true 'ugliness' of industrialism for Lawrence. Thus, Wiggiston is described in terms that accentuate its utilitarian sterility:

'The streets were like visions of pure ugliness; a grey-black, macadamised road, asphalt causeways, held in between a flat succession of wall, window, and door, a new-brick channel began nowhere, and ended nowhere. Everything was amorphous, yet everything repeated itself endlessly. ... The rigidity of the blank streets, the homogeneous amorphous sterility of the whole suggested death rather than life.' (p. 344)

In his description of the miners' subordination to the pit, 'the great mistress', uncle Tom Brangwen, the mine manager, paints a stark picture of the degree to which the industry has destroyed any sense of individuality in their lives: 'Every man his own little side show, his home, but the pit owns every man. The women have what's left of this man, or of that – it doesn't matter altogether. The pit takes all that really matters' (p. 348). In *The Rainbow*, this sense of the industrial machine as the only reality gains as we see its influence – and corrosive power – extend to other areas of life. For instance, disillusioned with her studies, Ursula has a vision of her College as a mere adjunct of commerce: 'It was a little apprentice-shop where one was further equipped for making money. The college itself was a little, slovenly laboratory for the factory' (p. 435). In *Women in Love,* Lawrence satirically extends his consideration of industry's dehumanising effect to reveal its influence upon the lives of the mine owners.

Women in Love is set in the years immediately preceding the First World War and, by concentrating upon two contrasted couples, it traces the prevailing mood of social and cultural crisis to the area of emotional and sexual relationships. Whilst it is a much bleaker work than *The Rainbow*, it too affirms the claims of instinctual over industrial life, but with the difference that the argument it offers for this is less arbitrary than that offered by its predecessor. Ursula's hopeful 'rainbow vision' provides *The Rainbow* with an up-beat ending that its social context does not really justify. Given the same context, the hope offered by the relationship between Ursula and Rupert Birkin in *Women in Love* is more coherent in that it depends upon their abandoning this context altogether: for them a new life, ultimately, beckons beyond the ties of home, family, and possessions. Such belief in an individual – rather than a social – code of conduct distinguishes Birkin from the other central male character in the novel, Gerald Crich. At the wedding reception of Gerald's sister, Laura, Birkin says that he should like people 'to like the purely individual thing in themselves, which makes them act in singleness. And they only like to do the collective thing'. Gerald replies that he 'shouldn't like to be in a world of people who acted individually and spontaneously' (p. 27), a response which allies him with Anton Skrebensky in *The Rainbow*, who tells Ursula: 'I belong to the nation and must do my duty by the nation' (p. 309). He sees himself as 'just a brick in the whole great social fabric' (p. 326).

In the 'Coal Dust' chapter of *Women in Love*, Gerald, the mine owner's son, is seen exerting a wilful mastery over the Arab mare he is riding as it tries to escape the clamour caused by an approaching colliery train. The nearer the train gets, the more frantic become the horse's struggles:

> 'She began to wince away, as if hurt by the unknown noise. But Gerald pulled her back and held her head to the gate. The sharp blasts of the chuffing engine broke with more and more force on her. The repeated sharp blows of unknown, terrifying noise struck through her till she was rocking with terror. She recoiled like a spring let go. But a glistening, half-smiling look came into Gerald's face. He brought her back again, inevitably.' (p. 103)

Of course, the horse is emblematic of the natural impulse that is quashed in the service of industry, whose relentlessness is perfectly captured in that post-positioned adverb, 'inevitably'. In *Women in Love*, Lawrence's concern extends beyond the plight of the mine-worker to include the nature of mine-management itself.

The presentation of the Crich family reveals the changing face of the industrial magnate as control of the mine passes from old Thomas Crich, a second-generation mine-owner, to his son, Gerald. Between them, father and son represent a crucial shift in the nature of the relationships between employer and employee. Thomas Crich's sentimental paternalism exists within an inherent contradiction: 'He wanted to be a pure Christian, one and equal with all men. He even wanted to give away all he had, to the poor. Yet he was a great promoter of industry, and he knew perfectly that he must keep his goods and keep his authority' (p. 219). By contrast, Gerald is not exercised by any such qualms – 'He abandoned the whole democratic-equality problem as a problem of silliness. What mattered was the great social productive machine' (p. 219) – instead, he is driven by the simple obsession to rationalise the mines and to make them more efficient:

'The working of the pits was thoroughly changed, all the control was taken out of the hands of the miners, the butty system was abolished. Everything was run on the most accurate and delicate scientific method, educated and expert men were in control everywhere, the miners were reduced to mere mechanical instruments. They had to work hard, much harder than before, the work was terrible and heart-breaking in its mechanicalness.' (p. 223)

But, in an amusing paradox, once he has 'converted the industry into a new and terrible purity', with himself as 'the God of the machine' (pp. 224, 220), Gerald finds that the 'machine' runs by itself: so successful has been his rationalisation that he has succeeded in making himself surplus to requirements. It is part of Lawrence's point about industrialism that Gerald is then shown to lack the inner resources necessary to sustain him.

With grim irony, the improved fortunes of the Crich's family business coincide with the deterioration of the family: Thomas Crich dies after a long, lingering illness. This association of business with death is central to Lawrence's presentation of Gerald, the industrial magnate *par excellence* in the novel: not only is Gerald responsible for the deaths of his brother (in a shooting accident) and sister (who drowns at the water party he is supervising), but he is repeatedly described in terms that emphasise his coldness – he is 'an arctic thing', 'a ray of cold sunshine', and so on (pp. 9, 105), and when he dies, it is in his 'element', in the snow-bound wastes of the Swiss Alps. This suggestion that business has, at its core, an inherent 'death-wish', is of a piece with the narrative suggestion that, taken to its extreme, industrial efficiency 'kills' the individual worker by reducing him to something mechanical. This idea might thus be construed as a bout of wish-fulfilment on Lawrence's part. None the less, in its presentation of the deleterious effects of industrialism in areas of life as diverse as sexual relations and art, *Women in Love* sees business as perpetuating the crisis of culture to which early 20th-century writers were responding. Thomas Hardy and D. H. Lawrence concentrate, respectively, upon rural and industrial economies, and thus, by and large, attend to this crisis of values 'from within' the milieu of English society: their works voice the sadness and anger at the breakdown of the pre-industrial way of life in *English* society. It was left to another writer, an immigrant, to offer a complementary view of this crisis 'from without' by placing it in an international context.

Conrad

Joseph Conrad (1857-1924) was the adopted, anglicised version of the name of Józef Teodor Konrad Korzeniowski. Born of ardent Polish patriots (his father was sent to a Russian penal colony for his views), Conrad left Poland at the age of 17 for Marseilles to become a trainee seaman in the French Merchant Service, before transferring to British ships in 1878 and working his way up through the ranks to obtain his Master's Certificate in 1886. A sailor in the last great age of sailing ships, Conrad's travels took him round the world and these experiences furnished him with material for the sea-fiction. After Conrad's sea career ended in 1894 (with a brief cross-Channel voyage on the *Adowa*), he committed himself to writing novels for a living and, although writing in his third language, he quickly earned his place among the foremost novelists of the age. Indeed, F. R. Leavis saw Conrad as the successor to Jane Austen, George Eliot, and Henry James in the 'great tradition' of the English Novel.

In his early novels, Conrad, like Hardy, describes humanity as a prolongation of the natural world. Conrad's first novel, *Almayer's Folly* (1895), earned him the sobriquet 'the Kipling of the Malay Archipelago'.[27] In *Almayer's Folly*, Conrad uses trade to pass an ironic comment upon Dutch colonialism. Set in the village of Sambir, the fictional counterpart of Tanjong Redeb on the Berau River in North Borneo, the novel charts the declining fortunes of the resident Westerner, Kaspar Almayer, a failed trader who is outsmarted by his native counterparts. Almayer's assumed cultural superiority leads him to dismiss the natives as inferior, yet Conrad reveals how the same impulses motivate both the European and the Malays, and the image of Almayer, towards the end of the novel, in an opium daze and being led about by his pet monkey provides a humorous picture of the would-be supremacist descending the evolutionary ladder.

Almayer's Folly might be thought of as a debasement of the theme of *Madame Bovary*: the novel offers a study in disintegration in the person of the *declassé* Almayer, whose cheap dream of riches makes of him a metaphor for failure. Ironically, Almayer's plan to flee Sambir and to introduce his daughter, Nina, into Amsterdam society entails a journey into the interior to collect gold and

---

[27] Unsigned review in *Spectator*, 19 October 1895, p.530.

diamonds. Thus, Almayer hopes to assert his Dutch identity by travelling deeper into the heart of Borneo! The link between commerce and cultural diversity is best made when Abdulla, who has quickly become the foremost trader in Sambir, visits Almayer with an offer to buy Nina as 'a favourite wife' for his nephew, Reshid.[28] Whilst the proposal itself deeply offends Almayer's assumed cultural superiority, the material advantages that Abdulla promises hint at the very connotators of European civilisation for which Almayer yearns:

> 'You know, Tuan,' he said, in conclusion, 'the other women would be her slaves, and Reshid's house is great. From Bombay he has brought great divans, and costly carpets, and European furniture. There is also a great looking-glass in a frame shining like gold. What could a girl want more?' (p. 45)

Part of Conrad's point in the novel is the blindness of colonialism to the shabbiness of its own motives. Thus, the reader and not the protagonist is aware of Abdulla's vested economic interests and how these are ranged against Almayer, outsmarting him at every turn. According to Cedric Watts, this provides the novel with a 'covert plot'.[29] I suggest that this idea of naked financial interest parading as something finer becomes something of a feature of Conrad's presentation of business and money in his subsequent novels.

In *Heart of Darkness* (1899), colonial expansion itself is exposed as little more than European greed masquerading as philanthropy. Drawing upon his own visit to the Congo Free State in 1890, Conrad paints a grim picture of imperialism that, by drawing attention to the cruelty of its methods, stresses its purely economic basis:

> 'It was just robbery with violence, aggravated murder on a grand scale, and men going at it blind – as is very proper for those who tackle a darkness. The conquest of the earth, which mostly means the taking it away from those who have a different complexion or slightly flatter noses than ourselves, is not a pretty thing when you look into it too

---

28 Joseph Conrad, *Almayer's Folly*, London: J. M. Dent and Sons, 1923, p. 45.

29 See Cedric Watts, *The Deceptive Text: An Introduction to Covert Plots*, Brighton: Harvester, 1984, Ch. 5.

much. What redeems it is the idea only.'[30]

Within the narrative, the civilising 'idea' behind the venture is debunked by Marlow's observations of the lust for ivory in Africa. In a letter to Arthur Conan Doyle (dated 7 October 1909), E. D. Morel, the founder of the Congo Reform Association, called *Heart of Darkness* 'the most powerful thing ever written on the subject'.[31] It was first published in *Blackwood's* magazine, in serial form, from February to April 1899, and, subsequently, in book form, in *Youth: A Narrative and Two Other Stories*, in 1902. In other words, Conrad's novella, expressing disillusionment with the imperial achievement, is published against an historical backdrop which includes the death of Queen Victoria and the outbreak of the Boer War. At the time of publication, Britain was still the banker of the world: 'in 1901 the British were still considerably the world's largest exporters of manufactured goods and by far the leading trading nation, accounting for some twenty five per cent of the world's trade.'[32] However, in various ways, Britain was showing signs of vulnerability: the first stirrings of nationalism were making themselves felt in far-flung corners of the Empire whilst, economically, her maritime advantage was being eroded by America.[33]

In the novel, the idea behind European involvement in Africa is voiced by Marlow's aunt as 'weaning those ignorant millions from their horrid ways' (p. 59). The yawning divide between such superficial sentiment and the manifestation of business in its crudest form advertises the blindness of colonial enterprise. In an interesting reversal, whilst business is disguised as colonialism in *Heart of Darkness*, in Conrad's great metropolitan novel, *The Secret Agent* (1907), it is Verloc's small business that provides the cover for his activities as a double agent. In keeping with the fact that Verloc's

---

[30] Joseph Conrad, *Youth: A Narrative and Two Other Stories*, London: J. M. Dent and Sons, 1923, pp. 50-51.

[31] Quoted in Edmund Dene Morel, *History of the Congo Reform Movement*, ed. William Roger Louis and Jean Stengers, London: OUP, 1968, p. 205n.

[32] Ford (ed.), 1992, p. 5.

[33] For a discussion of this, see Jacques Berthoud's essay 'Introduction: Conrad and the Sea' in: Joseph Conrad, *The Nigger of the 'Narcissus'*, ed. Jacques Berthoud, Oxford: OUP, 1992, pp. vii-xxvi.

activities involve secrecy, his trade is in 'shady wares'.[34] In these narratives, it is as though Conrad is suggesting that business *per se* entails some degree of subterfuge. Inevitably, one thinks of *The End of the Tether* (1902), where Captain Whalley continues to pilot the 'Sofala', in order to provide for his daughter, even though his blindness makes him unfit to do so. A variation on the theme of subterfuge – which may well owe something to H. G. Wells's *Tono-Bungay* – comes in *Chance*, published in 1914, in which the central figure, Flora de Barral, is victimised largely because of the collapse of her father's business empire that is discovered to consist of little beyond the advertising:

> 'One remembers his first modest advertisements headed with the magic word Thrift, Thrift, Thrift, thrice repeated; promising ten per cent on all deposits and giving the address of the Thrift and Independence Aid Association in Vauxhall Road. Apparently nothing more was necessary. He didn't even explain what he meant to do with the money he asked the public to pour into his lap. Of course he meant to lend it out at high rates of interest. He did so – but he did it without system, plan, foresight or judgment. And as he frittered away the sums that flowed in, he advertised for more – and got it. During a period of general business prosperity he set up The Orb Bank and The Sceptre Trust, simply, it seems, for advertising purposes. They were mere names.'[35]

Capturing the mood of the time in which it was written, this is a novel about women's struggle to get their voices heard in a world dominated by men. Thus, the fact that the male world of her father's business, upon which the young Flora depends for her security, is shown to be a sham, is simultaneously a criticism of the world of business and the subjugation of women. Ironically, it was this tale of swindling that finally made Conrad's fortune with the reading public.

However jaundiced it may seem, Conrad's view of business and of the economic underpinning of daily life is never less than realistic. Conrad served as a sailor in the age when sailing ships were giving way to steamers, and the romance of his sea-fiction is underpinned by the gritty realism of employment and trade: the sailors are doing a job and the ship is sailing in service of the

---

[34] Joseph Conrad, *The Secret Agent*, London: J. M. Dent and Sons, 1923, p. 5.

[35] Joseph Conrad, *Chance*, London: J. M. Dent and Sons, 1923, pp. 78-79.

business. For instance, in *The Nigger of the 'Narcissus'*, the reader never discovers what freight the 'Narcissus' is carrying on her return voyage from Bombay to London, and so is tempted to identify this 'freight' as the insights about themselves gained by the crew. But Captain Allistoun's refusal to cut the masts during the storm scene is nonetheless subtly linked to the trade-ethic that 'time is money', even if this is partially obscured by the captain's own egotism:

> 'He loved his ship, and drove her unmercifully; for his secret ambition was to make her accomplish some day a brilliantly quick passage which would be mentioned in nautical papers. He pronounced the owner's name with a sardonic smile.'[36]

A more obvious instance of this is provided in *Typhoon* when Captain MacWhirr, the dour skipper of the 'Nan-Shan' sails through, rather than round, the 'dirty weather' predicted by the steady fall of his ship's barometer. Like the heroes of Hardy, Conrad's MacWhirr is at home in his environment and so, when confronted by a crisis, he is guided by his seaman's instinct rather than the 'storm strategy' he reads about in books. MacWhirr's explanation of his actions to Mr Jukes, his chief mate, is humorous at the Captain's expense whilst, simultaneously, emphasising that he is an employee whose working practice is monitored:

> 'If the weather delays me – very well. There's your log-book to talk straight about the weather. But suppose I went swinging off my course and came in two days late, and they asked me: "Where have you been all that time, Captain?" What could I say to that? "Went around to dodge the bad weather," I would say. "It must've been dam' bad," they would say. "Don't know," I would have to say; "I've dodged clear of it." See that, Jukes?'[37]

This tale, which was originally entitled 'Equitable Division', provides a good example of the manner in which Conradian fiction is grounded in economic reality. Whilst the eventual title directs the reader towards the typhoon itself, the consequence of the storm is that MacWhirr has to redistribute their money to the Chinese

---

[36] Joseph Conrad, *The Nigger of the 'Narcissus'*, London: J. M. Dent and Sons, 1923, p. 31.

[37] Joseph Conrad, *Typhoon and Other Stories*, London: J. M. Dent and Sons, 1923, p. 34.

workers, returning home from Fu-chau to their families after working abroad. Confronted by this problem, MacWhirr solves it just as he does the problem of the typhoon, by confronting it head on. The boxes containing the workers' savings break open during the typhoon so MacWhirr orders Jukes to gather up all the money to prevent them fighting for it below-decks. The storm over, MacWhirr resolves the problem of redistribution by sharing the money out equitably. As Jukes writes to his friend:

> 'He told me afterwards that, all the coolies having worked in the same place and for the same length of time, he reckoned he would be doing the fair thing by them as near as possible if he shared all the cash we had picked up equally among the lot. ... There were three dollars left over, and these went to the three most damaged coolies, one to each.' (pp. 101-02)

It is part of the point of the novel that Jukes, another 'reader' of the unimaginative MacWhirr's actions, doesn't fully appreciate the captain's actions – 'he got out of it very well for such a stupid man,' Jukes writes to a friend (p. 102) – instead, this is left to the chief engineer, Mr Solomon Rout, who informs his wife that the captain 'has done something rather clever' (p. 96), and then forgets to inform her what it is! In the light of Jukes's desire to alter the ship's course away from the typhoon for the benefit of 'passengers', MacWhirr's attitude seemed racist – 'Never heard a lot of coolies spoken of as passengers before. Passengers, indeed!' (p. 31) – yet, as subsequent events demonstrate, the captain's fairness throws into stark relief the false humanitarianism of his chief mate. The point is that, to the unimaginative MacWhirr, the workers *are* just so much cargo being conveyed from one port to another.

Conrad's most forceful and far-reaching comments on business, however, come in *Nostromo* (1904). This novel, set in the fictional South American republic of Costaguana, offers both an analysis of the relationship between business and politics, through the San Tomé silver mine, the 'imperium in imperio' in Costaguana, and, through the American tycoon, Holroyd, in particular, a prediction of global economics across the whole of the 20th century. It is thus fitting that I conclude this survey of representations of business in early-20th-century literature with this 'most anxiously meditated' novel, as Conrad described it is his 'Author's Note'.

Charles Gould, a young Englishman, returns to Costaguana, the country of his birth, with his new bride, Emilia, and reopens the San Tomé silver mine, that had been forced upon his father when Gould was about 14, under a 'perpetual concession' that stipulated immediate payment of 'five years' royalties on the estimated output of the mine' to the impoverished government, 'the fourth in six years'.[38] Against a volatile political backdrop of revolution and counter-revolution, Gould, a trained engineer, succeeds in working the mine to the point where it becomes *the* force in the land, and Gould himself earns the nickname 'King of Sulaco' (p. 93). The novel's chronological shifts serve to replicate, in the reading process, the interconnectedness of people, patterns, and events, as Conrad's true subject in the novel is made clear: in *Nostromo*, Conrad's concern is nothing less than the historical process itself. Amid the welter of forces that combine to create the history of Costaguana, the one point of fixity is the silver itself. This novel charts the obsession with material interests as, ultimately, the characters connect more with the silver than with each other.

In a conversation with his wife, Charles Gould links commerce to social stability, making it sound as if the mine will serve a finer purpose than crude materialism:

> 'What is wanted here is law, good faith, order, security. Any one can declaim about these things, but I pin my faith on material interests. Only let the material interests once get a firm footing, and they are bound to impose the conditions on which alone they can continue to exist. That's how your money-making is justified here in the face of lawlessness and disorder. It is justified because the security which it demands must be shared with an oppressed people.' (p. 84)

However, in order to preserve and protect the mine, Gould resorts, first, to bribery and, then, to financing a revolution to install Don Vincente Ribiera as 'President-Dictator', which in turn fuels further revolution, leading, ultimately, to the War of Separation through which the Occidental province becomes the independent State of Sulaco. Such emphasis upon Costaguana politics as a function of economics carries with it the suggestion that Conrad's is, in part at least, a Marxist reading of history. But if the silver does influence the politics of Costaguana, does the founding of the State of Sulaco

---

[38] Joseph Conrad, *Nostromo: A Tale of the Seaboard*, London: J. M. Dent and Sons, 1923, p. 53.

achieve the stability and order of which Gould spoke to Emilia? The novel concludes against a backdrop of increasing class conflict and with powerful Sulacans conspiring for the annexation of Costaguana. As Doctor Monygham tells Emilia Gould:

> 'There is no peace and no rest in the development of material interests. They have their law, and their justice. But it is founded on expediency, and it is inhuman; it is without rectitude, without the continuity and the force that can be found only in a moral principle. Mrs Gould, the time approaches when all that the Gould Concession stands for shall weigh as heavily upon the people as the barbarism, cruelty, and misrule of a few years back.' (p. 511)

By the end of the novel, then, the wheel has come full circle. In affluent, present-day Sulaco, the Communist Party is urging the workers to rise against their capitalist exploiters. Conrad's novel reveals the entrapment of the individual within the larger forces – such as politics and economics – which shape the age, but it shows, too, how material interest induces a blindness to the presence of these forces. For instance, when Gould threatens to blow up the silver mine rather than surrender it to Pedro Montero, his defiance might suggest control and independence, but he is, really, just a counter in the game of international capitalism, the toy of the American financier, Mr Holroyd.

The political identity of Costaguana is shaped by representatives of various nations, predominantly European, suggesting that, in *Nostromo*, Conrad returns to the theme of colonial expansion. In *Heart of Darkness*, the blame for colonialism is laid at the door of all Europe, not simply Belgium, as Marlow traces Kurtz's parentage: 'His mother was half-English, his father was half-French. All Europe contributed to the making of Kurtz' (p. 117). In *Nostromo*, Holroyd's similarly cosmopolitan parentage – 'German and Scotch and English, with remote strains of Danish and French blood' (p. 76) – apportions the blame for the *financial* colonialism of South America just as widely. By comparison with our previous novels, the sheer scale of *Nostromo* is daunting, and indicative of the ambition of the Modern Novel: rather than offering a simple representation of business, *Nostromo* addresses the very forces which shape business in the 20th century. At the beginning of Gould's adventure in Costaguana, Holroyd offers him a summary of the country's history in purely financial terms, and is then moved to speculate upon the nature of American involvement in the country in terms which, prophetically, define the nature of international business in the 20th century:

'Now, what is Costaguana? It is the bottomless pit of 10 per cent loans and other fool investments. European capital had been flung into it with both hands for years. Not ours, though. We in this country know just about enough to keep indoors when it rains. We can sit and watch. Of course, some day we shall step in. We are bound to. But there's no hurry. Time itself has got to wait on the greatest country in the whole of God's Universe. We shall be giving the word for everything: industry, trade, law, journalism, art, politics, and religion, from Cape Horn clear over to Smith's Sound, and beyond, too, if anything worth taking hold of turns up at the North Pole. And then we shall have the leisure to take in hand the outlying islands and continents of the earth. We shall run the world's business whether the world likes it or not. The world can't help it – and neither can we, I guess.' (pp. 76-77)

6

MID-LATE TWENTIETH-CENTURY:

'AN UNPRECEDENTED

MORAL QUAGMIRE'

John Morris

Brunel University

1. The Scene in the 1930s

'You gave a week of your life, every week, so that you might have a hovel for shelter, an insufficiency of food and five bob left over to clothe yourself and the missis in shoddy'.

Walter Greenwood, *Love on the Dole* (1933)

IT IS DIFFICULT TO FIND POSITIVE AND APPRECIATIVE IMAGES OF BUSINESS in 20th-century English literature. This is especially true in the period leading up to the Second World War. By then the entrenched feeling among many writers reflected the powerful influence of Charles Dickens to the effect that business – capitalism – was a dirty, disreputable, tarnished affair in practice. *Hard Times, Dombey and Son* and in particular *Our Mutual Friend*, which includes an unseemly struggle for the ownership of a heap of dirt near the waters of the Thames, were profoundly influential on a whole range of differing writers from H.G. Wells to T.S. Eliot (the latter even considering an alternative title to *The Waste Land* (1922) taken from Dickens's novel).[1]

But there were further, political, reasons why the world of

---

[1] 'He Do the Police in Different Voices.' Eliot was referring here to Sloppy's skill as a newspaper reader in *Our Mutual Friend* and also to Dickens's experimental technique in anecdotal reportage, for Eliot like the great novelist was giving a panoramic view of London and its society. See T. S. Eliot, *The Waste Land: A Facsimile and Transcript of the Original Drafts including the Annotations of Ezra Pound*, ed. V. Eliot, London:Faber and Faber, 1971, p. 23. See also Erik Svarny, *'The MEN of 1914': T. S. ELIOT and Early Modernism*, Milton Keynes and Philadelphia: Open University Press, 1988, p. 188.

business and finance should have received such a 'bad press' in creative writing. For by the 1930s literature had become increasingly polarised into Left and Right. For the Left, capitalism was seen as allied to fascism. Indeed, fascism was seen in Freudian terms as a kind of social-psychological disease whose financial wing was capitalist. There were those on the Left who considered fascism to be the last death-throe of capitalism faced by the advance of Marxist theory and practice.[2] Thus W.H. Auden's Miss Gee who wonders 'Does anyone care/That I live in Clevedon Terrace/On one hundred pounds a year?' and who as a frustrated spinster is doomed to die of cancer, is portrayed as a victim, literally carved up by Church and State.

> *Mr Rose he turned to his students,*
> *Said: 'Gentlemen, if you please,*
> *We seldom see a sarcoma*
> *As far advanced as this.'*
>
> *They took her off the table,*
> *They wheeled away Miss Gee*
> *Down to another department*
> *Where they study Anatomy.*
>
> *They hung her from the ceiling,*
> *Yes, they hung up Miss Gee;*
> *And a couple of Oxford Groupers*
> *Carefully dissected her knee.* [3]

Such Freudo-Marxist analysis of how a predominantly capitalist society with an established church can use 'the little people' may seem absurd now, but it was common in the 1930s when for many the Soviet Union and its policies offered the only fair financial

---

[2] John Strachey's *The Coming Struggle for Power* (1932) took such a view and is considered 'the most influential exercise in Marxism produced by the English Left'. See also Strachey's 'The Strangled Cry', *Encounter* XV, November 1960, and Richard Crossman (ed.), *The God that Failed: Six Studies in Communism*, London: Hamish Hamilton, 1950, especially Crossman's Introduction. Further information on Strachey and his influence is given in Sonia Orwell and Ian Angus (eds.), *The Collected Essays, Journalism and Letters of George Orwell*, Vol. 1, Harmondsworth: Penguin Books, 1970, p. 247, n. 53.

[3] W. H. Auden, *Selected Poems*, ed. E. Mendelson, London: Faber and Faber, 1979, p. 58.

prospects for the future. Stephen Spender's picture of capitalist England as 'the landscape of hysteria' similarly sees only exploitation and cruelty in a country where the profit motive is paramount. The passengers in an aircraft coming in to land

> ...*observe the outposts*
> *Of work: chimneys like lank black fingers*
> *Or figures frightening and mad: and squat buildings*
> *With their strange air behind trees, like women's faces*
> *Shattered by grief.*

And here too capitalism is seen as in league with the Church in depriving people while obscuring the reality:

> ...*larger than all the charcoaled batteries*
> *And imaged towers against that dying sky,*
> *Religion stands, the church blocking the sun.*[4]

'Images of Cultural Debasement'

Yet the writers of the Right, Yeats, Pound, Eliot, Wyndham Lewis scarcely saw business and capitalism more favourably, partly because from their lofty stand-point they considered the counting of pennies and the charging of interest beneath them, but also because as mass society became larger and more integrated and more the creature of applied science, industry and technology they felt that standards were being debased. Indeed, John Betjeman spoke for many both of the Left and the Right in his 1937 poem when he invited bombs to 'fall on Slough... and get it ready for the plough'. The 'air-conditioned, bright canteens', and the 'tinned beans' and 'tinned minds', images of cultural debasement, are portrayed as the direct result of 'The profits of the stinking cad'.[5] Similarly, Gordon Comstock repeatedly in George Orwell's 1936 novel, *Keep the Aspidistra Flying* (written as an attack on the worship of the 'Money-God'), welcomed the idea of destroying the products of capitalist consumerist society because of their debasing effects, while Orwell's own war-time diary echoed these sentiments:

---

[4] Stephen Spender, *Collected Poems 1928-1953*, London: Faber and Faber, 1955, pp. 56-57.

[5] *John Betjeman's Collected Poems*, (compiled by Lord Birkenhead), London: John Murray, 1959, pp. 21-23.

'Always, as I walk through the
Underground stations, [I am] sickened
by the advertisements, the silly
staring faces and strident colours...
How much rubbish this war will sweep away...'[6]

It might now seem strange to us that creative writers of both Left and Right, divided on so much else, should have shared anti-business feelings, especially as Eliot became a director of Faber and Faber, Pound a propagandist for Mussolini, and Yeats an established figure close to the rich and privileged. What was really happening, I think, was that a great realignment was taking place, notably foretold by the remarkable Peter F. Drucker in his book *The End of Economic Man* (1939). Orwell too was quick to realise the significance of Drucker's prediction and acknowledged it.[7] Economically and therefore ultimately politically, Fascism and Communism were moving ever closer. The development of industry, technology and mass communication which accelerated in the 1930s in the face of probable war led remorselessly to even more powerful state capitalism on both sides of the political divide and eventually to the Nazi-Soviet non-aggression pact of 1939.

There is a further reason why business and industry should have been so negatively portrayed in the decade that produced the Means Test and the Jarrow Crusade. One would have thought indeed that the hardship and squalor vividly depicted in Orwell's *The Road to Wigan Pier* (1937), written on behalf of the Left Book Club, would have encouraged the positive re-establishment of successful businesses properly financed and run so that the unemployment figure of 3,000,000 could be significantly reduced. Yet that is scarcely found in the literature of the time which concentrated instead on the exploitation of workers, the poor working conditions and the callousness and cruelty of those who had succeeded in the system. But this further reason mentioned above has more to do with literature than with society. The problem goes back to the advent of the Modernist era in the first two decades of the 20th

---

[6] Entry for 14 June 1940 in Orwell and Angus, *op. cit.*, Vol. II, pp. 395-96. *Cf.* George Orwell, *Keep the Aspidistra Flying*, Harmondsworth: Penguin Books, 1962, p. 21.

[7] In 'Notes on Nationalism' (1945): 'A few writers...such as Peter Drucker, foretold an agreement between Germany and Russia'. (Orwell and Angus, *op. cit.*, Vol. III, p. 413, Note.)

century. It has been argued that literature faced a schism in the early years of the century. Should it concentrate on 'the voyage without' or 'the voyage within'? Was important creative writing to be about 'the real world', the world say of Rudyard Kipling whose work deals with war, empire, business, and so on, or the world, say, of James Elroy Flecker, the world of imagination, dream and spirit? Undoubtedly these two worlds which a Chaucer, a Shakespeare, a Donne, could bring together had become by 1910 so separate that a fusion was unthinkable.

'Stream of Consciousness'

It was perhaps because of this 'dissociation of sensibility' – to use T.S. Eliot's term – that ideas of what literature was supposed to be about, its very justification, divided into two 'camps'. The more powerful and *avant-garde* of these became known as 'stream of consciousness' writers: those who believed that creative writing should portray the life of the mind. One of its foremost apologists was Virginia Woolf who argued that the worthwhile literature of the early decades of this century was written by those who believed that the act of thought was 'an event'. She referred to writers like James Joyce, T.S. Eliot and herself. Significantly, she illustrated what she meant by attacking writers like Wells, Shaw, Galsworthy and Bennett, that is, those who would claim they dealt with 'the real world': the world of business and money in particular, but also of politics and society. She argued that in a novel such as Arnold Bennett's *Hilda Lessways* (1911) we could not hear characters' voices, 'we can only hear Mr Bennett's voice telling us facts about rents and freeholds and copyholds and fines'.[8] She claimed that the 'Edwardian' novelists – Bennett, Wells, Galsworthy – had stressed only 'the fabric of things' and by so doing had been allowed to 'palm off' upon the reading public 'a version' of the living reality that constitutes a person's character and life: 'the Edwardians were never interested in character in itself; or the book in itself. They were interested in something outside.'[9] Neither Wells nor Galsworthy tried to portray the reality of a character of, for example, an ordinary woman you might see in a railway compartment:

---

8   See Virginia Woolf, *Mr Bennett and Mrs Brown*, London: The Hogarth Press, 1924, pp. 9-23.

9   *Ibid.*

'I do not think that Mr Wells in his passion to make her what she ought to be, would waste a thought upon her as she is. ... Burning with indignation, stuffed with information, arraigning civilisation, Mr Galsworthy would only see in [her] a pot broken on the wheel and thrown into the corner.'[10]

Perhaps Virginia Woolf's most fundamental criticism of these novelists is as follows:

'It is to express characters – not to preach doctrines, sing songs, or celebrate the glories of the British Empire, that the form of the novel, so clumsy, verbose, and undramatic, so rich, elastic and alive, has been evolved.'[11]

Those critics who, like Virginia Woolf, considered these 'naturalistic' writers inferior, would tend to bracket together business and politics for they believed that the writers concentrated on 'the voyage without' effectively derived from W.E. Henley and Rudyard Kipling 'the dream of unending progress through empire and machine'[12] even if the empire was not necessarily the British empire but rather one of future socialistic propaganda.

I think it is important to recognise these influences because the 'greatness' subsequently claimed by critics like F.R. Leavis for writers of whom Virginia Woolf approved – Joyce, Eliot, D.H. Lawrence – effectively denigrated those who dealt with the realities of the world of business, industry and politics. Not only would such a significant text as Tressall's *The Ragged Trousered Philanthropists* (1914) have been considered scarcely worth attention but even what are now seen to be novels of lasting importance – Wells's *Tono-Bungay* (1909) and Bennett's *Anna of the Five Towns* (1902), for example – received scant regard as serious works of literature.

Even though Leavis considered Wells a very inferior novelist and 'slapped down' Lord David Cecil for even mentioning Wells in the same breath as writers like Conrad and Lawrence,[13] other critics

---

[10] *Ibid.*

[11] *Ibid.*

[12] W. Y. Tindall, *Forces in Modern British Literature, 1885-1956*, New York: Vintage Books, 1956, p. 57.

[13] In *Early Victorian Novelists* (1934), Harmondsworth: Penguin Books, 1948, p. 22. Leavis

have been highly appreciative of him as not only the father of science fiction but also 'a great comic novelist' in the Dickensian tradition. Wells had also had experience of business which he portrayed in a number of novels: *Kipps* (1905), *Tono-Bungay* (1909) and *The History of Mr Polly* (1910), for example. It is true that, as a socialist, Wells portrayed business as haphazard, a lottery and destructive, but it was always done with gusto, humanity and a sense of fun. In *Tono-Bungay* we see Uncle Ponderevo fantasising about making a fortune by playing the stock market or cornering the market for a patent medicine like quinine, an antiseptic or cocaine. 'Rather a nuisance to the doctors,' remarks his nephew George, the hero, to which he receives the reply:

'They got to look out for themselves. By Jove, yes. They'll do you if they can, and you do them. Like brigands. That makes it romantic. That's the Romance of Commerce, George.'[14]

Looking back on this conversation with the wisdom of adulthood, George tells us with biting irony:

'I will confess that when my uncle talked of cornering quinine, I had a clear impression that anyone who contrived to do that would pretty certainly go to jail. Now I know that any one who could really bring it off would be much more likely to go to the House of Lords!'[15]

Yet despite his uncle's 'going bust' and frittering away George's inheritance, George cannot resist the attraction of helping his uncle to build a financial empire by advertising and marketing a patent medicine called Tono-Bungay that largely consists of distilled water. The activity is deeply satisfying and great fun:

'We really worked infernally hard, and, I recall, we worked with a very decided enthusiasm, not simply on my uncle's part, but mine. It was a game, an absurd but absurdly interesting game, and the points were scored in cases of bottles.'[16]

---

believed his 'great tradition' would exclude Wells and that there was an 'elementary distinction' to be made between those within the tradition and a writer such as Wells.

[14] H. G. Wells, *Tono-Bungay* (1909), London: Odhams Press (undated), p. 57.

[15] *Ibid.*, p. 57.

[16] *Ibid.*, p. 116.

Together they do succeed in building a financial empire – which subsequently crashes.

Arnold Bennett, too, as we have seen, was sneered at by those who considered themselves superior, in part because he portrayed the world of business. 'He was declared to be a vulgarian who "stank of brass" – in Virginia Woolf's word, a tradesman.' Yet Frank Swinnerton, whom I quote here, continued, 'In reality he was an artist...'. And of Bennett it has also been said, 'although he regarded literature as a business, his imagination never became corrupt'.[17]

Bennett had an extraordinary capacity for describing the workings of a factory process such as a pottery involves:

> 'Confronted with a piece of clay, the batting-machine descended upon it with the ferocity of a wild animal, worried it, stretched it, smoothed it into the width and thickness of a plate, and then desisted of itself and waited inactive for the flat presser to remove its victim to its more exact shaping machine. Several men were producing plates, but their rapid labours seemed less astonishing than the preliminary feat of the batting machine. ... Neither time nor space nor material was wasted in this ant-heap of industry. In order to move to and fro, the women were compelled to insinuate themselves past the stationary bodies of the men. ... Everyone exerted himself as though the salvation of the world hung on the production of so much stuff by a certain hour; dust, heat, and the presence of a stranger were alike unheeded in the mad creative passion.'[18]

Here, in my opinion, Bennett anticipated the kind of man-machine interface later to be portrayed in Eastern Europe by writers such as Zamiatin, Mayakovsky and Capek. Such prophetic futurism was not to be achieved by a workmanlike journeyman: there is real stylistic power here and, lest the reader does not make the proper connections, Anna, the eponymous heroine, who has just witnessed the awe-inspiring union of man and machine, ponders over 'the organising power, the forethought, the wide vision, and the sheer ingenuity and cleverness which were implied by the contents of this

---

[17] See Arnold Bennett, *The Journals*, ed. F. Swinnerton, Harmondsworth: Penguin Books, 1954, Introduction, p. 5. See also M. Seymour-Smith, *Guide to Modern World Literature*, New York: Funk & Wagnalls, 1973, p. 201.

[18] Arnold Bennett, *Anna of the Five Towns* (1902), Bath: Chivers Press, 1991, p. 113.

warehouse. ... It was a humble and deeply felt admiration'. The passage ends with the lightest touch of humour: '"You seem to make a fine lot of tea-sets," she remarked.'[19]

Business and Industry – Class Divisions

Finally in this discussion of how and why business was portrayed as it was in the period that was to lead to the Second World War, I will briefly touch on the work of three further writers: Galsworthy, Lawrence and Forster. They all reflect class divisions when business and industry are portrayed.

In Galsworthy's play *The Skin Game* (1920) there is a head-to-head confrontation between the landed gentry and a vulgar *nouveau riche* industrialist who justifies despoiling the countryside and breaking his promise not to evict people living in tied cottages on grounds of expediency: 'My works supply thousands of people, and my heart's in *them*. What's more, they make my fortune. ... Suppose I were to consider this and that, and every little potty objection – where should I get to? – nowhere!'[20] Yet all is not as clear-cut as it may seem for the battle between the two emblematically named rivals. Hillcrist, the gent, has a wife who manages mercilessly to expose the marital and moral irregularity in the family of Hornblower, the vulgar industrialist. When it comes to hitting below the belt the message seems to be that the upper classes are more than a match for the lower. Similarly, in *The Forstye Saga* it appears that the dynasty of property owners and lawyers is to be exposed. However, by the time the saga draws to its close, 'The Forstyes who have been the villains of the early novel now become its heroes'.[21]

That business and industrialism debase mankind is a recurrent message in the major fiction of D.H. Lawrence from *Sons and Lovers* (1913) through *The Rainbow* (1915) and *Women in Love* (1921) to *Lady Chatterley's Lover* (1928). Worse than that in Lawrence's view, the industrial emasculates mankind: it destroys what is vital and organic in him. It is significant in Lawrence's portrayal that the upper-class mill-owners are mechanical types

---

[19] *Ibid.*, p. 118.

[20] John Galsworthy, *Loyalties, with two other plays*, London: Pan Books, 1953, p. 157.

[21] M. Seymour-Smith, *op. cit.*, p. 200.

like Gerald Crich and Sir Clifford Chatterley. Gerald 'glistens' like a machine, the word 'mechanical' is constantly used in reference to him and during his wrestling bout with the 'organic' Rupert Birkin, Gerald's power is described as 'plastic', 'frictional' and 'mechanical' and his appearance as 'gleaming'.[22] Conversely, Birkin, the schoolteacher, is throughout *Women in Love* portrayed as vulnerable flesh which yet, unlike Gerald Crich's, has the power to grow. Birkin, however, is constantly threatened by the mechanical:

> 'Birkin fixed the iron handle of the sluice and turned it with a wrench. The cogs began slowly to rise. He turned and turned like a slave. ... Ursula looked away. She could not bear to see him winding heavily and laboriously, bending and rising mechanically like a slave, turning the handle.'[23]

Of course, Lawrence's was an extreme view of industry and commerce but not one to be totally separated from other writers: some of Lawrence's ideas and images are anticipated in the work of William Morris and even carried on in the poetry of T.S. Eliot.

Lawrence's admirer, E.M. Forster, also portrayed social types whose characteristics are directly related to questions of wealth, class and business. There is the 'anger and telephones' type (successful businessman), the 'ancestral wisdom' type (one spiritually remote from the concerns of business, commerce and technology), and the lower or lower middle-class semi-cultured type (one in danger of falling into poverty and therefore out of 'society'). *Howards End* (1910) clearly displays these types but it has to be said that whatever the social satire and indeed moral condemnation involved in the portrayal of Henry Wilcox's behaviour, there is tacit acceptance that 'anger and telephones' – that is, successful business practice – pays the mortgage even though Wilcox's advice to Leonard Bass concerning finance and employment is an absolute disaster. On these matters, as on the Empire, Forster's portrayal had an ambiguity which some find teasing and others irritating.

Indeed, overall, many writers of different *genres,* different political persuasions and different social opinions were ambiguous

---

22 D.H. Lawrence, *Women in Love*, London: Ace Books, 1960, pp. 212-16.

23 *Ibid.*, p. 145.

about business in the pre-war period and of course many have been since. 'A necessary evil' might suggest something of a general approach to those who wished to write, be published and succeed as an influence in an age where patronage was increasingly scarce and where market size was increasingly developing in the direction of mass audiences, this being made possible and ultimately inevitable as the media industry accelerated towards what was to become an explosion in the post-war years.

2. The Post-War Era: The Business of Death and its Aftermath

> *If we are more than groping pain,*
> *If we are more than soldiers,*
> *Can we separate desire and death?*
> *And must these streets form scabs,*
> *The smiling fields grow sick*
> *While little shops hoard luxuries, and avarice*
> *Gleams in the commercial eye?*
>
> Emmanuell Litvinoff, *Garrison Town*
>
> *Ah, were I courageous enough*
> *To shout* stuff your pension!
>
> Philip Larkin, *Toads*

WHAT WAS THE WAR FOUGHT FOR? For many British writers it was *not* fought to restore the *status quo* with its inequalities of class and wealth. But although 'fairer shares for all' might encapsulate the mood and wishes of many ex-military, ex-combat, writers and indeed the general mood, it was by far from clear which economic system would or should prevail. The land-slide victory for Labour in 1945 ushered in a government which, within the space of a few years, had taken into state ownership the Bank of England and the coal, gas, electricity, iron and steel and transport industries. By the early 1950s a planned, nationally run, integrated industrial policy had been set in place, giving clear advantages as far as the co-ordination of services and capital investment were conceived. There were undoubtedly improvements in working conditions and in facilities such as hospitals and schools for many, yet those in charge, those in managerial and executive positions, tended to be from the same background as before the war: upper-middle class, privately educated, Oxbridge. Attlee's massive programme of nationalisation and the creation of a National Health Service were brought in by a Cabinet nearly all of whom had been to Eton, Harrow or similar schools. Eighty per cent of the country's industry remained in private ownership. Thus, whatever socialist policies had achieved in the reorganisation of industry, little had been done to transform the character and structure of British society.

Yet had not George Orwell in 'My Country Right or Left', while patriotically applauding 'the military virtues' and lambasting the 'boiled rabbits' of the Left, acknowledged that if necessary 'the red militias' should be billeted at the Ritz and 'the London gutters run with the blood' to bring in a New Britain after the war?[24] There is a sense in which the term 'business as usual' took on for many writers an ironic and even pessimistic meaning in the 'Forties and 'Fifties. For what had really changed after all? Unless you were lucky or very talented you were in hock to a commercial or state-capitalist organisation, working your life away to make the rich richer and the powerful even more so. Such sentiments may seem a travesty and, indeed, those without a job, despite the advent of the Welfare State, would have recognised them as such, yet particularly in the writing fraternity the sense that this war had not delivered economically and socially any more than the Great War, was to continue powerfully at least until the 1970s.

During the war, and for a while after, there appeared a series of books called *English Story* edited by Woodrow Wyatt. Many were 'Services Editions' and must have been read by thousands of serving men and women. The Fourth Series includes 'Fancy Free', a story by James Hanley. Ostensibly it is a graphic account of a drunken pub-crawl told in the present tense by a newly disembarked sailor in search of alcohol and female company. Yet it is also about death and money and the connection between the two. For the sailor meets a man whose job it is to stand behind a grille all day and dole out wages to sailors' wives. The job had reduced him to a scarcely human shadow: 'that was his place in this city ... being pressed down and fated to wear a grey suit forever.'[25] In the convivial

---

[24] Orwell and Angus, *op.cit.*, Vol. I, pp. 591-92.

[25] James Hanley, 'Fancy Free', in *English Story: Fourth Series*, ed. Woodrow Wyatt, London: Collins, Services Edition, 1945, p. 12.

atmosphere of the pub with its liquor and buxom barmaids, the man seems a harbinger of coldness and death, 'a fish-eyed feller' dressed in grey whose incongruous appearance 'tickles [the sailor] to death'.[26] And in a monologue worthy of a plebeian character in *The Waste Land* the sailor pictures the man as symbolic of the spiritual death of someone who is caged daily to count out money:

'Pass down between great walls, marvellous walls these, might be walls leading into Paradise, and doors everywhere, all shining, and clink and clank of office machines, and ringing of telephones, and they're not the only bells that ring. Go far down this corridor, always keeping to ... the left-hand side, and we come to a hole in the wall, iron grille there. You're behind that. ...you're behind a grille. You pay out coin to sailors' women, you have your hands dug into mountains of money, it might be sand or sugar or rubbish to you, so used to having your hand in it. Isn't that right?...this grille's finely woven, you might be a priest behind your confessional, you can't see anybody or anything except the face that's sort of flowed up to you, another thing, you never look up. That's right, isn't it? ... Now if you pushed your head through this grille, which you never do, and might be frightened to do, if you did, you'd see a fair long line of sailors' women, all drib and drab and shuffling up to your hole, and leaning about the walls and whispering, and never talking too loud, and edging up, by the mere inch, and one at a time they come to your grille ...and you dive into the mass of money and hand some out, never say good day, never say thanks, say nothing at all. That's you isn't it? Sun might be pouring in all over that place, still you say nothing...Saying nothing's a duty to do, and you do your duty. ...[You] believe in nothing except figures, your head's full of them, full of nothing else. ...How you break away from them at day's end, I don't know, and God knows where you go to, but here you are and I can tell at a glance that you push yourself around all evening, crushing into this and that pub, all the time aiming to get away from your Figures, dancing in your head. ...following you around everywhere. ...That's tough on you, but blame the grille. ...'[27]

Shortly after, when he comes face to face with the vibrant barmaid Susie, 'she looks hard at him' and he vanishes 'just like he was shadow and not man'.[28]

---

[26] *Ibid.*, pp. 12-14.

[27] *Ibid.*, pp. 15-17.

[28] *Ibid.*, p. 17.

War and Business

This positively Kafka-esque (or perhaps Dickensian) figure brings to mind a recurrent idea in 20th-century literature to the effect that money and money-counting are not just degrading and dirty but also deathly. Such feelings were undoubtedly reinforced by both world wars, partly because they were *industrial* wars which acted inevitably as catalysts for the accelerating development of scientific and technological research and of commercial and state-capitalist expansion. The idea that war was a business was further reinforced by the increasing involvement of civilians not only in the war effort but also of course in the suffering of war, its death and destruction. The Blitz made London, the financial capital of the world, a front-line city and its areas of devastation are clearly anticipated in George Orwell's novel *Coming Up For Air* (1939) and echoed in his last book *1984* (1949). Similarly, our greatest poet of the Second World War, Keith Douglas, who clearly saw war literally as diabolic and that to take part involved being in league with 'the devil', portrayed the commercial detritus that litters a battlefield:

> ....*by a day's travelling you reach a new world*
> *the vegetation is of iron*
> *dead tanks, gun barrels split like celery*
> *the metal brambles have no flower or berries*
> *and there are all sorts of manure, you can imagine*
> *the dead themselves, their boots, clothes and possessions clinging to the*
> *ground, a man with no head*
> *has a packet of chocolate and a souvenir of Tripoli.*[29]

As Peter Drucker has argued, the 'devils' of hyperinflation and unemployment had haunted the Weimar Republic leading to Germany's need for a *homo magus* or 'witch doctor' to purge all ills by violence or war if necessary. (And were such ideas not already confirmed by the anthropological research of Malinowski among the Tobriand Islanders?) In a real sense, therefore, total war was big business 'gone mad', an idea later to be confirmed with lacerating humour in Joseph Heller's *Catch-22* (1961).

---

[29] 'Cairo Jag', in *I Burn for England: Anthology of the Poetry of World War II*, selected and introduced by Charles Hamblett, London: Leslie Frewin, 1966, p. 91.

A British novel which also deals with these ideas and which deserves to be better known is Alex Comfort's *The Power House* (1944). Set in Northern France before and during the German occupation, the early part of the novel is dominated by La Virginie, a huge steam-engine which operates looms. The machine is so large and powerful it attracts the admiration and loving commitment of those who operate and tend it – or perhaps one should say 'her'. But La Virginie is also a murderess who crushes the unwary who work near her in her 120-foot embrace. At her heart is a 'cauldron of moving parts'.

La Virginie is part of an industrialised complex that includes mills, works, a chemical plant, a plastics factory and a slaughterhouse. Each has its own machines, smells, noises, pollution and dangers. Apart from industrial accidents there are the appalling conditions in which many work. It is the time of socialist and communist rallies and of pitched street battles with fascists just before the collapse of the Popular Front. And, of course, the 'phoney war' is soon to become very real with the German invasion. Against this background we follow the lives of the employees, their hopes and fears, jealousies, sexual and emotional problems, the squalors and satisfactions of their working days. A good example of the two-way tug of employment is the case of Uncle Pecquard who loves and takes pride in the work that destroys his health – anticipating perhaps our current ambiguous attitude to the decline in Britain's coal-mining industry since 1980.

'Uncle Pecquard was having a bath, standing upright in it, his whole remarkably deformed body exposed to view. His forearms were bent into semicircles, and his thighs bowed as if he had stood upon them when they were soft, and so bent them. His skin was surprisingly white, and his face, from the enlargement of his skull and his lower jaw, was concave and triangular. He held it on one side, so as to look out of the corner of his eyes, the other side being gradually obscured by a cloud which had come over it during the last six months. He could still pick up a bale by its cord with the crane hook, however, by looking sideways. He walked sideways also, like a crab. He was soaping himself slowly, his bent arms working, and his body white from the shoulders down. His face was black with coal dust, except for white circles where he had knuckled his eyes, and a black patch covered the part of his back that his deformity prevented him from reaching. The markings on his face, the bent arms, made him resemble an erect

Himalayan bear, peering through the steam to see who was opening the door.'[30]

Comfort's style – especially when he describes workers and their machines – owes something perhaps to Arnold Bennett and before him to Emile Zola, though he also writes with the eye of a surgeon. Uncle Pecquard, who works as a crane-operator, not only because of financial need at a time of growing unemployment, but because of intense pride in the job, is in his misfortune a symbol of the callousness of capitalist industry which will use, ruin and then discard. When found to be unfit for work he is given a small pension:

> 'Old Pecquard bit his moustache and tried not to sob, since the dust from the ore and the rubbing of his eyes had made him tearless, so that all he could show of grief was a grimace. From then on he sat in his chair. When [his family] wanted him removed they pushed the chair with Uncle Pecquard in it.'[31]

But something even bigger than these industrial concerns is taking place in his novel. For La Virginie, despite being for some positively voluptuous in her attractions, together with her fellow machines, comes to symbolise the plight of industrial man trapped in a system he cannot control that is in due course taken over by the Nazi army of military machine-men who reduces those captured further to slaves or even animals which, like those in the slaughterhouse, are dispensable once they have served their purpose. The pre-invasion scene was just a preparation for what was to follow. The novel, however, ends on a note of desperate fight, anarchy, subversion and passionate idealism:

> 'Throughout continents, sickness and deformity are coming to be valuable. ... We're the weak. We're bombed, starved, taxed, jailed, conscripted, shot or frightened. ...We are the enemies of society, and we must learn disobedience. ...You carry your freedom inside your skull and your ribs. ...Therefore we hang to life like crabs to a piece of bait till they pull our legs off one at a time. ...There is only one

---

[30] Alex Comfort, *The Power House*, London: Readers Union, George Routledge & Sons, 1945, p. 8.

[31] *Ibid.*, p. 76.

responsibility – to the individual who lies under your own feet. To the weak, your fellows.'[32]

It is perhaps significant that the novel was prefixed with a German quotation whose translation is 'killing is a form of our continuing bereavement'.

The American Connection

There is a further reason why business became associated with death both before and during the Second World War: the American connection. American influences on British culture had grown steadily since their significant advent during and after the Great War. However, following the Great Crash in 1929, American writing that portrayed business increasingly pictured commerce as destructive of talent and humanity: equally hard on those who were creative and those who were vulnerable. Even before the Wall Street crash, Scott Fitzgerald had portrayed the death of the eponymous Gatsby as a product of his financial and social success while the fact that no-one attends his funeral and his empty mansion is surrounded by ashpits takes on a symbolic value. And again in *The Last Tycoon* (published posthumously in 1941), the glittering tinsel world of Hollywood is seen to mask a cruel world of money versus art in which the talented and romantic hero Monroe Stahr is crushed by the power of the profit motive. Deceit and death also dominate the plays of Arthur Miller which portray business, like *All My Sons* (1947) and *Death of a Salesman* (1949). The 'little guy' is callously swept aside by forces which even the victim himself, in this case Willy Loman, fails to recognise because he sentimentally harks back to the brave America of opportunity he had been brought up on. As Biff tells his father, he has been bred in an atmosphere of self-deception:

> 'I never got anywhere because you blew me so full of hot air...I am not a leader of men, Willy, and neither are you! You were never anything but a hard working drummer who landed in the ash-can like all the rest of them.'[33]

---

[32] *Ibid.*, p. 318-19.

[33] Arthur Miller, *Death of a Salesman*, Act II, London: Pocket Book Edition, The Cresset Press, 1952, pp. 116-17.

Images of death, such as ashes, are recurrent in mid-century American portrayal of the business world. One of the most telling and ironic, perhaps, is Kenneth Fearing's brilliant evocation of a funeral (eerily reminiscent of Gatsby's heartless end, though here at least are some nameless pallbearers):

'Dirge'

*1-2-3 was the number he played but today the number came
3-2-1;
bought his Carbide at 30 and it went to 29; had the
favourite at Bowie but the track was slow –*

*O, executive type, would you like to drive a floating
power, knee-action, silk-upholstered six? Wed a
Hollywood star? Shoot the course in 58? Draw to
the ace, king, jack?
O, fellow with a will who won't take no, watch out
for three cigarettes on the same, single match;
O democratic voter born in August under Mars,
beware of liquidated rails –*

*Denouement to denouement, he took a personal
pride in the certain, certain way he lived his own,
private life,
but nevertheless, they shut off his gas;
nevertheless, the bank foreclosed; nevertheless
the landlord called; nevertheless, the radio broke,*

*And twelve o'clock arrived just once too often,
just the same he wore one grey tweed suit, bought
one straw hat, drank one straight Scotch, walked
one short step, took one long look, drew one deep
breath,
just one too many,*

*And wow he died as wow he lived,
going whop to the office and blooie home to sleep
and biff got married and bam had children and oof
got fired,*

zowie did he live and zowie did he die,
With who the hell are you at the corner of his
casket,
and where the hell we going on the right hand
silver knob, and who the hell cares walking second
from the end with an American Beauty wreath
from why the hell not.

Very much missed by the circulation staff of the
New York Evening Post; deeply, deeply mourned by
the B.M.T.,

Wham, Mr Roosevelt; pow, Sears Roebuck; awk,
big dipper; bop, summer rain;
bong, Mr, bong, Mr, bong, Mr, bong.[34]

Even 'jokey' writers like e.e. cummings make connections between money and death:

suppose
Life is an old man carrying flowers on his head.

young death sits in a café
smiling, a piece of money held between
his thumb and first finger[35]

Cummings also wrote memorably: 'a salesman is an it that stinks to please'.[36] Moreover, while he too links money and death, Ogden Nash in 'Bankers are just like Anybody Else, Except Richer' has the following:

Most bankers dwell in marble halls,
Which they get to dwell in
because they encourage deposits and discourage withdrawals.[37]

---

[34] *The Penguin Book of Sick Verse*, ed. George MacBeth, Harmondsworth: Penguin Books, 1963, pp. 323-24.

[35] e.e. cummings, *selected poems 1923-1958*, Harmondsworth: Penguin Books, 1965, p. 6.

[36] *Ibid.*, p. 53.

[37] In the original text the word is 'withdralls'; *The Pocket Book of Ogden Nash*, with an

In the trivialisation of banks, the suggestion of small-mindedness, Nash is following a well-established tradition of humour that had been seen also in the novels of Thornton Wilder:

> 'I'm closing up my account,' he said. 'I'll draw out everything except the interest.'
>
> 'I beg your pardon?'
>
> 'I'll take out the money,' he repeated, raising his voice as though the cashier were deaf, 'but I'll leave the interest here.'
>
> The cashier blinked a moment, then began playing with his coins. At last he said in a low voice: 'I don't think we'll be able to keep your account open for so small a sum.'
>
> 'You don't understand. I'm not leaving the interest here as an account. I don't want it. Just turn it back into the bank. I don't believe in interest.'
>
> The cashier began casting worried glances to right and left. He paid out both sum and interest across the counter, muttering '...the bank...you must find some other way of disposing of the money.'
>
> Brush took the five hundred dollars and pushed the rest back. He raised his voice sharply and could be heard all over the room saying, 'I don't believe in interest.'
>
> The cashier hurried to the president and whispered in his ear. The president stood up in alarm, as though he had been told that a thief was entering the bank. He went to the door of the bank and stopped Brush as he was about to leave.
>
> 'Mr Brush.'
>
> 'Yes.'
>
> 'Might I speak to you for a moment, Mr Brush? In here.'
>
> 'Certainly,' said Brush, and followed him through a low door into the presidential pen.
>
> Mr Southwick had a great unhappy head rendered ridiculous by a constant adjustment of various spectacles and black ribbons. His professional dignity rested upon an enormous stomach supported in blue cloth and bound with a gold chain. They sat down and gazed at one another in considerable excitement.
>
> 'Mm......mm..... you feel you must draw out your savings, Mr Brush?' said the president softly, as though he were inquiring into a private and delicate matter.

Introduction by Louis Untermeyer, New York: Pocket Books, Inc., 1955, p. 163.

'Yes, Mr Southwick,' replied Brush, reading the name from a framed sign on the desk.

'....and you're leaving your interest in the bank?'

'Yes.'

'What would you like us to do with it?'

'I have no right to say. The money isn't mine. I didn't earn it.'

'But your money, Mr Brush, - I beg your pardon, - your money earned it.'

'I don't believe that money has the right to earn money.'[38]

The Technology of Control Systems

But at some point the 'funny' aspects of business and finance inherent perhaps in the Keynesian idea that the stock market was 'a lottery' became subsumed in its deathly aspect. Perhaps it was the advent of British futuristic novels such as *Brave New World* and *1984* where state controls meant that any fluctuation or movement in currency would be *intended.* Certainly the technology of control systems permeates the picture of a future society in Kurt Vonnegut's *Player Piano* (1952) where that society is divided into three groups: the professional managers (qualified people who operate the system), the proletariat, the 'Reeks and Wrecks' (those with redundant or non-existent skills who are forced into the reconstruction and reclamation corps), and thirdly the machines (computers and computerised techniques) which control the system. What is portrayed is a financial and commercial society which, however competitive, entails the cultural death of man. For social engineering has meant that a

'union of the country's manufacturing facilities under one council has taken place...Similar councils had been formed for the transportation of raw materials, food and communication industries... The system had so cut waste and duplication, that it was preserved after the war and was often cited as one of the few concrete benefits of the war'.[39]

Indeed, 'waste and duplication' are eliminated through rationalisation and techniques of social control while future qualified workers

---

[38] From Thornton Wilder's *Heaven's My Destination* (1935); quoted in G. C. Thornley (ed.), *Further Practice in English*, London: Longman, 1970, pp. 12-13.

[39] Kurt Vonnegut, *Player Piano*, London: Flamingo Books, 1992, p. 45.

are placed into professional and social slots by 'grading machines'. The struggle of the emblematically named Paul Proteus, the arch-hero and 'rebel observer', is set against the remorseless development of civilisation 'towards a techtopia where humanity is subordinated to its own mechanical means'.[40] Significantly, it is clear that behind this novel lies the epoch-making early study of computer and cybernetic power and its social implications, *The Human Use of Human Beings* by Norbent Wiener, itself a precursor of the disturbing study by Joseph Weizenbaum, *Computer Power and Human Reason.*[41]

When we look back now in the early 2000s we can see that business and finance and their computerisation, let alone society, are no more predictable and subject to real controls than quasars and black holes would have been fully in accordance with the laws of physics as taught in the early 1950s. But it has to be said that the dystopian look at finance and business set an important literary and cultural trend to the effect that those who work within the system need to use it before it uses them.

In Britain by the mid-1950s all that has been discussed above was established as an influence on the rising generation: those who were likely to have been called up at the tail-end of the war or involved in National Service. University education was being widened socially and attracted on a much greater scale those who came from working- and lower middle-class backgrounds. They knew that business was unscrupulous and cut-throat: many came from families that had been personally involved in its effects. They knew too that money was dirty: 'filthy lucre'; 'where there's muck there's brass'. Indeed, there was and is a cultural and literary tradition that links money to excretion: it can be found in Swift, Dickens, William Morris, D.H. Lawrence and right through to Martin Amis. The new generation were aware too of the dangers of work reducing one to a kind of automaton. Yet in general they wanted what is now called 'part of the action' and their wants and requirements were, in Britain, to a significant degree class-driven. Key texts to support these claims are John Braine's *Room at the Top* (1957), Kingsley

---

[40] See David Porush, *The Soft Machine: Cybernetic Fiction*, New York and London: Methuen, 1985, pp. 90-92.

[41] Vonnegut, *op. cit.*, p.22. The books by Wiener and Weizenbaum date from 1950 and 1976 respectively.

Amis's *Lucky Jim* (1954), Alan Sillitoe's *Saturday Night and Sunday Morning* (1958), and the poetry of Philip Larkin. Other writers of that period would be associated: John Wain and Stan Barstow, for example, while Muriel Spark and Stevie Smith wrote in part from their experience of business and commerce, the former publishing *The Girls of Slender Means* in 1963. Some of these writers are also associated with the group which became known as the 'Angry Young Men' following Walter Allen's review of *Lucky Jim* in 1954.[42] 'Angry' for a while some of them may have been in the sense that their social and financial origins debarred their progress to 'The Fame and The Girl and The Money' but 'rebels' they were not, despite being called so in some contemporary studies. On the contrary, in general it could be said that they were knocking at the door of success, if not the Establishment, and asking to be let in.

Room At the Top contains the essence of what we are concerned with here. Indeed, it came to typify the *genre* as did the name of its hero, Joe Lampton. 'Working-class boy makes good' is an insufficient *cliché*, however, to do justice to the fierceness and, yes, anger with which Joe sets about his quest. Behind the fierceness and anger is the question of class, but it is not as simple as that because the hero has a hard-eyed, calculating quality that informs his aspirations. His lust to succeed is directed by awareness, experience and education. It is interesting that Joe comes to talk in terms of grades and of bridging the gap between grades as if here too in Warley, an industrial northern town that is significantly superior socially to his home town of Dufton, the kind of mechanical system had developed which predetermines status. We are not as far as it might seem from Kurt Vonnegut's *Player Piano*. Here in my opinion is the most important passage which encapsulates and anticipates what the novel is about:

'Then... something happened which changed my whole life. ...

Parked by a solicitor's office...was a green Aston-Martin tourer...a beautiful piece of engineering...; it wasn't the sort of vehicle for business or for family outings but quite simply a rich man's toy.

---

42 *New Statesman and Nation*, Vol. 47, 30 January 1954: reprinted in Gene Feldman and Max Gartenberg (eds.), *Protest*, London: Quartet Books, 1973, pp. 299-300.

As I was admiring it a young man and a girl came out of the solicitor's office...

The ownership of the Aston-Martin automatically placed the young man in a social class far above mine; but that ownership was simply a question of money...This seems all too obvious; but it was the kind of truth which until that moment I'd only grasped theoretically...

For a moment I hated him...I tasted the sourness of envy. Then I rejected it. ...This didn't abate the fierceness of my longing. I wanted an Aston-Martin, I wanted a three-guinea linen shirt, I wanted a girl with a Riviera suntan – these were my rights, I felt, a signed and sealed legacy. ...I remembered the second hand Austin Seven which ...Dufton's Chief Treasurer had just treated himself to. That was the most the local government had to offer me; it wasn't enough. I made my choice then and there: I was going to enjoy all the luxuries which that young man enjoyed. I was going to collect that legacy. It was as clear and compelling as the sense of vocation which doctors and missionaries are supposed to experience though in my instance of course the call ordered me to do good to myself not others.'[43]

And, of course, Joe Lampton does get the girl and the job and the money, sufficient no doubt eventually to buy an expensive car. He does it by courting (and in the end almost raping) Susan Brown, the daughter of his future boss, the major local industrialist who realises what has happened and with grudging admiration for Joe's success and determination is prepared to admit him to the family and a good job with his company despite Joe's lack of pedigree: 'See her tomorrow and get it done with, I'll not have it put off anymore.' When Joe inquires why he resisted the match earlier, old Brown says: 'You should have seen to it that your parents had more brass.'[44]

It is 'brass' that determines events in the novel and defines a kind of harsh morality. The discarded mistress, Alice Aisgill, already into early middle age, kills herself in a horrific intentional motor accident that leaves her crawling half-dead in her own blood. Yet the overall effect is less one of pity for her than the inevitability and in a sense rightness of her destruction. She was in the way. She had played around with too many men, we are told, and anyway as her

---

[43] John Braine, *Room at the Top*, London: Methuen, 1983, pp. 29-31.

[44] *Ibid.*, p. 228.

former girl friend tells our hero: '...it was all for the best. She'd have ruined your whole life.'[45] Thus Alice symbolises in her demise the ruthlessness of the business ethic, although I am not sure that John Braine would have seen it quite in this way. As with the other novelists of this genre there was a definite ambivalence concerning those who succeeded in making money. When Joe muses 'honour, like freedom, is a luxury for those with independent incomes',[46] I suspect it is the author speaking, and yet of course much of the evidence which the novel itself provides would contradict this statement.

'The Angry Young Man – A World of Absurdity'

It is true that the early novels, poems and plays of the 'angry young men' were 'egotistical' in the Keatsian sense – that is, that their work recreated their own world. Like Jim Dixon, Kingsley Amis had experienced working as a young university lecturer on probation. That world through Amis's uncanny gift for humorous invention seems to be transformed into something 'rich and strange': a world of absurdity, of at times 'Alice in Wonderland' dimensions, though I can vouch for the fact the universities have indeed gone through absurdist periods, largely due to government interference! In *Lucky Jim* there are strange pre-echoes of the plot of *Room at the Top* in that when Jim is invited to the ridiculous weekend party at his Professor's house he meets his odious, pretentious son Bertrand (pronounced in the French manner) whose beautiful girlfriend, Christine, Jim instantly falls in love with. As in the case of Jack Wales, Susan Brown's former intended in John Braine's novel, the anger felt by the protagonist is fired to white-hot proportions by the snobbish superiority of the upper-class, public school-educated rival for the lady's hand – although other parts of her body attract most of his attention. Once again the ex-grammar schoolboy wins through, getting the girl and the job and an *entrée* into money and privilege. Jim's career as a university lecturer ends farcically when he collapses drunkenly while giving a public lecture on 'Merrie England' before an audience that includes the Principal and most of the College Council. But his dismissal is well

---

[45] *Ibid.*, p. 256.

[46] *Ibid.*, p. 233.

compensated for when he is taken on as a well-paid private secretary to Christine's wealthy uncle, Julius Gore-Urquart.

Arthur Seaton in Alan Sillitoe's *Saturday Night and Sunday Morning* is another central character with a job which in many ways he despises. Like his creator he had worked at a piece-work rate on the production line in a Nottingham cycle factory. Monday, for him, is 'back to the treadmill'. Although Arthur is a joker with an eye for the girls and a passion for beer, a man full of vitality, he communicates memorably the deathly, mind-numbing repetitiveness of his work. Not inappropriately, D.H. Lawrence springs to mind when we read the following:

> 'The minute you stepped out of the factory gates you thought no more about your work. But the funniest thing was that neither did you think about work when you were standing at your machine. ...The noise of motor-trolleys passing up and down the gangway and the excruciating din of flying and flapping belts slipped out of your consciousness after perhaps half an hour, without affecting the quality of the work you were turning out. ...You went off into pipedreams for the rest of the day. And in the evening, when admittedly you would be feeling as though your arms and legs had been stretched to breaking point on a torture-rack, you stepped out into a cosy world of pubs and noisy tarts that would one day provide you with the raw material for more pipedreams as you stood by your lathe.'[47]

He works of course just for the money; his job means that half his life is lived vicariously. Can, could such a means of employment be socially, indeed humanly, justified? And yet, rebel that he seems to be in some ways, Arthur too wishes to join, to be engaged, in the very set-up that the novel satirises. In an interesting and revealing passage near the end of the novel while Arthur is fishing by the canal, he compares himself to the fish:

> 'As soon as you were born you were captured by fresh air that you screamed against the minute you came out. Then you were roped in by a factory, had a machine slung around your neck, and then you were hooked up by the arse with a wife.'

---

[47] Alan Sillitoe, *Saturday Night and Sunday Morning*, London: Pan Books, 1960, p. 31.

And then Arthur continues: 'It meant death for the fish, but for a man it might not be so bad. Maybe it was only the beginning of something better in life...'[48]

Most revealing of all are Arthur's final thoughts:

> 'Slung into Khaki at eighteen, and when they let you out, you sweat again in a factory, grabbing for an extra pint, doing women at the weekend and getting to know whose husbands are on the night-shift, working with rotten guts and an aching spine, and nothing for it but money to drag you back there every Monday morning.'

Yet he continues immediately: 'Well, it's a good life and a good world, all said and done, if you don't weaken...'[49] *That* is the prime characteristic of the 1950s novels of this *genre*: defiant optimism despite the moaning (some would say whining) about the job, the money, the system. If they can, the heroes want to be inside and climb towards success and happiness.

Arthur's foreman is called Robboe which suggests indeed that here too the author was aware that factory office employees were being treated like machines (robots) with the implication that in the future the identification between man and machine could become even closer. Even in the poetry of Philip Larkin there are such suggestions: that an employee becomes programmed to respond to just this or that situation in the workplace, recognise this face and ignore that. Sometimes the stimuli are mechanical or electronic as in the superb 'Aubade':

> *.........we can't escape,*
> *Yet can't accept. One side will have to go.*
> *Meanwhile telephones crouch, getting ready to ring*
> *In locked-up offices, and all the uncaring*
> *Intricate rented world begins to rouse.*[50]

Frequently the imprisonment in work – in Larkin's case at a university – is inseparable from money and the need for it with

---

[48] *Ibid.*, p. 189.

[49] *Ibid.*, p. 191.

[50] Philip Larkin, *Collected Poems*, edited with an Introduction by Anthony Thwaite, London and Boston: The Marvell Press and Faber and Faber, 1988, p. 209.

which, as is the case of so many writers, especially of the post-war period, he had an ambiguous relationship. 'Money' or its equivalent as an image or epithet is recurrent in this verse (from 'Neurotics'):

> *The mind, it's said, is free:*
> *But not your minds. They, rusted swift, admit*
> *Only what will accuse or horrify,*
> *Like slot machines only bent pennies fit.*[51]

In 'Modesties' he spoke of 'Thoughts that shuffle round like pence' and in 'Arrival' of shovelling 'faces like pennies down the back of mind'. And most potently of all, in the poem 'Money' he speaks of the futility of our dependence on it:

> *...however you bank your screw, the money you save*
> *Won't in the end buy you more than a shave.*
>
> *I listen to money singing. It's like looking down*
> *From long French windows at a provincial town,*
> *The slums, the canal, the churches ornate and mad*
> *In the evening sun. It is intensely sad.*[52]

The famous 'Toads' is ostensibly about 'work' but of course the need to do it – to be trapped and crushed by it – is inseparable from the need for money:

> *Ah, were I courageous enough*
> *To shout* stuff your pension!
> *But I know, all too well, that's the stuff*
> *That dreams are made on.*
>
> *For something sufficiently toad-like*
> *Squats in me, too. ...*[53]

And in 'Toads Revisited' work, and therefore money (a.k.a. 'toad'),

---

[51] *Ibid.*, p. 22.

[52] *Ibid.*, p. 198.

[53] *Ibid.*, p. 89.

are appropriately equated with death:

> *... ...give me my in-tray*
> *My loaf-haired secretary,*
> *My shall-I-keep-the-call-in – Sir:*
> *What else can I answer,*
>
> *When the lights come on at four*
> *At the end of another year?*
> *Give me your arm, old toad;*
> *Help me down Cemetery Road.*[54]

3. The 'Sixties and Beyond

> *Money, it's a crime.*
> *Share it fairly, but don't take a slice of my pie.*
>
> Pink Floyd, *'Money'* (1973)
>
> *Money is the only thing we have in common.*
> *Dollar bills, pound notes, they're all suicide notes.*
>
> Martin Amis, *Money* (1984)

THE 1960s HAS BEEN CALLED 'THE SWINGING DECADE': one in which 'having fun' now and not considering the morrow was fashionable and one which even spawned quasi-oriental philosophies that were anti-work, anti-business and anti-profit. The influence of hippie-dom harked back to the beatniks of the 'fifties. Yet some of those who appeared most in support of such a life-style ended up becoming – to use a later term – 'seriously rich'.

During the late 1960s money and its application in society became quite suddenly trendy. The Beatles – who helped to power the financial success of Carnaby Street and The King's Road – Mary Quant, Terence Conran and many others effectively focused an explosion of talent and creativity that were unmistakably marketable. And yet the picture we get of business, finance and money itself in the writing of the 1970s and indeed into the succeeding decades is one of mockery and guilt with increasingly a note of hysteria and death – just as if the legacy of the Second World

---

[54] *Ibid.*, p. 148.

War, far from abating, intensified. Moreover, when one thinks of the accelerating impact of new technology on industry and the money markets, all this is hardly surprising.

The topic of money was certainly 'in the air' by 1972 – or perhaps I should say 'on the air' because of the phenomenal success of the film version of *Cabaret* and its hit song 'Money, money, money'. The musical had a strange history which takes us back to the 1930s, the period at which this essay begins, for although the musical was based on John van Druten's play *I am a Camera* which had also been made into a successful film in 1955, its real genesis was Christopher Isherwood's semi-autobiographical novel *Goodbye to Berlin* (1939).

The Role of Money: the 'Mad' Christie Malry

The role of money in society and the ethics of the situation have always interested writers, of course, but by the early 1970s we are firmly in the run-up to massive computerisation and globalisation of money systems – a process which still continues and whose effects can alarm and surprise even seasoned observers. In 1973 appeared an extraordinary novel called *Christie Malry's Own Double-Entry* by B.S. Johnson. There is something rather 'mad' about the work, but then in the era of *Monty Python*, which targeted institutions like the BBC, Universities, Government Departments and Banks, such a quality seems singularly appropriate – the novel even has the characteristic of referring to itself as a novel just as in *Monty Python* you get characters saying: 'What a way to end a sketch!' This novel moves us firmly into the era 1970-90, that was to produce such revealing and often absurd – in the literary sense – pictures of the commercial world as David Hare's *Plenty*, Martin Amis's *Money* and Caryl Churchill's *Serious Money,* of which works more discussion later.

The novel begins: 'Christie Malry was a simple person. It did not take him long to realise that he had not been born into money,' and soon continues: 'He therefore decided that he should become a bank employee. I did tell you Christie was a simple person.'[55] While working at the bank Christie finds he is increasingly irritated by colleagues whose acts of wrong towards him as he sees them

---

[55] B.S. Johnson, *Christie Malry's Own Double-Entry*, Harmondsworth: Penguin Books, 1984, p. 11.

need, in his opinion, recompense. During his evenings Christie studies Accountancy and becomes aware of the system of Double-Entry which leads to his 'Great Idea': that is that he should draw up a double-entry account with 'THEM': other people in the world. Every offence he considers he has received is shown as a debit on his account with 'THEM' which duly receives a recompense to be credited to the other column of the account. For example, the Bank's General Manager is unpleasant and £1.00 is debited, but a small kindness from a female colleague results in 28p credit. Soon Christie is getting his recompense by scratching the façade of an Edwardian office-block or leaving his mother's funeral bill unpaid.

Much of the early part of this novel is farcical or absurd – but there is an interesting undertone of serious disturbance suggesting desperation that the mad world of society (and its transactions) is not recognised for what it is. These matters are focused by the author through his device of Christie Malry's double-entry. For example, when leaving his mother's funeral the clergyman who has officiated at the service hands him a leaflet. Christie's reaction is to write the following letter to the Borough of Hammersmith Weights and Measures Department:

'Dear Sirs:

re St Jude's Church.

You will note that the organisation publishing the enclosed leaflet claims to have the answer to all problems, personal, political and international?

I would be grateful if you would check upon the factual accuracy of this claim and, if you find it to be in any way false or exaggerated, I trust you will institute proceedings under the relevant section of the Trade Descriptions Act.

Yours sincerely,

Christie Malry.'[56]

The action of the clergyman and the letter are recorded in Christie's account with 'THEM' and appear in the significantly titled 'The First Reckoning'.

---

[56] *Ibid.*, pp. 34-35.

After leaving the bank Christie works for Tapper's, an organisation that 'had been manufacturing sweets and cakes for a mere eighty-three years', where he becomes an invoice clerk. We are close to the world of Reginald Perrin and 'Sunshine Desserts', and indeed the entire workings, organisation and set-up of Tapper's sweet-factory is comically and satirically portrayed through the device of Christie's double-entry. This passage indicates, in more than one sense, the flavour of this part of the novel:

> 'Christie could see the sheen of professional passion in Tiny's [the Foreman's] eyes as he savoured the bashing the baths of chocolate took. And he was not slow in indicating his favourite, either, Tiny: the dark brown bath. ... There were those to whom it was given to like plain chocolate, said Tiny, the connoisseurs, the cognoscenti, the true aristocrats; and there were the rest, the others, the chocolate *lumpen-proletariat. ...*
> Tiny kept a Georgian handled gill glass by this one royal bath, and from this he periodically...supped his beloved nectar to ascertain whether or not it had reached its apogee. "A fortunate man, thought Christie"; and it crossed his mind that the right kind of foreign body could well yield a handsome credit.'[57]

Tiny's enthusiasm and Christie's sharp eye for potential double-entry targets are put into perspective when employees are given bags of 'misshapes of their own' and the Sector Head cries, 'I wouldn't eat this firm's muck if you paid me!' The situation produces some superb throw-away lines as when one colleague complains that his girl-friend who works in the Wages Section will not reveal the salary of the Head of the Typing Pool. 'Would you credit it?' he says. 'I'd have to think about it,' replies Christie.[58]

The novel moves remorselessly towards terrorism and a kind of justification for it that significantly is underpinned by criticism of a heartless money-system of profit and loss – as Christie sees it. As part of his recompense for injustices received he blows up the local tax office, killing several people. Here is a bit of his 'justification':

> 'I have no right to kill people. No one has, according to all the arguments.

---

[57] *Ibid.*, p. 65.

[58] *Ibid.*, pp. 67-70.

Yet people are killed. There are even licensed killers of people, of several kinds.

Despite the overwhelming concurrence with the canon regarding the absolute sanctity of human life, in fact society saw that human life was in fact a very expensive, plentiful and easily-disposable asset. Of all things, human life was the easiest to replace. A machine would be difficult, costly...

Human life is cheap, dirt-cheap, according to this society...despite its pious mouthings. What it does in practice is not what it says it does. It does not care for human life: it shortens that life in pursuit of mere profit, it organises wars from which it is certain mass killings will result. ...

Christie could go on.'[59]

In the Third Reckoning the Credit or Recompense column contains the sum of £110.10 for the Tax Office bombing 'calculated at the rate of £1.30' for each body 'being an allowance of the commercial value of the chemicals contained therein: plus damage to property etc.' By the time we reach the Fourth Reckoning Christie has succeeded in poisoning 20,479 'innocent West Londoners' similarly charged for at the same rate and producing a credit of £26,622.70. We may be reminded of N.F.Simpson's *One Way Pendulum* (1959) but the effect of the humour here is macabre and by the Final Reckoning Christie has died, his body riddled with cancer. Shortly after the novel's publication the author committed suicide.

The Attack on Thatcherism

Mrs Thatcher came to power in 1979 and, rightly or wrongly, that era is still seen by many as one in which it became socially acceptable to be not only vulgarly rich but to laud one's wealth over others less fortunate. Harry Enfield's character, Loadsamoney, became not just an amusing joke: he could be seen as an exaggeration of the reality. In any case, the atmosphere of the period with its working-class jobbers sporting garish braces and driving Porsches was to many preferable to the ethos associated with the 'Winter of Discontent'. The stereotyped images created by the media gathered strength during the 1980s and of course increasingly dominate today with a power which alarms some observers. Yet this

---

[59] *Ibid.*, pp. 115-16.

heady brew of computer-generated image and profit that was to make tycoons in the multi-media business even more fabulously rich – while leaving others penniless, bankrupt and hopelessly in debt – this whole approach to life was significantly and in a sense prophetically attacked on the eve of Thatcherism in David Hare's major play *Plenty* (1978), which was subsequently made into a film.

The key figure in *Plenty* is Susan Traherne, one of the David Hare heroines the author admires 'but whom the audience dislikes'.[60] She is an idealistic young woman who has never been able to free herself emotionally – perhaps I should say psychologically – from her wartime activities as an agent operating in occupied France. She has no admiration or respect for the accepted social mores of post-war Britain and in particular for the English 'Establishment'. She is fiercely devoted to her primitive, atavistic ideas of what is right and what is wrong: ideas which served her well during her time as an agent. Consequently, despite periods in which she tries with success to live an appropriate life with her diplomat husband, the experience takes her ever closer to mental breakdown.

The play opens with a scene set in a Knightsbridge flat at Easter 1962. Susan is leaving her husband Raymond Brock and has, unknown to him, rented the flat to Alice, a hippy bohemian who helps unmarried mothers. Raymond, the former diplomat turned City insurance broker, is lying asleep naked and 'covered in dried blood'. How all this has come about is revealed scene by scene as we see a series of flashbacks commencing in occupied France in November 1943 and taking us right up again to Easter 1962.

The nub of the play is the borderline between right and wrong for Susan. She will not compromise. Is this moral behaviour on her part? Or self-indulgence as her husband claims? When she is pressed into a corner to face the consequences of her actions she becomes violent. For example, she decides she wants a child but wants it by a man who is nothing to her. When after 18 months of failing to cause a pregnancy Mick, the would-be father, remonstrates with Susan, saying that he wants to humanise the relationship, that he feels dirty and used, she fires a revolver at him. Aware that she

---

[60] David Hare, *Plenty*, London: Faber and Faber, 1978, p. 87. 'A Note on Performance by the Author'.

has damaged her husband's career as a diplomat she goes to the senior staffing officer of the Diplomatic Corps to plead for his promotion and, when she gets negative reactions, threatens to kill herself if he is not promoted in six days. Susan is clearly an 'impossible' person – and yet we still have the nagging feeling she might be right.

This is what brings us to money and the concept of 'selling out'. Lurking behind Susan's actions are deeply established ideas of the sanctity of life and of natural morality, perhaps expressed in Christianity as 'Man doth not live by bread alone but by every word that proceedeth out of the mouth of God'. We sense that somehow – however bizarre this idea might be – this 'mad' woman Susan has some channel that links her with divine good – whatever her behaviour might suggest to the contrary.

As the play progresses we realise that Susan is fundamentally and, in various senses, dangerously opposed to what British society represents economically and politically because she sees it as a hypocritical charade – even the Britain of Attlee's post-war government. The 'invoices go back and forth, import, export...'[61] When Alice asks Raymond Brock whether he has lots of money he replies: 'I find it moderately easy to acquire. I seem to have a sort of mathematical gift. The stock exchange. Money sticks to my fingers I find. I triple my income. What can I do?'[62] At the end of this scene, after an argument about the insulting and dismissive way Susan refers to Raymond's boss Leonard Darwin in front of Alice ('he would not trust him to stick his prick into a bucket of lard'), Raymond says it is time he was 'pushing off home'.[63] After another exchange in which Susan accuses Raymond of using such expressions which do not 'belong', he admits that the diplomatic world is dull, stuffy and dead but adds that it is the only world he has. When he urges Susan to visit him in Brussels she uses the excuse of her hated job to prevent her coming: '...the shipping office is very important to me. I do find it fulfilling. And I just couldn't let Mr Medlicott down.' This is a lie, but in a strange way the comment is genuine for Susan knows she is not good for

---

[61] *Ibid.*, p. 30.

[62] *Ibid.*, p. 33.

[63] *Ibid.*, pp. 35-36.

Raymond. Yet we feel they are doomed to remain together in a future which offers, in Alice's ironic words, 'peace and plenty'.[64]

The remainder of the play is in a sense concerned with Susan divesting herself of worldly goods. She compares the 'glittering lies' she told as an undercover agent in France with her present job of 'lying for a living', producing what her 'masters call good copy' to sell 'some rotten shoe'. When she asks Alice what the point of her existence is she is told that she has 'sold out'.[65] His diplomatic career ruined, Brock also sells out, getting an insurance job in the City, ruefully reflecting 'we can cope in a smaller sort of flat. Especially now we don't have to entertain...I can't help feeling it will be better, I'm sure. Too much money. I think that's what went wrong. Something about it corrupts the will to live. Too many years spent sploshing around'.[66] It should not be forgotten that 'selling out' in the sense in which it is used in this play does not only mean offering yourself as a purchasable package in a capitalist market but also 'giving up', retreating from ideals. Thus Brock's 'selling out' is of a different and minor order compared to what Susan, in her own mind, risks. For Susan 'selling out' would become death. She gives £200.00 to one of Alice's protegees to pay for an abortion, remarking 'Don't thank us. We're rotten with cash', and subsequently 'giving' Brock's flat to Alice so that she can continue her work for unmarried mothers. The last we hear of Susan is that she has dropped out of the society she hates, is on drugs and has been, albeit briefly, reunited with her Second World War mentor and idol code-named Lazar – a man who, ironically, ashamedly admits to giving in (selling out): 'I gave in. Always. All along the line. Suburb. Wife. Hell. I work in a corporate bureaucracy...'[67] The last we hear of Raymond Brock is that he had had to fight to get his house back from Alice.

I consider this play to be a very significant text on the question of the representation of capitalist corporate society because it portrays in human terms the effects on people and their ideals, especially as they appeared immediately before the Thatcher era, the Big Bang

---

[64] *Ibid.*, pp. 37-38.

[65] *Ibid.*, p. 44.

[66] *Ibid.*, p. 74.

[67] *Ibid.*, p. 83.

and the Alice in Wonderland world of Soros and Leeson that the high-tech globalisation of the money-markets was to create. It is also notable that the one political event in the play that is closely examined – the Suez Crisis – reveals that Eden's government and the Foreign Office 'sold out' on the question of honour, thus betraying the ideals of their staff: 'the entire war is a fraud cooked up by the British as an excuse for seizing the canal.' For Susan Traherne the linked financial and political systems are irredeemably corrupt and she refers to the situation wistfully as the 'death-rattle of the ruling class'.[68]

The 'Money-Conspiracy'

The 1980s inevitably brought a growing sense of money and business being innately corrupt, dirty and 'mad' and nowhere in contemporary creative writing was this clearer than in Martin Amis's novel *Money* (1984). This astonishing, rambling *picaresque* work has as its central theme the fact that the world is increasingly governed by the 'money-conspiracy'. In a video conversation with Ian McEwan recorded soon after the publication of *Money*, Martin Amis speaks at length on the historic sense of money as sordid, dirty and 'smelly' and in doing so echoes almost word for word the sentiments of John Self, the anti-hero in his financially eponymous novel.[69] The sentiments are all the more powerful in that they are to a large extent guilt-ridden for both character and author. Money, with its associations of drugs, fast-food, sex, instant-access credit, computers, faxes, fruit machines, and so on, is seen as the key to unlocking an ever-powerful force of addiction (chemical, mechanical, electronic) that enslaves and debases the world in mindless self-indulgence. Money is the key to this power but is also controlled by it: it is a cyclical self-reproducing process in which 'advanced' financial societies are trapped.

Here are two quotations from the novel, written incidentally as a kind of confessional diatribe.

---

[68] *Ibid.*, p. 51.

[69] The video is from the series *Writers in Conversation* and was produced for the Anthony Roland Collection of Films on Art by the ICA. In the interview Amis covers, among other topics, 'Money in literature, folklore and history' and 'Money in the twentieth century'. Interestingly, another topic is the 'Unspoken threat of annihilation informing contemporary thought'.

'*Money,* money stinks. It really does. Dah, it stinks. Pick up a wad of well-used notes and fan them out in your face. Pick it up. Fan it. Do it. Little boys' socks and porno headache tang, old yeast batch, larders, damp towels, the silt from purses' seams, the sweat of the palms and the dirt in the nails of the people who handle this stuff all day, so needfully. Ah, it stinks.'[70]

'With dry lips and voodoo heat in his eyes Felix told me that all America was interflexed by computer processors whose roots spread ever outward from the trunks of skyscrapers until they looped like a web from city to city, sorting, clearing, holding, okaying, denying, denying. Software America sprawled on a humming grid of linkup and lookout, with display screens and logic boards of credit ratings, debt profiles. And now all the States were keying in my name, and the VDUs were all wincing like spooked electro-encephalograms. America played space-invaders with the words john self. I was a money enemy. And the tab police were on my tail.'[71]

The quotations come from near the end of the novel when John Self discovers he has been the victim of a financial 'sting' that could only be possible in the unreal fantasy world that the money markets have become. It is interesting to note that the subject matter and imagery in the latter passage echo or anticipate the work of William Gibson and in particular his *Neuromancer* (1984), while of course the electronic world portrayed looks forward to such recent cinema thrillers as *The Net*.

The novel, delivered in the first person in a kind of rambling, yet strangely incisive, tirade littered with expletives, portrays the life of John Self, who like his creator, is taking stock of life and self at the half-way point: age 35. His life-style which receives his constant contempt but from which he cannot break free is one of the consumption of addictive additives:

'My clothes were made of monosodium glutimate and hexachlorophene. My food is made of polyester, rayon and lurex. My rug lotions contain vitamins. ...My brain is gimmicked by a microprocessor the size of a quark, and costing ten pee and running the whole deal. I am made of – junk, I'm just junk.'[72]

---

[70] Martin Amis, *Money*, Harmondsworth: Penguin Books, 1985, p. 389.

[71] *Ibid.*, pp. 350-51.

[72] *Ibid.*, p. 265.

The humour, as exhibited here, can be extremely funny but it is always tinged with the sick and the black, while the reversals and exaggerations give the visions of London and New York a quality that reminds me of Allan Ginsberg's *Howl.* The junk world portrayed symbolises, and is the product of, the often mentioned 'money-conspiracy': 'If time is money, then fast food, saves both.' Moreover, John Self's 'job', making pornographic films, takes him to the centre of a pointless existence of futile self-gratification. Even when he laughs at himself the laughter contains horror and self-contempt. Here he is suddenly realising who is pictured in a home-made pornographic video:

> 'A fat pale guy was giving a bronzed blonde the treatment on a wobbly iron bed. ...Quite quickly I realised that the girl was Butch Beausoleil. A little later I realised that the man – the man was John Self. Me, in other words. ...this fat actor or extra or bit-part player, his pocked back, juddering beerbelly and tumescent throat – no it wasn't the body (we all have *bodies*), it was the face. Ah! The face! The shame and fear of its bared gums, its elderly winces, its terrible surprise. ...'[73]

John Self had just performed this act with one of his leading actresses (Butch Beausoleil) only to find that she had secretly filmed it. The horror of what he sees is all the greater since it is characteristic of the 'junk' lifestyle he cannot resist. When he subsequently does form a stable relationship based on affection with Martina Twain he finds himself unable to perform sexually and betrays her with an old flame who has maliciously arranged for them to be caught *in flagrante delicto.*

One could argue that linking these moral obscenities with money – let alone business – is tendentious and contrived. But Amis is clearly convinced by his vision of what is wrong with the world – the more so perhaps because he is caught up in the 'conspiracy'. Businesses that deserve to succeed fail and vice-versa, the whole affair seen as a global lottery in which winners and losers are chosen at random. John Self's uncle Norman, with whom he lived from seven to 15, tried 'to make it big' during those years in America, 'a land with success in its ozone, a new world for the go-getters and new-broomers, a land where fortune grins and makes the triple-ring sign...Yeah. Or not?' In practice, despite hard work and enterprise,

---

[73] *Ibid.*, p. 280.

he repeatedly failed and ultimately has to return penniless to Britain. Such stories of cruel market forces were not new to fiction, of course, as we have noticed with regard to *The Great Gatsby* and *Death of a Salesman*, but by the 1980s the literal inhumanity which controlled those forces (that is, that they derived from non-human powers linked to technology on a global scale) was taking the picture, the scene, into a new and frightening dimension. John Self also talks about the unemployed, the no-hopers:

> 'I came of age in the Sixties, when there were chances, when it was all there waiting. Now they seep out of school – to what? To nothing. ... The dole-queue starts at the exit to the play-ground. ...Life is hoarded elsewhere by others. Money is so near you can almost touch it, but it is on the other side – you can only press your face up against the glass...You can't drop out any more. Money has seen to that. There's nowhere to go. You cannot hide out from money. ...'[74]

And of course, to use a monetary metaphor, the other side of the coin is the wealth of those who randomly succeed in the lottery that the business and financial world has become:

> 'They are all shapes and colours, innocent beneficiaries of the global joke which money keeps cracking. They don't do anything: it's their currencies that do things.'[75]

John Self is in fact financially ruined by a 'scam' which itself symbolises the operation of the global 'money-conspiracy'. The backers for his film – incidentally also called *Money* – are former actors. All the expenses he claims, all the documents he signs, all the cheques he endorses which he thinks are paid for out of the financial resources provided by his backers are in fact creating a huge debt that is down to him to repay. As Martin Amis himself (who appears as a character in this novel!) explains to John Self:

> 'You signed a lot of documents. My guess is that you signed them all twice. Once under Co-signatory, once under Self. It was your name. The company you formed wasn't Goodney & Self. It was Self & Self. It was Self. The hotels, the plane tickets, the limousines, the wage bill,

---

[74] *Ibid.*, p. 153.

[75] *Ibid.*, pp. 153-54.

the studio rental. You were paying. It was you. It was you.'[76]

The novel is subtitled *A Suicide Note.* The suicide of John Self never materialises despite a spirited – if that is the word – attempt near the end. But Martin Amis, the author rather than the character, suggests in a short Preface that the Note is addressed to us, to the readers, to ourselves, and that we are part and parcel of the suicide, that in a sense it is our suicide too. There is indeed a quirky neo-romanticism approaching sentimentality in Amis's final portrayal of John Self – a kind of down-market junk-fed Candide – representing by his name all of us, *un homme moyen sensuel,* who instead of cultivating his garden as a means of survival, just continues to be his imperfect self, living from day to day but on a much smaller scale than before. Indeed, he is mistaken for a beggar while waiting for his new girlfriend, Georgina. Seeing the tenpence piece lying in his cap he tells us:

> 'Well, you've got to laugh. You've got to. There isn't any choice. I'm not proud. Don't hold back on my account. Now here's that Georgina at last moving clear of the crowd; her smile is touching and ridiculous – delighted yet austere, and powerfully confident – as she ticks towards me on her heels.'[77]

The Obscenity of 'Serious Money'

The outrageous crudity, the sheer obscenity, that jaundiced observers, particularly those of the 'Old Left', considered they saw in Thatcherite, monetarist Britain received massive exposure in the media and in creative writing during the late 1980s and nowhere was this more clearly expressed than in *Serious Money,* Caryl Churchill's play, first performed at the Royal Court Theatre in 1987. Indeed, such is the fidelity with which the crude and the obscene are reproduced, that 'the parody becomes the thing parodied'.[78]

The play is set in the City following 'The Big Bang': 'The financial world won't be the same again because the traders are

---

[76] *Ibid.,* p. 378.

[77] *Ibid.,* p. 394.

[78] Stephen Spender on Eliot's imitation of jazz lyrics in 'Sweeney Agonistes', quoted in V. de S. Pinto, *Crisis in English Poetry 1880-1940,* London: Hutchinson, 1972, p. 157.

coming down the fast lane.'[79] 'White Knights' and corporate raiders have invaded the square mile. A cartel is plotting a hostile take-over of an unsuspecting, old-fashioned company called Albion with the help of the new breed of arbitrageurs and 'oiks': those who use junk bonds and 'greenmail'. But things go wrong when Jake Todd, a commercial paper dealer, is shot dead and the Department of Trade and Industry begins to investigate.

What is portrayed is a heartless, ruthless world of industrial espionage, 'dirty tricks' and greed of unparalleled vulgarity, yet written in the kind of verse which T.S. Eliot had successfully adapted for the stage in such plays as *The Cocktail Party* and *The Confidential Clerk.* Here Corman, a corporate raider, and Brown, an industrial spy, are planning their take-over of Albion:

CORMAN

The analysts reports are satisfactory,
Predicting high industrial synergy.
I'll have to close the chocolate biscuit factory.
The management lacks drive and energy.
Tell me what you learnt about the company.

BROWN

I spent a month posing as a secretary.
The working atmosphere is very pleasant.
A shock to the chairman would be salutary,
His presence at his desk is just symbolic,
He disappears to fish and shoot pheasant. ...

CORMAN

Excellent, they'll put up no resistance.
I'll sack them all, put in new staff, maybe promote a few of their assistants.
Too late for them to make the company over,
Because I am going to take the company over.
Now to the larger and still more inviting
Albion Products. Fuck the analysts,

---

[79] Caryl Churchill, *Serious Money*, London: Methuen, 1987, p. 25.

What do they know? It's much more exciting.
Is their chairman gaga too and their managing director always pissed?

SMITH

No, he's sober and quite competent.
Duckett runs a rather happy ship......
...they all seem quite efficient.
Employees feel considerable loyalty.
The factory has been visited by royalty.

CORMAN

Albion is obviously deficient
In management. Old-fashioned and paternal.
These figures stink. I can make it earn a lot
more for its shareholders, who are
The owners after all. It will be far
Better run, streamlined, rationalised,
When it forms part of Corman Enterprise.
(And anyway I want it.)
Right. Both targets will be hit.
Now summon my war cabinet.[80]

The crudeness of the language illustrated above symbolises of course the crudeness in moral and perhaps aesthetic terms of the world portrayed. And the greed I mentioned is not just simple greed for wealth and nice possessions: it is also greed for success upon success in the world of money. Meanwhile the unsuspecting Duckett, chairman of Albion, one of the 'old school', is thinking of turning profit into new possessions:

DUCKETT

I'm Duckett. I enjoy the Financial Times.
It's fun reading about other people's crimes.
My company Albion's price is looking perky.
I think I'll buy that villa in the south of Turkey.[81]

---

[80] *Ibid.*, pp. 37-38.

However, the obscenity of the language and the crudeness of the rhythm reach their apotheosis in the Futures Song sung from the floor of L.I.F.F.E.[82] It finishes:

> *Money-making money-making money-making money-making*
> *money-making money-making money-making money-making caper*
> *Do the fucking business do the fucking business do the fucking business*
> *And bang it down on paper*
>
> *So L.I.F.F.E. is the life for me and I'll burn out when I'm dead*
> *And this fair exchange is like a rifle range what's the price of flying lead?*
> *When you soil your jeans on soya beans shove some cocoa up your head*
> *You can never hide if your spread's too wide, you'll just fuck yourself*
> *instead.*[83]

T.S.Eliot's theatrical career began in fact with two 'aristophanic fragments' called *Sweeney Agonistes* which portray a reduced crude world of sex and violence and, above all, death.   In my opinion Caryl Churchill has had considerable success in using and updating Eliot's techniques in creating the moral and cultural vacuum that she sees the City to be.

A sense of theatrical and cultural history is also shown in Caryl Churchill's use of a scene from the late 17th-century playwright Thomas Shadwell – considered something of a joke by his contemporaries for his vulgarity.   Such a speech sets the tone of what is to follow:

HACKWELL

Look thee, brother, if it be to a good end and that we ourselves have no
share in the vanity of wicked diversion thereof by beholding of it but only
use it whereby we may turn the penny, always considered that it is like to
take and the said Shares will sell well; and then we shall not care....[84]

---

[81] *Ibid.*, p. 39.

[82] London International Financial Futures and Options Exchange.

[83] *Ibid.*, p. 62.

[84] *Ibid.*, p. 13.

London, it seems Caryl Churchill is saying, has returned to the vulgarities and obscenities of the past though now they are systematised and amplified in the new technologies of globalisation. As Zac, a banker, puts it:

> *Sure this is a dangerous system and it could crash any minute and I*
> *sometimes wake up in the bed*
> *And think is Armageddon Aid, nuclear war or a crash, and how will I end*
> *up dead?*
> *(But that's just before breakfast.)*
> *What really matters is the massive sums of money being passed round the*
> *world, and trying to appreciate their size can drive you mental.*
> *There haven't been a million days since Christ died.*
> *So think a billion, that's a thousand million, and have you even tried*
> *To think a trillion? Think a trillion dollars a day,*
> *And that's the gross national product of the USA. ...*
> *Naturally there's a whole lot of greed and*
> *That's no problem because money buys freedom...*
> *...the Conservatives romped home with a landslide victory for five more*
> *glorious years.*
> *(Which was handy though not essential because it would take far more*
> *than that for Labour to stop us.)*[85]

Thus the play ends with an uncanny anticipation of Blairite economic policy – at least I think that is what Caryl Churchill would say. And as for the murder of Jake? It appears that the government probably used MI5 or the CIA to silence his awkward questions and anyway no-one really cares as long as the scam of international finance continues. A scapegoat (Greville Todd) is sent to prison 'to show the government was serious' and then things carry on as before. It all illustrates what could be taken as the play's subtitle: 'Do others before they can do you.'[86]

---

[85] *Ibid.*, p. 109.

[86] *Ibid.*, p. 108.

4. Final Thoughts

'Here we go. Here we go. Here we go.'

AS THE CENTURY ENDED it was apparent that life in 'the advanced world' had become an unprecedented moral quagmire. To use a word such as 'unprecedented' may seem excessive – after all the idea that the 'love of money is the root of all evil' dates back to the origin of currency in the third millennium BC.[87] But it is now money – and its use in business and in leisure as deployed in a world dominated by computers – that has created the situation which horrifies and, disturbingly, excites the imagination of so many gifted contemporary writers. Whether you read Tom Wolfe's *The Bonfire of the Vanities* (1988), Gordon Burn's *Alma Cogan* (1989), Will Self's *My Idea of Fun* (1993), Bret Easton Ellis's *American Psycho* (1991) or Julie Birchall's *Ambition* (1990), you find repeated the characteristic ingredients of a yuppiedom whose 'meaningless' machine-ridden existence is spiced-up by artificial – often drug-induced – excitement of the most powerful and dangerous residual emotions: violence, greed, despair, death-wish, megalomania, hollow laughter, distortion of reality, and total abandonment of any moral sense. The brooding feel of death and the relentless domination of technology which began to appear in the portrayal of business before the Second World War accelerated, as we have seen, during the 1970s and 1980s in the work of, among others, B.S. Johnson and Martin Amis. This *genre,* if we can call it that, would also include the work of lesser literary figures like James Herbert and Jeffrey Archer: writers who inevitably see themselves as much businessmen as authors, part of the process, producers of a potential package of book, film, video and even, perhaps, tee-shirt. However, the trend in writing I have discussed, in which in a sense business has been both subject and villain, seems to be approaching an apotheosis. Let us hope it is that and not an apocalypse.

---

[87] See Jonathan Williams (ed.), *Money: A History*, London: British Museum Press, 1997, p. 16.

Government: Whose Obedient Servant?

A Primer in Public Choice

Gordon Tullock
Arthur Seldon
Gordon L. Brady

In *Government: Whose Obedient Servant?*, three economists provide an account of the theory of public choice and its applications without the technical jargon which makes it difficult for newcomers to appreciate the importance of this branch of economics.

The authors are three leading exponents. Professor Gordon Tullock is one of the founding fathers of public choice theory and has been responsible for many of the most imaginative ideas and the most significant advances in the subject.
Dr Arthur Seldon, for many years the Editorial Director of the Institute of Economic Affairs, was one of the first to recognise the importance of public choice and has been a principal contributor to the development of the subject in Britain.
Dr Gordon Brady has written extensively about ways in which public choice theory can be applied to some of the most pressing issues of our time.

Sir Antony Jay, joint author of *Yes, Minister* and *Yes, Prime Minister* contributes a Foreword in which he explains how his experiences led him, by a different route, to the same conclusions as those of this 'admirable book'.

The Institute of Economic Affairs
2 Lord North Street, Westminster, London SW1P 3LB
Telephone: 020 7799 3745 Facsimile: 020 7799 2137
E-mail: iea@iea.org.uk Internet: http://www.iea.org.uk

ISBN 0-255 36482-2

£10.00

Regu'
Thr
The De

John Blundell
Colin Robinson

The rising tide of government regulation in most countries is provoking a reconsid
extent to which the state should lay down rules for others. Self-regulation and other to.
voluntary rule-setting are being examined as substitutes for regulation by government.

Readings 52 begins with a paper by John Blundell and Colin Robinson which analyses the forces
behind government regulation, its shortcomings and the scope for voluntary regulation. Seven
papers by distinguished commentators on regulation then examine Blundell and Robinson's
conclusions.

Contents

The Institute of Economic Affairs
2 Lord North Street, Westminster, London SW1P 3LB
Telephone: 020 7799 3745 Facsimile: 020 7799 2137
E-mail: iea@iea.org.uk Internet: http://www.iea.org.uk   ISBN 0-255 36483-0

£10.00